P O R T A B L E

California
Wine Country

1st Edition

W9-BEQ-975

by Erika Lenkert and Matthew R. Poole

with John Thoreen

Macmillan • USA

ABOUT THE AUTHORS

A native San Franciscan, **Erika Lenkert** spends half her time in Los Angeles and the other half traveling throughout the state. She's currently a contributing writer for *Los Angeles* magazine and dozens of guides to California as well as the restaurant editor for *California Homes* magazine. Erika is pleased she actually gets paid to force her opinions onto others—something she'd done pro bono for years.

Freelance travel writer and photographer **Matthew R. Poole** has authored 17 travel guides to California and abroad. He currently lives in San Francisco and is an ardent fan of Ravenswood zinfandels. You can reach him at mrpoole@sirius.com.

In addition to this guide, Erika and Matthew coauthor a number of other Frommer's guides to California, including *Frommer's California, Frommer's San Francisco from $60 a Day,* and *Frommer's Memorable Walks in San Francisco.*

MACMILLAN TRAVEL

A Simon & Schuster Macmillan Company
1633 Broadway
New York, NY 10019

Find us online at **www.frommers.com**.

ISBN 0-02-862137-9
ISSN 1093-9776

Editors: Cheryl Farr and Leslie Shen
Production Editor: Tony McDonald
Photo Editor: Richard Fox
Production Team: Eric Brinkman, David Faust, Heather Pope, and Karen Teo
Design by Michele Laseau
Digital Cartography by Roberta Stockwell and Jim Moore

SPECIAL SALES

Bulk purchases (10+ copies) of Frommer's and selected Macmillan travel guides are available to corporations, organizations, mail-order catalogs, institutions, and charities at special discounts, and can be customized to suit individual needs. For more information write to Special Sales, Macmillan General Reference, 1633 Broadway, New York, NY 10019.

Manufactured in the United States of America

Contents

List of Maps

AN INVITATION TO THE READER

When we first started writing for Frommer's, we'd call our editors after each of our books was published and excitedly ask, "Any reader mail?" We were just dying to learn whether folks were enjoying our books—or actually reading them, for that matter. We were disappointed when we hadn't received any mail, but our editors assured us that it was a compliment; most people write only to complain, so we must be doing something right. But the fact is, we want to hear what you think. What did you love? What did you hate? What was over- or underrated? Did you find a hotel, restaurant, bar, attraction—whatever—that we should have included? Tell us your opinion, so we can share the information with your fellow travelers in upcoming editions. That way, perhaps we'll stop accosting and questioning poor, innocent visitors when we see them carrying our guides through the towns of northern California. C'mon, drop us a note. Write to:

Erika Lenkert & Matthew R. Poole
Frommer's Portable California Wine Country, 1st Edition
c/o Macmillan Travel
1633 Broadway
New York, NY 10019

AN ADDITIONAL NOTE

Please be advised that travel information is subject to change at any time—and this is especially true of prices. We therefore suggest that you write or call ahead for confirmation when making your travel plans. The authors, editors, and publisher cannot be held responsible for the experiences of readers while traveling. Your safety is important to us, however, so we encourage you to stay alert and be aware of your surroundings. Keep a close eye on cameras, purses, and wallets, all favorite targets of thieves and pickpockets.

FIND FROMMER'S ONLINE

Arthur Frommer's Outspoken Encyclopedia of Travel (www.frommers.com) offers more than 6,000 pages of up-to-the-minute travel information—including the latest bargains and candid, personal articles updated daily by Arthur Frommer himself. No other Web site offers such comprehensive and timely coverage of the world of travel.

WHAT THE SYMBOLS MEANS
✪ Frommer's Favorites

Our favorite places and experiences—outstanding for quality, value, or both.
The following abbreviations are used for credit cards:

AE	American Express	ER	enRoute
CB	Carte Blanche	JCB	Japan Credit Bank
DC	Diners Club	MC	MasterCard
DISC	Discover	V	Visa

The Best of the Wine Country

*W*hether you're on a budget or blowing your annual bonus, there's no way around it: a Wine Country experience epitomizes indulgence. Literally all that's expected of you is to eat, drink, relax—and then do it all over again. The rest—wine tastings, spa treatments, hot-air balloon rides, horseback tours—is mere icing on an already idyllic itinerary. In fact, you don't even have to like wine to love the Wine Country; anyone who enjoys lounging in a hammock on a warm summer's day will succumb, because the Wine Country is just that: the country. The verdant expanses of rolling hills patterned with grape-garnered trellises, hued with mustard and wildflowers, and dotted with farmers plowing the soil and vintners tending to their vines is country life at its picture-perfect best.

Of course, there's a whole lot more: wineries both great and small producing some of the world's finest wines, nationally renowned chefs serving exceptional cuisine, luxury resorts catering to the rich and famous, and soothing mineral hot springs priced for the rest of us. Yes, the world may be falling apart elsewhere, but not here—for this eternal Eden of indulgence is where we go when we feel the need to be pampered, when it's time to whip out the charge card for that $100 dinner or a 1994 Silver Oak cabernet sauvignon and say, "Frankly, my dear, I don't give a damn."

Which is why you're holding *Frommer's Portable California Wine Country.* Consider it your personal passport to the best that the Napa and Sonoma valleys have to offer. Follow our suggestions and you'll know why this is one of our favorite vacation spots on the planet; in time, it's bound to become one of yours, too.

1 The Best Wineries

- **Domaine Chandon** (Yountville, Napa Valley): Founded by Moët et Chandon, the valley's most renowned sparkling winery has all the grandeur of a world-class French champagne house. Strolling with a glass of bubbly in hand through this estate's beautifully manicured rose gardens—complete with swan pond—is a quintessential Wine Country experience. See page 66.

- **PlumpJack Winery** (Oakville, Napa Valley): The proprietors of San Francisco's PlumpJack restaurant and wine shop have transformed the former Villa Mount Eden's winery into a hip, playful, energetic place—a welcome diversion from the attitude you'll come to expect from Napa Valley wineries. But it's not just about atmosphere: They're making some very impressive wines here, including some killer cabernets. No tours or picnic spots are available, but this refreshingly stylized and friendly facility will make you want to hang out for a while nonetheless. See page 68.

- **V. Sattui Winery** (St. Helena, Napa Valley): Nowhere else can you taste small-volume wines (only sold here), stock up on gourmet lunch supplies (free tastes!), and join in on a huge ongoing picnic all at the same time. Crowds are mighty here, but like the saying goes: If you can't beat 'em. . . . See page 75.

- **Joseph Phelps Vineyards** (St. Helena, Napa Valley): Intimate, comprehensive tours and knockout tastings make this one of our favorite wineries to visit. An air of seriousness hangs heavier than harvest grapes when you first arrive, but the mood lightens as your knowledgeable guide explains the ins and outs of wine making as you taste five to six wines ranging from sauvignon blanc and to what's bound to be terrific cab (*Wine Spectator* regularly awards Phelps's cabernets and blended reds with scores in the high 90s, and aficionados have been known to come close to brawling over bottles of the coveted 1994 Insignia cab). Don't forget to reserve ahead; tours and tastings are by appointment only. See page 76.

- **Prager Winery & Port Works** (St. Helena, Napa Valley): If you want a real down-home, off-the-beaten track Wine Country experience, this place can't be beat. Pass the oak barrels and you'll quickly come upon a cozy clapboard tasting room where owner/winemaker Jim Prager, a sort of modern-day Santa Claus, will pour you samples of his yummy after-dinner wines and a few other selections (including a very good chardonnay and cab). The whole experience is so wonderfully unique that it makes the $5 tasting fee seem like a bargain. See page 77.

- **Clos Pegase** (Calistoga, Napa Valley): Viewing the art at this temple to wine is as much the point as tasting the wines themselves. Renowned architect Michael Graves designed this incredible oasis, which integrates an impressive modern art collection—including a sculpture garden—with a state-of-the-art winemaking facility that features 20,000 square feet of aging caves.

The Wine Country

The **Hess Collection** winery also houses a noteworthy display of museum-quality artwork that's worth checking out. See page 64.

- **Gloria Ferrer Champagne Caves** (Carneros District, Sonoma Valley): Gloria is the grande dame of the Wine Country's sparkling wine producers. On a sunny day, it's impossible not to enjoy sipping a glass of dry Brut on the terrace of this palatial estate as you take in the magnificent views of the vineyards and valley below. If you're unfamiliar with the *méthode champenoise,* make time for the 30-minute tour, which takes you past the fermenting tanks, the bustling bottling line, and into the dark caves brimming with rack after rack of fermenting wine. See page 140.

- **Gundlach-Bundschu Winery** (Sonoma, Sonoma Valley): Gundlach-Bundschu is the quintessential Sonoma winery: nonchalant about appearance, obsessed with wine. Oenophiles in the know covet G-B's reds, particularly the zinfandels, which are remarkably inexpensive for such well-crafted wines. Tours include a trip into their 430-foot cave (the longest in California, they claim). They also have the best picnic grounds in the valley here. And if you're in the valley on a summer weekend, plan on catching one of the Shakespearean plays staged at the winery's outdoor theater—they're loads of fun. See page 141.

- **The Benziger Family Winery** (Glen Ellen, Sonoma Valley): As soon as you arrive here, you'll know you're at a family-run winery—in fact, you'll be instantly made to feel as if you're part of the Benziger clan. This low-volume, high-quality winery offers an exceptional self-guided tour, a free 40-minute tram tour through its pastoral grounds, free tastings, and many excellent, reasonably priced wines. See page 145.

- **Matanzas Creek** (Santa Rosa): It's not technically in Sonoma Valley, but if there's one winery that's worth the drive up to Bennett Valley, it's Matanzas Creek, one of the prettiest wineries in California (particularly when the lavender fields are in bloom). And their wines are pretty spectacular, too: Their Journey 1990 chardonnay has been hailed by wine critics as the finest chardonnay *ever produced in the United States*—and we think their merlot is easily the finest you'll taste in the Wine Country, too. See page 150.

2 The Best Winery Tours for First-Timers

- **Domaine Chandon** (Yountville, Napa Valley): Not only are the grounds sublime, but the comprehensive tour walks you through the high-tech facilities and the entire champagne-making process, from the history of the winery to the cellars, riddling room, and bottling line. Tours are free and no reservation is necessary, but if you want to taste, it'll cost you: $3.50 to $5.75 for a full glass (sorry, no free sips). Come during high season, though, and you can supplement your bubbly with a few appetizers and kick back on their garden-front patio. See page 66.

- **Robert Mondavi Winery** (Oakville, Napa Valley): As one of the most prominent wineries in the valley, it's only appropriate that Robert Mondavi would offer a guided tour for every sort of wine taster. The basic 1-hour comprehensive production tour covers all aspects of the wine-making process and gives you a look at the destemmer-crusher, the tank room where fermentation is done, the bottling room, and the vineyard, all accompanied by a top-notch narrative—the guides are great at making sure you know what you're looking at. Your reward at the end? A free tasting, of course. If you find yourself inspired, you can then move on to one of the other offered tours, such as the 3- to 4-hour advanced wine-growing tour. Make your reservations in advance, if possible; these tours get booked up, especially in high season. See page 67.

- **St. Supéry Winery** (Rutherford, Napa Valley): This straightfor-ward winery is a great place for first-time tasters to learn more about oenology. Their nifty self-guided tour comes complete with "SmellaVision," an interactive display that teaches you how to identify different wine aromas and attributes; there's also a dem-onstration vineyard that you can wander through to learn about growing techniques. See page 70.

- **Kornell Champagne Cellars** (Calistoga, Napa Valley): While this isn't the Wine Country's most comprehensive tour, it may be its most unintimidating one. Staff members Dennis, Bob, Chris, and Rich will do practically anything to maintain their self-proclaimed reputation as the "friendliest winery in the valley"—and that includes taking the time to explain *anything* you want to know about wine. They also serve you all the bubbly you want, guarantee you'll never wait more than 10 minutes to take the 20-minute tour, and even offer up a great story about Marie Antoinette's champagne-glass design. See page 81.

- **Schramsberg** (Calistoga, Napa Valley): The label that presidents serve when toasting with dignitaries from around the globe also serves up the Wine Country's best introduction to the méthode champenoise process of making sparkling wine. The excellent tour is both comprehensive and unintimidating, and an experience you won't soon forget; the highlight is the visit to the 2¹/₂ miles of hand-carved champagne caves—you'll feel like you've landed in the middle of a *Tom Sawyer* adventure. And the tasting room is positively gothic. Be sure to book a spot on the tour in advance, as they fill up quickly. See page 82.

- **Sterling Vineyards** (Calistoga, Napa Valley): This dazzling white Mediterranean-style winery, perched high above the rest of the valley atop a rocky knoll (you'll arrive via aerial tram), offers the most comprehensive self-guided tour in the entire Wine Country. It's great for getting to know the entire wine-making process at your own pace. See page 83.

- **The Benziger Family Winery** (Glen Ellen, Sonoma Valley): *Wine Spectator* magazine hailed this family-run winery as having "the most comprehensive tour in the wine industry." The exceptional self-guided tour, which includes a free 40-minute tram ride, is both informative and fun; it winds through the estate vineyards before making a champagne-tasting pit stop on a scenic bluff. Tour tickets are a hot commodity, so be sure to plan ahead for this one. See page 145.

- **Sonoma Mountain Estate Hopyards & Brewery** (Glen Ellen, Sonoma Valley): Okay, it's not a winery—but it's just as fascinating. Nowhere else in America will you find a brewery so dedicated to educating the public on the entire beer-making process, from barley field to bottle. Founded by the famous Benziger clan—one of the most famous names in Sonoma wine making—the brewery uses its very own mountain spring water that flows beneath the property to produce one of the best amber ales we've ever tasted. See page 146.

3 The Best Experiences Beyond the Wineries

- **Hot-Air Ballooning over Napa's Vineyards:** Admit it: Floating over lush green pastures in a hot-air balloon is something you've always dreamed of but never got around to actually doing. Here's your best chance, because Napa Valley is the busiest hot-air balloon "flight corridor" in the *world*—and what more romantic place to sail up, up, and away? For recommendations on the best Napa hot-air balloon companies, see page 85.

- **Spreading Out Your Picnic Blanket for a Gourmet Alfresco Feast:** You've been with the crowds all day—sitting with them in traffic and sipping elbow-to-elbow in the tasting rooms. If the thought of joining the masses for a meal after all that seems about as romantic and relaxing as a New York subway ride, cancel your restaurant reservations and pack a picnic instead. Both Napa and Sonoma have some of the most spectacular picnic spots on the planet, not to mention excellent places to fill your basket, including the legendary **Oakville Grocery Co.** (☎ 707/944-8802), a West Coast outpost of New York's **Dean & DeLuca** (☎ 707/967-9980), and the **Sonoma Cheese Factory** (☎ 707/996-1000), which offers more kinds of house-made jack cheeses than you ever imagined were possible. See page 131 for details on picnicking in Napa, page 176 for Sonoma picnicking tips.

- **Pampering Yourself at a Spa:** The Wine Country is the perfect place to relax—so what better place to indulge in a tension-relieving massage, a purifying facial, or a rejuvenating body wrap? Our favorite spots to spa it are St. Helena's **White Sulphur Springs Retreat & Spa** (☎ 707/963-4361) and **Health Spa Napa Valley** (☎ 707/967-8800), and the **Sonoma Mission Inn & Spa** (☎ 800/862-4945). See pages 108 and 152.

- **Horseback Riding through the Wine Country:** If you like horses and venturing through cool, shaded forests, then consider seeing the countryside from the saddle. **Napa Valley Trail Rides** (☎ 707/996-8566) will lead any level of rider on a leisurely ride (with the occasional trot thrown in for excitement) through beautiful Bothe–Napa Valley State Park. On the other side of the hills, the **Sonoma Cattle Company** (☎ 707/996-8566) will take you through lovely Jack London State Historical Park. Both companies also offer sunset, full-moon, barbecue, and box-lunch rides as well. See page 154.

- **Touring Sonoma's Wineries on Two Wheels:** With quiet, gently sloping country roads and lots of bucolic scenery, Sonoma is perfect for cycling. **Goodtime Bicycle Company** (☎ 888/525-0453) can take you on one of their organized excursions to Kenwood-area wineries or to south Sonoma's wineries; not only do they provide a gourmet lunch featuring local Sonoma foodstuffs, they'll also carry any wine you purchase and even help with shipping it home. They'll happily rent you a bike and point you to easy trails if you'd rather set out on your own. See page 136.

- **Getting Your Thrills in the Skies:** If you're the thrill-seeking type, catch a panoramic ride in an authentic 1940 Boeing-built Stearman biplane with **Aeroschellville Biplane & Glider Rides** (☎ 707/938-2444), which depart from the south end of

Sonoma Valley. You can also try a glider ride, which will take you soaring over the vineyards—simply breathtaking. See page 151.

4   The Best Luxury Hotels & Inns

- **Auberge du Soleil** (Rutherford, Napa Valley; ☎ 707/963-1211): This spectacular Relais & Châteaux member is quiet, indulgent, and luxuriously romantic. The bathrooms alone are celestial—as are the views. This is one of our favorite places on earth—and always our first choice in the Wine Country. See page 101.

- **Meadowood Napa Valley** (St. Helena, Napa Valley; ☎ 800/458-8080): Tucked away in its own private valley is this ultraluxurious resort, a favorite retreat for Hollywood celebs and corporate CEOs. Spend your days hiking the private trails or playing golf, tennis, or croquet, and follow up with a trip to the health spa and whirlpool. Top it all off with dinner in the excellent restaurant, and you'll have a tough time finding a reason to leave. A place of towering charm and style. See page 103.

- **Sonoma Mission Inn & Spa** (Sonoma, Sonoma Valley; ☎ 800/862-4945): Another popular retreat for the wealthy and the well-known, this multimillion-dollar resort is the last word in spa luxury. Naturally heated artesian springs are the place's coup de grace. Sauna, steam room, whirlpool, outdoor exercise pool, weight room, tennis courts, a whole menu of spa treatments—you can pamper yourself in myriad ways, and retire to your superluxe suite when the day is done. Excellent restaurant, too. See page 156.

- **Gaige House Inn** (Glen Ellen, Sonoma Valley; ☎ 800/935-0237): When we visited this gorgeous inn, we were not merely impressed—we didn't want to leave. This is the finest B&B in the Wine Country. First-class service, an abundance of amenities, luxurious rooms outfitted with top-quality goods—everything you'd expect from an outrageously expensive resort, but at much more reasonable prices (and with a much more intimate atmosphere). See page 161.

- **Kenwood Inn & Spa** (Kenwood, Sonoma Valley; ☎ 800/353-6966): The honey-colored, Tuscan-style buildings, flower-filled flagstone courtyard, and pastoral views of vineyard-covered hills are enough to make any northern Italian homesick. The lavishly done rooms come with just about every extra you could want (except TV, which would interfere with the tranquil ambiance), the full-service spa is to die for, and the staff is as friendly and welcoming as they can be. See page 163.

5   The Best Moderately Priced Accommodations

- **Wine Country Inn** (St. Helena, Napa Valley; ☎ 707/ 963-7077): This attractive wood-and-stone hideaway, complete with a French-style mansard roof and turret, offers lovingly and individually decorated rooms and copious amounts of hospitality. It's also very well priced, considering the outrageous rates usually charged in St. Helena. One of the inn's best features is its attractively landscaped outdoor pool (heated year-round); in fact, the whole charming place overlooks a pastoral landscape of Napa Valley vineyards. See page 106.

- **Deer Run Bed & Breakfast** (St. Helena, Napa Valley; ☎ 800/ 843-3408): If romantic solitude is a big part of your vacation plan, this place had better be on your itinerary—regardless of your budget. Each of the wood-paneled rooms looks onto innkeepers Tom and Carol Wilson's 4 acres of forest; each one comes outfitted with gorgeous antiques and a slew of amenities, not to mention all the solitude you could possibly desire. The ultimate heavenly hideaway. See page 107.

- **White Sulphur Springs Retreat & Spa** (St. Helena, Napa Valley; ☎ 707/963-8588): This woodsy hideaway is a short winding drive away from downtown St. Helena. Established in 1852 and set among 330 acres of creeks, waterfalls, hot springs, hiking trails, and redwood, madrone, and fir trees, White Sulphur Springs claims to be the oldest resort in California; it's geared toward nature-retreat types, who will appreciate both the cozily rustic cabins and the untrammeled surroundings. A full menu of spa treatments rounds out the relaxation. See page 108.

- **Cottage Grove Inn** (Calistoga, Napa Valley; ☎ 800/799-2284): This romantic cluster of cottages is our top affordable pick for doing the Calistoga spa scene in comfort and style. Each brand-spanking-new cottage comes complete with a wood-burning fireplace, homey furnishings (perfect for curling up in front of the fire), cozy quilts, and an enormous bathroom with a skylight and a deep, two-person Jacuzzi tub. See page 109.

- **El Dorado Hotel** (Sonoma, Sonoma Valley; ☎ 800/289-3031): Designed by the same folks who put together Napa's ultraexclusive Auberge du Soleil, this place may look like a 19th-century Wild West relic from the outside, but inside it's all 20th-century deluxe. French windows offer lovely views of the courtyard, which features a heated lap pool. Breakfast, served either inside or out in the courtyard, is heavenly. See page 159.

- **Glenelly Inn** (Glen Ellen, Sonoma Valley; ☎ 707/996-6720): With verdant views of Sonoma's oak-studded hillsides, this former 1916 railroad inn is positively drenched in serenity. This place has everything you'd expect from a Wine Country retreat: bright, immaculate rooms with old-fashioned claw-foot tubs and Scandinavian down comforters adorning the firm beds, a hearty country breakfast served beside the large cobblestone fireplace, and a long veranda where you can curl up in a comfy wicker chair to admire the idyllically bucolic view. See page 163.

6   The Best Restaurants

- **Oakville Grocery Café** (Oakville, Napa Valley; ☎ 707/944-0111): Fervent foodies fought for tables at this roadside cafe as soon as wine wizard Joseph Phelps opened its doors in late 1997. This breakfast-and-lunch–only spot isn't fancy, nor is it expensive—but after one bite of the melt-in-your-mouth salmon, watercress, and herb aioli sandwich, you'll happily put up your dukes for a table, too. See page 117.
- **The French Laundry** (Yountville, Napa Valley; ☎ 707/944-2380): If you've got the cash and you're a serious food lover, you have no choice: You must dine here and find out for yourself why chef/owner Thomas Keller was voted 1997's "Chef of the Nation" by the James Beard Foundation. Dinner at this intimate restaurant is an all-night affair, and when it's finally over, you'll be ready to sit down and do it all over again—it's that good. But make your reservations well over a month in advance, or you may not even get in the door. *Tip:* Cut your bill in half by coming for lunch instead of dinner. See page 118.
- **Pinot Blanc** (St. Helena, Napa Valley; ☎ 707/963-6191): One of our favorite newcomers to the Wine Country is owned by L.A.'s celebrity chef Joachim Splichal (of L.A.'s Patina dynasty). Here, he leaves the cooking to executive chef Sean Knight, whose masterful preparations of Splichal's signature French bistro–style fare are served in one of the most sophisticated dining rooms in the region. See page 124.
- **Catahoula** (Calistoga, Napa Valley; ☎ 707/942-2275): Celebrity chef Jan Birnbaum runs one of the best restaurants in the Wine Coun-try. Catahoula is both funky and fun, and the Southern food that comes out of the wood-burning oven—such as the gumbo ya ya with andouille sausage—is spicy and exciting. You'd

have to travel all over Louisiana to find another place like this. See page 129.

- **Babette's Cafe** (Sonoma, Sonoma Valley; ☎ 707/939-8921): After it was voted the "Best Best-Kept Secret" by the *San Francisco Bay Guardian* and got the thumbs-up from *Gourmet* magazine, this quaint little French place soon became one of the hottest places to dine in Sonoma. Thankfully, it still manages to maintain its homey atmosphere despite the rave reviews. Chef Daniel Patterson's five-course fixed-price dinner is worth saving room for; we suggest starting your feast with the fresh goat cheese on toast with endive-and-herb salad, and crowning it with the delectable warm-peach-and-blueberry napoleon (yum!). See page 166.

- **The Grille** (Sonoma, Sonoma Valley; ☎ 707/938-9000): Jeffrey Jake, a wondrously talented chef with a reputation for turning no-name restaurants into award-winning success stories, had done it again. One bite of his corn risotto flavored with wild mushrooms and molten Reggiano Parmigiano cheese, and you're sure to agree. About half of Jake's California menu is spa-conscious, which makes this a great choice for those who don't want to overindulge. See page 166.

- **Lo Spuntino** (Sonoma, Sonoma Valley; ☎ 707/935-4743): For a quick gourmet lunch in Sonoma, there's no better place to go than Lo Spuntino. This suave deli and wine bar, run by the same people responsible for the success story that is Viansa Winery, is the sexiest thing going in Sonoma. It's a visual masterpiece, with shiny black-and-white–checkered flooring, long counters of Italian marble, and an enticing display of cured meats and cheeses. Start by sampling Viansa Winery's finest, and end your meal at the gelateria, where you can wrap up with some intense Italian ice cream. Service is deli-style: Order at the counter, then scramble for an empty seat; the most coveted are outdoors overlooking the plaza. See page 171.

- **The Girl & The Fig** (Glen Ellen, Sonoma Valley; ☎ 707/938-3634): The cuisine at this modern, attractive cafe is nouveau-country with French nuances—and, yes, figs: They appear in such wonderful creations as the winter fig salad made with arugula, pecans, dried figs, and Laura Chenel goat cheese, tossed in a fig-and-port vinaigrette. Nonfiggy dishes include pan-roasted medaillons of lamb served with a fresh mint sauce (When's the last time you had fresh mint sauce?) and a hearty winter vegetable stew. Both tourists and locals pack the place nightly, so try to reserve ahead. See page 172.

2

The Wine Country Experience

by John Thoreen, Wine Tutor at Meadowood Napa Valley

Over the past 20 years, John Thoreen has built an international reputation as wine lecturer and writer. Presently he is Director of the Wine Center at the prestigious Meadowood Napa Valley resort. You can reach John at Meadowood at ☎ 707/967-1205 or online at **vintuteur@aol.com**.

*S*eeing the Wine Country can be an enormously pleasant day trip. However, investing at least a full day in each valley will reward you with multiple hedonistic dividends—and put you near the head of the class in understanding the ultrapremium wines of California. In the pages that follow, we'll give you a head start on your trip by introducing you to the Napa and Sonoma valleys and the exciting world of wine making.

1 Introducing the Napa & Sonoma Valleys

If you see San Francisco as a charming yet congested metropolis, the two rural valleys just an hour to the north, Sonoma and Napa, offer a delightfully calming and rustic retreat. In the Wine Country, the focus is mainly on gastronomy: adventures with wine and food augmented by a setting of charming villages and towns, sunny afternoons, striking mountain landscapes, carefully presented works of art and architecture, and seas of the world's tidiest vineyards.

The mix of sophistication and rusticity can be peculiar: Dusty pickups park outside some of the finest restaurants in the country. Vintners clad in denim jackets carry bottles of First Growth Bordeaux Chateaux into local bistros. Barns both small and large are more likely to house wine barrels than bales of hay. In the Napa Valley town of St. Helena, a debate recently raged about a use permit for Saks Fifth Avenue. Saks lost. Sonoma just approved—although not without a battle—a posh 150-room hotel just blocks from the historic town square. Many of the homes that pepper the region, tucked back among the vines or perched on hillsides, appear in the pages of Architectural Digest. And these are small towns!

While Napa and Sonoma view each other as competitors (Sonoma produced a bumper sticker that reads "NAPA makes auto parts, SONOMA makes wine"), and while you can sense a difference in attitude traveling from one valley to the other, together as the Wine Country they differ from any other region in California. This uniqueness is based on several factors: a tumultuous geology comprised of 50 or 60 perfectly poor soils; a colorful yet disjointed historical record; a climate unique to growing world-class grapes; legions of entrepreneurs who have often misunderstand the wine business; resilient farmers who once grew wheat and prunes before switching to grapes; and you, one of five million folks who visit each year. (Some years ago, a journalist claimed that Napa is second only to Disneyland as a tourist attraction—an exaggeration that has been perpetuated ever since.)

QUALITY, NOT QUANTITY   In the odd jargon of marketing, "premium" refers to those wines selling for under $7, "super premium" wines run between $7 and $14, and "ultrapremiums" cost $15 and up. The majority of California's premium wines come not from Napa and Sonoma, but from the state's vast Central Valley—still, most of America thinks of Napa and Sonoma as *the* Wine Country. In fact, the seemingly endless spread of vines in Napa and Sonoma comprise only a small part of California's total vineyard acreage. Because the yields per acre here are much lower than in the Central Valley, Sonoma produces only about 7% of the wine made in the state; Napa makes only around 5%. In short, the Wine Country north of San Francisco gained its fame not from quantity, but quality.

Though the Wine Country's total acreage is small, the intensity of its wine-making activity is remarkable. Sonoma Valley claims to be home to 150 wine producers, Napa Valley to 250, which places almost *half* of California's 900 wine producers in just two relatively small regions. Even more remarkable is the fact that many of the hot boutique labels selling for $50 or more per bottle are housed as "tenants" in larger wineries and are not counted as wineries per se. When you combine the wineries you can visit with those that thrive as "labels," Napa and Sonoma are probably home to 60% or 70% of the ultrapremium labels in California. Thus, when you visit the Wine Country, you're sure to experience many of the very best wines that California has to offer.

THE KEY: GEOGRAPHY

Why does the Wine Country produce such a disproportionate amount of the ultrapremiums in the state? What makes the wines of Sonoma and Napa so good? Mother Nature can take most of the credit: The local climate and geology are the primary factors for the region's wine-making success. Beyond these fortuitous geographical features, the flow of history and twists of politics also come into play, though to a much lesser degree. If not for the ocean, the mountain ranges, the earthquakes, and the volcanoes, the valleys of Napa and Sonoma would never have been formed.

Heading into the Wine Country from San Francisco, you traverse a range of Mediterranean-like climates; each differs significantly based on its distance from the ocean or San Francisco Bay, and on its proximity to the small mountain ranges that parallel the coast and block the passage of cold ocean air inland. Grapes love this particular climate, as do numerous other crops ranging from olives, walnuts, apples, and citrus fruits to wild herbs like fennel, bay, sage, and mustard.

The climatic differences are subtle, yet significant. While the Wine Country will never know such weather extremes as the snows of Buffalo, New York, or the humidity of Washington, D.C., everyone who lives here knows that Napa, the city, is cooler by 10 or more degrees on a warm summer day than Calistoga, 20 miles to the north. Because the south end of the Wine Country—referred to as the Carneros District—is cooled by the breeze off the bay, it works best for chardonnay and pinot noir, delicate grapes of Burgundy that cannot thrive in hot climates. Farther north, around Kenwood in Sonoma and St. Helena in Napa, the warmer climate suits Bordeaux grapes such as cabernet sauvignon, merlot, and sauvignon blanc.

THE IMPORTANCE OF PLACE: APPELLATIONS   In both Sonoma and Napa, the latest refinements occurring in the wine world involve discovering a "sense of place" for each style of wine. This critical understanding of soils and slopes happened years ago in Bordeaux, Burgundy, Chianti, and other classic wine-growing regions. Those areas' legally recognized, specific place names say "This soil planted to this grape on this hillside makes a distinctive style of wine." The United States started such a system only recently. As a result, "Napa" was recognized as an appellation, a "named place," in 1981; the area designated "Sonoma" received its approval in 1983. Finer distinctions have sliced these larger regions into smaller pieces, each of which makes further claims to unique qualities in their wines. Today, Sonoma has 11 subappellations; Napa has 10. Thus, you might see a wine label that reads: "Kenwood

Vineyards, Cabernet Sauvignon, Sonoma County, Sonoma Valley," the terms becoming increasingly more specific about the source of the grapes. In Napa it might be "Saintsbury, Pinot Noir, Napa Valley, Carneros."

Over the last 10 years, players in the local wine scene have debated the merits of appellations and subappellations. One school says that the words "Napa" and "Sonoma" carry tremendous good will, and that diluting them with numerous new terms will only confuse the consumer, who's often confused enough already about wine. The visionaries argue that as long as "Napa" and "Sonoma" appear on the label, additional specifics will only help the wine drinker. Only time will tell in this latest twist in the history and politics of the Wine Country.

A LOOK AT THE PAST

Sonoma and Napa valleys were latecomers to the California vineyard scene. Around 1780, Franciscan missionaries, establishing the first of their 21 missions in California, planted the first vineyard in the state near San Diego. The first commercial vineyards were established in Los Angeles around 1825. Around the same time, the 21st and last Franciscan mission, Mission San Francisco Solano, planted its vines near present-day Sonoma; the same vines became the first commercial vineyard in the region about 15 years later, when the missions became secularized. Napa saw its first vineyards in 1838, but had yet to produce commercial wine until 1858, when Charles Krug made a few gallons for John Patchett.

Los Angeles continued to dominate California's wine industry until the 1870s, when Sonoma took over the leadership in total acres around 1875. In turn, Napa replaced Sonoma in acreage a decade later. Not only did Napa and Sonoma grow in size, but tasters noticed their wines were demonstrably superior simply because the climates of Sonoma and Napa were (and still are) distinctly cooler than those in the Los Angeles region.

Somewhat sadly, in terms of today's viticultural and winemaking successes, the delightfully colorful history of wine of early California is rather short-lived. In one sense, the wine business in California is only 30 or 40 years old. Unlike Europe and other New World wine-growing regions, which have enjoyed continuous generations of wine making, we lived through a terrible break in our development—Prohibition—and had to start all over again.

Most of California's wineries shut down during Prohibition, though a few remained in operation to produce wine for sacramental and medicinal purposes. But in the years of temperance, the United States had all but lost whatever palate it had acquired for dry table wines, those which we now buy in abundance from supermarket shelves. For 35 years after Prohibition, more than half the wine consumed in this country was dessert (a.k.a. "fortified") wine, so-called ports and sherries, which contain 18% to 20% alcohol and loads of sugar.

Of course, this perversion of good taste has since been reversed, but oddly so. Each wine generation has been dramatically shorter than its predecessor: The first lasted almost 100 years (1825–1919), the second (after the break for Prohibition) only 30 years (1934–1965), and the third just 15 years (1966–1980). From hereon the path swerves from wine making to growing grapes, and necessarily slows down, as the Wine Country has—albeit cautiously—hit its stride.

THE FIRST GENERATION (1825–1919)   This fascinating period in wine making involves the entangling of a variety of ethnic groups over several generations: Spanish Fathers, native Americans, European immigrants (the first settlers in Napa and Sonoma were mostly Germanic, followed later by Italians and French), and Chinese (the main labor force; even today you can see the miles of stone walls they built and visit caves they carved out with picks). One of the major struggles of this generation involved breaking away from the grape variety used by the missions (and therefore called "Mission"), but only a few growers possessed such vision: Count Agoston Haraszthy at Buena Vista, T. Belden Crane and Charles Krug in St. Helena, Jacob Schram at Schramsberg (a historical monument now making champagne), and, later, Gustaf Niebaum at Inglenook (now Niebaum-Coppola).

Between 1870 and 1890, Sonoma and Napa wines won medals with some frequency in international competitions; most of the region's wines, however, were not even bottled at the wineries but rather sold in bulk to merchants, who often blended them badly. Not infrequently, they were even labeled with European names for sale on the East Coast! Regardless, these years laid a solid basis for a regional wine industry: In 1889, Sonoma could claim around 100 wineries, Napa around 140.

Unbeknownst to wine makers, however, a disaster was in the works. A plant louse the size of a pinhead, *phylloxera vastatrix*, began attacking vineyards in the 1880s. As a result, Napa lost roughly 75% of its acreage in the 1890s.

The Looming Shadow of Prohibition   The business managed to hold its own after the turn of the century, only to encounter a far more formidable foe—the cries of Carrie Nation and the Temperance Movement, whose Prohibition stance had been gaining ground with the moral majority in the last decades of the 19th century. Even in Napa, the Anti-Saloon League made inroads with voters as early as 1912, 7 years before Prohibition became a national fact. During this dry era, the number of wineries dwindled from 600 to a few remaining stragglers. (Ironically, the grape acreage *exploded* to satisfy the need for home wine makers across the country who could legally make 200 gallons per household. Unfortunately, the thick-skinned grape varieties that ship well in railcars do not make fine wine.)

THE SECOND GENERATION (1934–1965)   Whoopee! After 13 years of speakeasies, bathtub gin, and phony sherry, Americans could legally drink real wine!

Well, not at first. The few hundred entrepreneurs who rushed in to make a killing in wine found they had essentially no market, and quickly went bankrupt. Americans had almost no interest in dry European-style table wines. A few producers who had made wine during the last years of Prohibition and aged it throughout the Prohibition period had some success. Growers such as Louis Martini and Cesare Mondavi had survived and flourished by shipping their grapes to home winemakers (legal during prohibition), and were ready to start promoting their California wines in the late 1930s and early 1940s.

In trying to revive the wine business, one of the major battles was fought over varietal labeling—the labeling system we now take for granted that makes the name of the grape variety (cabernet sauvignon, chardonnay, and so on) the most important word on the label after the name of the producer. All through the 19th century and fully into the 1960s, huge volumes of wine were called Burgundy, Chablis, Chianti, Rhine Wine, and such, referring wistfully to some vague growing region or type of grape, and usually delivering wine that only accidentally resembled the stated product. One grower argued vociferously against the new labeling because if the law passed, he would have to actually put some Riesling grapes in his wine labeled "Riesling." To him, Riesling was just a style or a marketing tool. Who cared if it actually tasted like Riesling?

It was a pretty grim era for American wine making in general, and California's Wine Country wasn't fairing much better. In 1937, Napa had 37 wineries, while Sonoma was flush with 91. Collecting accurate statistics is a challenge, but apparently the number of Napa wineries decreased from 47 in 1945 to 25 in 1960. According to one source, only 12 wineries of those 25 made enough wine to sell outside of Napa County; the same source reports that Sonoma's count had dwindled to seven wineries in 1950 and grew only to nine by 1960. If these numbers are even close to reality, it's clear that recovery from Prohibition was painfully slow, backsliding a few times along the way.

Nonetheless, a handful of well-grounded wineries sailed through this sluggish period, and a few of their wines can still be appreciated today. Most came from Napa, including Inglenook, Beaulieu, Beringer, Christian Brothers, and Louis Martini. Sonoma, in contrast, had a stronger bulk wine-making tradition and a more casual attitude about the role of wine in the good life (subsequently, long-winded arguments have been—and probably always will be—held about the casual Italian-Sonoma approach versus the more northern-European, image-conscious, award-bent Napa approach).

Ironically, in recent years, Sonoma has been touting its ability to garner more gold medals. Whatever the significance of a wall festooned with ribbons and awards, Sonoma has certainly caught up with Napa when it comes to making fine wines.

THE THIRD GENERATION (1966–1980)   It's impossible to draw hard lines in the flow of time, but no other single event marks the modern era of wine making like Robert Mondavi's 1966 move away from Charles Krug, a family-owned winery since 1943, to found his own winery in Oakville. Joe Heitz had launched his own label in 1961 and, in Sonoma in 1959, James Zellerbach at tiny Hanzell had revived traditional Burgundian wine-making techniques. At around the same time, Peter Newton acquired the first land holdings for Sterling Vineyards. But unlike his peers in the field, Mondavi combined a push toward new wine-making technology with an aggressive marketing flair that has grown ever since, and now extends to several brands and international alliances.

Compared to previous generations of wine makers, third-generation vintners looked like grade-schoolers, a bunch of kid wine makers (many of whom were graduates of U.C. Davis or Fresno State) in their playgrounds filled with new toys: stainless-steel tanks, small oak barrels, a panoply of yeast cultures to ferment their wines, new vineyards planted to the best grape varieties, and, in several senses, the freedom to play and experiment. In 1972 and 1973, a remarkable cluster of wineries came on the Napa scene: Chateau

Montelena, Clos du Val, Burgess Cellars, Mt. Veeder Vineyards, Silver Oak, Caymus, Diamond Creek, Stag's Leap Wine Cellars, Carneros Creek, Franciscan, Silver Oak, Trefethen, Clos du Val, Stonegate, Joseph Phelps, and Domaine Chandon. These seasoned players now share a quarter of a century of wine-making experience—and the beginnings of a legacy.

In Sonoma Valley, Kenwood, Chateau St. Jean, and St. Francis all sprang up in the early 1970s. For these wineries, and the many that followed, the 1970s can be considered the decade that wine makers discovered their styles of wine. With all the new wine-making equipment and new vineyards, styles changed almost annually: one year a crisp, appley chardonnay with moderate oak; the next, a very fleshy, soft wine dominated by a heavy oak bouquet. In the third year, a third style. The poor consumer took a wild ride through these years, but as wine makers matured, their styles stabilized.

Napa and Sonoma had been often comparing their wines with international benchmarks, and favorably so. The French pooh-poohed the comparison; that is, until an English wine merchant staged a tasting in Paris in 1976. There, French wine experts on French soil gave top places in a blind tasting to the chardonnay from Chateau Montelena, as well as the cabernet from Stag's Leap Wine Cellars. The results shocked France and tickled the California Wine Country. At last, they were approaching the big leagues.

THE FOURTH GENERATION (1980–PRESENT)   The most recent phases of change in the Wine Country have been marked by signs of caution—both in the vineyard and in the marketplace—mingled with a few fantastic vintages. Since 1990, we have lived in a golden age of good vintages and astonishing sales, especially for more expensive wines ranging from $50 to $100 per bottle. Throughout the 1980s and 1990s, the number of new labels has grown steadily, as if there were no problems and never will be. Wine creates optimists, and always has.

Wine sales leveled off in the early 1980s, when both Napa and Sonoma vintners discovered that phylloxera, scourge louse of the 1880s and 1890s, had returned, requiring replanting of most acreage in both counties. (Actually, phylloxera was never really exterminated; it's permanently in the soil. Rather, the solution to fix the problem went awry.) The prospects of pulling out 70% to 80% of the vines hit growers and wineries hard, both emotionally and financially. A vineyard is a long-term investment, taking 30 to 40 years to fully mature—and that's only if nature, always a temperamental partner, behaves. Add to that the staggering costs—$20,000 to $25,000 per acre to plant a vineyard—and you'd best tell your banker you need another $2,000 per year per acre just to cover farming costs before you get a full crop in 4 or 5 years. Most growers worked out the financing; by the late 1990s, over half of the replanting had been finished. Now, with thousands of acres coming on stream, a few voices talk about overproduction. Welcome to the ever-cyclical wine business.

While Napa and Sonoma make both white wines and red wines extremely well, the 1990s have seen a breakthrough in the styling of reds, a higher level style change than those of the 1970s and early 1980s. Using a couple of techniques that you'll likely hear discussed on tours (for example, "presoaking" and "extended maceration"), wine makers are coming up with richly flavored wines that are supple and approachable, even when young. One enthusiast of the new style, Dennis Johns at St. Clement Vineyards, says he wants his red wines to be "sweet, round, and juicy, even in the barrel." Don't look for these wines to have true sweetness. The difference lies in their having a very fine grade of tannin, which in the past could make wines so puckery they went down like liquid nails. If a decade ago you were ever turned off by red wines, it's time to retaste—and hopefully, enjoy.

2 Wine Making 101

MAKING WINE

In the flush of today's golden age of California's Wine Country, one might forget that California, let alone Napa and Sonoma, did not invent wine. Credit for this discovery goes to a woman who probably lived around 7,000 years ago: At least one cultural anthropologist suggests that a food-gathering, cave-dwelling woman brought into her cave clusters of wild grapes and put them in a concavity on a rock ledge. Her child, or children, walked over them a few times (or, worse, sat on them), breaking open many berries. The busy cave keeper neglected the grapes for a few days. When she finally noticed the pool of juice (caves *are* dark, after all), it was frothing and giving off strange, but not unpleasant, aromas. It's hard to imagine why she would cup the juice in her hand and drink it, but she did—and it affected her most strangely. Let's assume it was pleasantly tasty, if not a little bit too sweet. In any case, she'd discovered wine—and

Sonoma and Napa, as well as the rest of the world, owe her a debt of gratitude.

Amazingly, her techniques saw only a few improvements in the next millennia. First, wine makers learned that wine must be stored in sealed containers—clay amphora or wooden barrels—or it spoils, turning into vinegar. Second, cool storage also prevents spoilage, hence the use of caves and cellars. The wines of the Greeks and Romans were probably as good, or as bad, as those made by monks in the Middle Ages, and only a bit improved by secular wine makers from the Renaissance to the Industrial Revolution.

The science called "enology," which has given the world the highest overall quality of wine ever, was developed after Louis Pasteur's work with fermentation and bacteriology around 150 years ago. Only in the last few generations have wine makers acquired very technical training and earned Ph.D.'s in viticulture (the science of grape growing) in a concentrated effort to understanding wine and vineyards.

Even with this recent development of science applied to wine, the catch phrase today for many wine makers in Sonoma and Napa is "I want the wine to make itself." The desired image is wine maker as midwife, whose role is to merely assist the mother (grape) in a very natural process—not much different from the cave dweller and her young assistants. It sounds so simple: 1) harvest ripe grapes; 2) put the juice from the grapes in a container with some yeast; 3) watch the juice ferment into wine; 4) clarify and age the new wine; and 5) drink!

Obviously, making wine is much more complex than that. From arguing about the very meaning of "ripe" to controlling the "ferment" in order to affect flavors and textures of the wine, the contemporary "natural" wine maker must incorporate his or her knowledge of fermentation, microbiology, and even such vagaries as the proper barrel (French, American, or Hungarian oak) for aging. These wine makers enjoy the powerful position of being able to make wine simply, naturally, and without spoilage simply because they know, scientifically, what can go wrong. Our cave dweller didn't have a clue.

On your tours of wineries, you'll hear differing stories about the "right" way to make wine, for each vintner harbors strong opinions—almost like a creed—on his or her wine styling. Be prepared for some inconsistencies; ferreting them out can be half the fun. To help you sort through the claims, here's a brief but broad sketch of the ABCs for making white wines, red wines, and sparkling wines.

WHITE WINES   For white wines, the wine maker wants only the juice from the grapes. (For red wines, both the juice and skins of the grapes are essential; using the white-wine–making technique, you can make a *white* wine from a *red-skinned* grape—white zinfandel, for example.) Grapes are picked either by hand or machine and brought to the winery as quickly as possible. Just as a sliced apple turns brown when left on the kitchen counter, grapes oxidize—and can even start fermenting—if not processed quickly. At some wineries, the clusters go through a "destemmer-crusher," which pops the berries off their stems and breaks them open (not really crushing them). The resulting mixture of juices, pulp, and seeds—called "must"—is pumped to a press. At other wineries, the whole clusters are put directly into a press (a new and widely used technique called, logically, "whole cluster pressing").

Most presses these days use an inflatable member, like a balloon, and gently use air pressure to separate the skins from the juice, which is then pumped into fermenting vessels. In the recent past, most white wines were fermented in stainless-steel tanks fitted with cooling jackets. Cool, even cold, fermentations preserve the natural fruitiness of white grapes. More recently, many Napa and Sonoma producers have begun using small wooden barrels for fermentation of white wines, especially chardonnay. This practice reverts to old-style French wine-making techniques, and captures, so it's believed, fragrances, flavors, and textures not possible in stainless steel. Barrel fermentation is labor intensive (each only holds 45 to 50 gal. for fermentation), and the barrels are expensive ($600 to $700 each for French barrels, $250 to $300 for American barrels).

After white wines are fermented, they are clarified, aged (if appropriate), and bottled, usually before the next harvest. For the simpler white wines—chenin blanc, Riesling, and some sauvignon blancs—bottling occurs in the late winter or early spring. Most sauvignon blancs and chardonnays go into the bottle during the summer after the harvest. A few white wines, mostly chardonnays, take the slow track and enjoy 15 to 18 months of aging in small barrels with prolonged aging on the lees, the sediments from the primary fermentation. Those treatments are unusual, but they produce chardonnays that are richly flavored, complex, and expensive.

RED WINES   The chief difference between white wines and red wines lies simply in the red pigment that's lodged in the skins of the wine grapes. So while for white wines the juice is quickly pressed away from the skins, for rosés and reds the pressing happens after the right amount of "skin contact." That can be anywhere from 6 hours—yielding a rosé or very light red—to 6 weeks, producing a red that has extracted all the pigment from the skins and additionally refined the tannin naturally occurring in grape skins and seeds.

Almost all red wines are aged in barrels or casks for at least several months, occasionally for as long as 3 years. In the past, casks in California were usually made from redwood and were quite large (5,000 gal. to 25,000 gal.). Only a few wineries still use redwood today. Most of the wooden containers—collectively called "cooperage"—are barrels now made of American or French oak, holding roughly 60 gallons each.

The aging of red wines plays an important role in their eventual style, because several aspects of the wine change while in wood. First, the wine picks up oak fragrances and flavors (yes, it is possible to "overoak" a wine). Second, the wine, which comes out of the fermenter murky with suspended yeast cells and bits of skin, clarifies as the particulate material settles to the bottom of the barrel. Third, the texture of the wine changes as puckery compounds called "tannins" interact and round off, making the wine more supple. Deciding just when each wine in the cellar is ready to bottle challenges the wine maker every year. And, to make the whole process even more challenging, every year is different.

Unlike white wines, which are usually ready to drink shortly after bottling, many of the best red wines will improve with aging in the bottle. Napa and Sonoma cabernet sauvignons, for example, often reach a plateau (try not to think "peak") of best drinking condition that ranges from 7 to 12 years after the vintage, the year that appears on the label. However, there are no rigid rules. Some self-proclaimed cabernet freaks prefer their reds rather rough and ready. Only by tasting, tasting, tasting will you find your own comfort zone. Such a trial!

SPARKLING WINE & CHAMPAGNE   In Sonoma and Napa, sparkling wine plays the role of a serious specialty—serious enough to have drawn major investments from four of the best-known French houses from Champagne as well as two from Spain, in addition to 10 or 12 local producers.

Whether the bubbly wine in the fancily dressed bottle is called "sparkling wine" or "champagne" (it *is* legal for wineries in America to call their product "champagne," though it galls the French, pun intended), the key to the pervasive high quality of all these wineries lies in their using the *méthode champenoise* as their production technique. In Champagne, it takes the form of step-by-step regulations that, for the most part, codify practices learned by trial and error for making the best wine. Those regulations have no force here, but the best producers follow most of them and put the words "méthode champenoise" on their labels. For quality assurance, those are the words to look for (as opposed to "bulk" or "Charmat" process).

There is no better way to understand the fascinatingly intricate "champagne method" than to see it firsthand, to walk through the process with a knowledgeable guide. The harvest begins in August in Napa and Sonoma with the picking of pinot noir, chardonnay, pinot blanc, and pinot meunier, the grape varieties of Champagne. The grapes are picked a bit underripe by "still" (nonbubbly) wine standards, both to retain crispness and to avoid excessive body and flavors. The grapes are then pressed and the juice fermented into plain—austere, in fact—still white wines. That takes 2 weeks. By November and December, the new wines (each variety and vineyard kept as a separate lot) are clear, or "bright."

Now the wine makers *really* go to work, because they need to blend the new wines in preparation for a second fermentation—this one taking place right in the bottle, the very bottle that eventually comes to your table. That's how we get the bubbles!

The second fermentation takes 4 to 6 weeks. After that, we have primitive champagne, 90 to 100 pounds per square inch of carbon dioxide (CO_2) in each bottle. And we also have a yeasty sediment in each bottle. That's a bit of a mess and must be cleaned up eventually. But for now—and perhaps for as long as 3 to 7 years—it's a benign mess. Yeast plays two virtuous roles in making sparkling wine: first, it produces the bubbles; second, as the dead yeast cells decompose over time (yuk!), they release flavor products that give sparkling wines made by méthode champenoise their special fragrances and flavors. The amount and depth of flavor varies widely from producer to producer. Each house has its own style, light or heavy, and tries to replicate it each year. That's why people say, "I'm a Mumm drinker," or "I'm a fan of Krug."

Making fine sparkling wine, and making it well, constitutes the ultimate wine-making challenge. The general rule among wine makers is that great white wines and great red wines are derived mostly from their place of origin: the right grape planted in the right soil and right climate. Sparkling wine involves artifice and finesse at every step, making it all the more remarkable that we drink it so freely, at times even carelessly. But the producers wouldn't have it any other way—if only we would drink more of it.

GROWING GRAPES

Somehow wine making seems much more glamorous than growing grapes. Growing grapes is farming; it's dusty and hard manual labor. In contrast, wine making is almost ethereal (except for rolling and stacking barrels around and hosing grape skins out of the press).

In truth, most wine makers in Sonoma and Napa spend more time in the vineyards than at the winery. It took 20 or 30 years to learn that quality starts, absolutely, in the vineyard, and that the wine maker can do nothing to compensate for bad fruit. There's simply so much to learn about wine making that decisions can be revised, even reversed, annually; not so with vineyard decisions.

MODERN GROWING AS GARDENING   Just as wine makers had worked their way up the learning curve for wine making, and as winery owners had turned to acquiring vineyards as the next source of quality control, everyone in the Wine Country learned that the *phylloxera vastatrix*, a soil-based plant louse, would be wiping out most of the vineyards, just as it had done a century ago, first in Europe and then in California (for more on this, see "A Look at the Past" earlier in this chapter). The "fix" was to plant rootstocks that resisted phylloxera and to graft desirable grape varieties above the soil, which worked for several decades.

Unfortunately, it seems that the choice for the principal rootstock was somewhat vulnerable, or phylloxera mutated and developed new appetites, or perhaps a combination of both occurred. Since the mid-1980s, replanting has been a major focus, almost a preoccupation. In hindsight, phylloxera might be seen as a small (but enormously expensive) blessing. It has indeed refocused our attention to the soil; it's no exaggeration to say that today much of the excitement in Napa and Sonoma lies in the vineyards. And we're showing that farming here isn't agribusiness; rather, it could almost be called microfarming. Warren Winiarski, founder of Stag's Leap Wine Cellars, eloquently insists that for himself and the others in Napa, grape growing is not agriculture, it's horticulture—gardening.

As you drive through Sonoma and Napa, you'll pass hundreds of experimental "gardens." If you look closely at the shape of the vines, the density of the planting, the height of the trellis system, even the orientation to the compass, you'll perceive a playground in the earth just as the wine makers of the 1970s had a playground of fancy wine-making toys. It's too early to assess the results of this replanting, but the "silver lining" attitude common to farming sees higher grape quality than ever, and thus higher wine quality.

CLIMATE CONTROL   Because you will visit the Wine Country for a day or two in one particular season, you might want to know how the Wine Country looks in other seasons. While the climate is benign, the changes from season to season still have a drama about them. In the winter, the rainy season in Mediterranean climates, the nights can be cold, dropping to 30°F to 40°F, but a sunny winter day sees highs in the 60s—picnic weather if you're wearing a light wool sweater.

Winter also can be confused with spring elsewhere. Camellias might bloom on New Year's Day, azaleas shortly thereafter, along with the blue and yellow acacias. From December through April, the vines are dormant, stark outlines of trunks and arms, but the valley floors and hillside are lush green with common weeds and a few seeded ground covers. One of the common weeds is mustard: In good years, you'll find acres and acres of bright-yellow mustard, celebrated each season with the Napa Valley Mustard Festival.

The vines burst from dormancy in mid-March for the earliest varieties (chardonnay, pinot noir, gewürztraminer) and in April for the later blooming varieties (cabernet sauvignon, zinfandel). The growth is rapid, sometimes almost an inch a day. Until mid-May, there's a danger of frost. By late May and early June, the new shoots, called "canes," have grown 3 or 4 feet in length; flower clusters start to blossom. The success of the "bloom and set," as it's called, makes for some nervous moments: uncontrollable elements such as hot weather and rain can compromise the crop. But, especially compared with the vagaries of weather in continental Europe, the benign Mediterranean weather goes sour only occasionally.

In midsummer, usually around late July, the first signs of color show up in red grape varieties, a pretty blush at first that in a couple weeks becomes a deep purple, a sure sign that the grapes are ripening. White grapes change from a lime green to a golden green as they ripen. They get delectably sweeter and sweeter until the wine maker decides they are ripe for the picking, as the saying goes.

From August through October, you will likely witness every available hand in the Wine Country harvesting the grapes. For a single vineyard it takes only a day—perhaps just a few hours—to pick the grapes, since they need to be as fresh and cool as possible. Once the grapes are harvested, the vines hopefully have the chance to grow for a few more weeks, now storing energy in the form of carbohydrates that will sustain them to the next spring.

After cold nights in November and December, the first winter rains knock and blow the vibrant-colored leaves off the vines, which then go dormant until March and April, when they'll start the cycle again.

THE LIFE OF THE VINE   Unless soil problems or vineyard pests intervene, a vineyard should have a commercial life of 30 to 40 years. In Sonoma, a number of producing vineyards are approaching the 100-year mark, and though the quantity of the harvest falls off in old vines, the quality seems to improve. As the Italian proverb goes, "You plant a vineyard for your son; you plant an olive grove for your grandson." Regardless of the latest technological advances in viticulture, vineyards will not be rushed—which gives much-needed consolation to grape growers, and a sense of permanence to the Wine Country.

3   How to Wine-Taste Like a Pro

Stopping at tasting rooms to sample the goods, otherwise known as wine tasting, ranks as one of the top rituals in Wine Country touring. It provides pleasure for everyone, as well as the chance to learn why the wines of Sonoma and Napa rank high among the wines of the world.

Precautionary notes would say "taste moderately," for there are literally 200 or so tasting rooms, and the virtues in wine take time to notice. Most of the attendants in tasting rooms know that, generally speaking, Americans drink very little wine (20% of the population drinks over 80% of the wine consumed). Because we're all on a very pleasant learning curve, our goal as wine educators is to help you discover wine at many levels. If you should encounter a winery staffer with "attitude" (unfortunately, it happens), don't buy *any* of that wine and simply move on to the next stop.

The time-honored techniques for tasting wine involve three steps: a good look, a good smell, and a good sip of each wine. You'll learn about wine most quickly if you compare them, ideally side by side. Almost any comparison will reveal features of wines you might not see by tasting one wine at a time. You might think of it as the wines talking to one another ("I'm smoother than you are"; "I'm way more puckery than all of you"). By listening to these little conversations, you can discover just how smooth or how puckery you want your wines to be. Tasting rooms in Napa and Sonoma have their own regimens, usually offering a series of wines; when it seems appropriate, and when the tasting room is not too busy, ask your host if you can do some comparisons.

THE VISUALS OF WINE

Take a moment to look at the wine for its clarity and for its hue. With just a couple of glances, you'll see that red wines reveal many shades of red: ruby, garnet, purple, and variations. White wines also differ in hue, from white gold to straw to dark gold, sometimes laced with a light green. For the most part, wines ought to be clear, even brilliant, though a few unfiltered wines now bear a light haze as a badge of courage that says, "I was not heavily filtered." (Filtration for clarification is standard practice and benign if not overdone.)

Color can be a sign of a wine's condition, of its health, even of its age. White wines that show any browning might be going "over the hill" and have a musty, baked smell. Red wines that show a lot of rusty red might also be past their prime, while reds that show a lot of purple are probably young.

THE AROMAS & BOUQUET OF WINE

Some wine professionals will tell you the olfactory aspect of wine is more important than the taste. Saner heads remind you that wine is a *beverage,* not a perfume; it comes home to rest in the mouth. It's true that our noses work better as tools of perception than our mouths. We can smell several thousand scents, but can taste only four: sweet, sour, bitter, and salty. But it's also true that we are smelling the wine (via the retro nasal passages) when it passes through our mouths.

A decently shaped wineglass will direct a lot of aromas to your nose. Swirling the glass helps excite the fragrances. Comparing the "nose" of two or three wines can be very revealing, but possibly a bit frustrating, too: You "see" differences with your nose, but might stumble when you try to describe them. The words are on the tip of your tongue, if there at all. What comes to mind may seem silly: "apple," "coconut," "cherries," "mushrooms," "dirt," "cheese," and the like.

If this is the case, then you've hit the Wall of Wine Tasting: **vocabulary.** It's not easy to describe the fragrances and flavors in wine. We are mostly reduced to similes and metaphors, to comparing wines with more familiar substances. A lot of wine writing is inadvertently humorous; some of it qualifies as bad poetry. That's neither your fault *nor* the fault of the wine. We must simply get over the inadequacies of language to describe wine—and get on with our tasting. Have fun with your verbal fantasies!

For all the ambiguity in wine descriptors, the words "aroma" and "bouquet" do possess widely recognized, distinct meanings (though on the street we use them almost interchangeably). **Aroma** points to the characteristic smell of the various grape varieties, which can be quite distinct. Just as you would probably not confuse a Pippin apple with a Golden Delicious, once you are familiar with sauvignon blanc, it will not remind you of chardonnay. **Bouquet,** in the academy of wine, refers to fragrances that come from sources other than the grapes, such as the vanillalike fragrance of French oak.

During your trip to the Wine Country, you can learn the basics of aroma simply by comparing a sauvignon blanc side by side with a chardonnay. Or, in terms of bouquet, a younger cabernet beside an older cabernet. Not every tasting room will be able to arrange all the comparisons, but you will find many opportunities.

THE TASTE OF WINE

Tasting wine—literally putting it through our mouths—can be seen as something quite different from *drinking* other beverages. (Of course, we can drink wine, too. Indeed, *most* of the time we should just drink wine.) Tasting, as opposed to drinking, has built-in dynamics. In fact, it helps to focus on the wine moving through the mouth: something that happens in a measured sequence, like listening to a musical phrase. It's not like taking a snapshot—"Click, I've got it."

One of the legendary tasters in California at the turn of the century, Henry Lachman, merchant and international judge of wines, wrote a monograph in which he discussed each sip of wine as having "a first taste, a second taste, and the good-bye." That's a cute way of dealing with the physiology of our mouths: In the front of the mouth we **taste for sweetness** and **feel the body** of the wine; in the middle we find **acidity** and the **flavors** of the grape; and in the back, the **finish** or "good-bye," which can be long or short, supple or astringent. Imagine a tasting as having checkpoints in your mouth: front, middle, and back.

In the abstract, wine dynamics sound odd. With practice, however, especially as you compare the taste of two or three wines, they become obvious, and the observational skills quite easy to pick up. After you see how a wine can be full and lush in the front of your mouth, then turn fresh and tasty, and finally linger nicely (or fail to linger), it remains for you to decide what "shapes" you prefer in your wines.

Red wines in particular show fairly clear **shapes.** One of the additional challenges in tasting red wines lies in knowing that the shape changes with age. Rough, puckery young red wines can age into supple, subtly flavorful, pleasing liquids. Which red wines will age well and over what period of time is, again, something you can learn by comparison. It's best done by arranging a "vertical" tasting: several vintages of the same wine. ("Horizontal" tastings are several producers tasted from the same vintage.) Even three to five wines from vintages spread over, say, 10 years will give you a good idea of how much age you want to have on your red wines. Tasting rooms often have "Reserve" wines or "Library" wines that you can acquire for tasting.

Tastings of several wines—either vertical or horizontal tastings—make for marvelous evenings of gourmandizing when you return home. Have a few friends over to taste the wines "blind" (without labels visible). Get everyone's preference. Then sit down to dinner and finish them off, now with the labels in full view. Inevitably, opinions will change, often in amusing reversals.

It's up to you to decide how seriously you want to engage the Wine Country. If it's a first visit, consider it an introduction. You can't do it all in a single visit, of course, which is all the more reason to schedule a return trip to the Wine Country.

Finally, two important tips for a healthy day in the Wine Country: Be moderate in your wine tasting and generous in drinking water. Cheers!

4 The Chief Grape Varieties

by Erika Lenkert and Matthew R. Poole

CABERNET SAUVIGNON   This transplant from Bordeaux has become California's most well-known varietal. The small, deep-colored, thick-skinned berry is a complex grape, yielding medium- to full-bodied red wines that are highly tannic when young and usually require a long aging period to achieve their greatest potential. Cabernet is often blended with other related red varieties, such as merlot and cabernet franc (see below), into full-flavored red table wines. Cabernet, whose most distinctive character is a lush black-currant aroma, is best matched with red-meat dishes and strong cheeses. If you're looking to invest in several cases of wine, cabernet sauvignon is always a good long-term bet.

CHARDONNAY   Chardonnay is the most widely planted grape variety in the Wine Country, producing exceptional medium- to full-bodied dry white wines. In fact, is was a California chardonnay that revolutionized the world of wine when it won the legendary Paris tasting test of 1976, beating out France's top white burgundies. You'll find a range of chardonnays in the Wine Country, from delicate and crisp wines that are clear and light in color to buttery, fruity, and oaky (no other wine benefits more from the oak aging process) wines that tend to deeper golden hues as they increase in richness. This highly complex and aromatic grape is one of the few grapes in the world that doesn't require blending; it's also the principle grape for making sparkling wine. Chardonnay goes well with a variety of dishes, from seafood to poultry, pork, veal, and pastas made with cream and/or butter.

CHENIN BLANC   Mainly planted in France, chenin blanc runs the gamut from cheap, dry whites with little discernible character to some of the most subtle, fragrant, and complex whites in the world. In the Wine Country, the grape is mostly used to create fruity, light- to medium-bodied and slightly sweet wines. Chenin blanc lags far behind chardonnay and sauvignon blanc in popularity here, though in good years it's known for developing a lovely and complex bouquet, particularly when aged in oak. It's often served with pork and poultry, Oriental dishes with soy-based sauces, mild cheeses, and vegetable and fruit salads.

MERLOT   Traditionally used as a blending wine to smooth out the rough edges of other grapes, merlot has gained popularity in California since the early 1970s—enough so that wineries such as Sonoma's St. Francis are best known for producing masterful merlots. The merlot grape is a relative of cabernet sauvignon, but it's fruitier and softer with a pleasant black-cherry bouquet. Merlots tend to be simpler and less tannic than most cabernets and drinkable at an earlier age, though these wines, too, gain complexity with age. Serve this medium- to full-bodied red with any dish you'd normally pair with a cabernet (it's great with pizza).

PINOT NOIR   It has taken California vintners decades to make relatively few great wines from pinot-noir grapes, which are difficult to grow and vinify. Even in their native Burgundy, the wines are excellent only a few years out of every decade, and are a challenge for wine makers to master. Recent attempts to grow the finicky grape in the cooler climes of the Carneros District have met with promising results. During banner harvest years, California's pinot grapes produce complex, light- to medium-bodied red wines with such low tannins and such silky textures that they're comparable to the finest reds in the world. Pinots are fuller and softer than cabernets and can be drinkable at 2 to 5 years of age, though the best will improve with additional aging. Pinot noir is versatile at the dinner table, but goes best with lamb, duck, turkey, game birds, and semisoft cheeses.

RIESLING Also called Johannisberg Riesling or white Riesling, this is the grape from which most of the great wines of Germany are made. It was introduced to California in the mid-19th century by immigrant vintners and is now used mainly to produce floral and fruity white wines of light to medium body, ranging from dry to very sweet (it's often used to make late-harvest dessert wine). Well-made Rieslings, of which California has produced few, have a vivid fruitiness and lively balancing acidity, as well as a potential to age for many years. Suggested food pairings include crab, pork, sweet-and-sour foods, and anything with a strong citrus flavor.

SAUVIGNON BLANC Also labeled as **fumé blanc,** sauvignon blanc grapes are used to make crisp, dry whites of medium to light body that vary in flavor from slightly grassy to tart or fruity. The grape grows very well in the Wine Country, and has become increasingly popular due to its distinctive character and pleasant acidity; indeed, it has recently become a contender to the almighty chardonnay. California's premier maker of sauvignon blanc (at least in our opinion) is Napa's Grgich Hills. Because of their acidity, sauvignon blancs pair well with shellfish, seafood, salads, olive oil–based dishes, and vegetarian cuisine.

ZINFANDEL Zinfandel is often called the "mystery" grape because its origins are uncertain. The first "Zinfandel" label appeared on California labels in the late 1800s; hence, it has come to be known as California's grape. In fact, most of the world's zinfandel acreage is planted in the Napa Valley, though the best zinfandel grapes grow in cool coastal locations. Zinfandel is by far the Wine Country's most versatile grape, popular as blush wine (the ever-quaffable **white zinfandel,** a lighter, more fruity wine, usually served chilled), as dark, spicy, and fruity red wines, and even as a port. Premium zins, such as those crafted by Ravenswood winery in Sonoma (the Wine Country's Zeus of Zins), are rich and peppery, with a lush texture and nuances of raspberries, licorice, and spice. Food-wise it's a free-for-all, though premium zins go well with beef, lamb, venison, hearty pastas, pizza, and stews.

Here are also a few lesser-known grape varieties that you might encounter as you explore the Wine Country. In addition to these, California's wine makers are beginning to experiment with a number of French varietals from the Rhône region and the Italian **sangiovese** grape with some success.

CABERNET FRANC   A French black grape variety that's often blended with and overshadowed by the more widely planted cabernet sauvignon, cabernet franc was actually recently discovered to be one of the parent grape species that gave rise to cabernet sauvignon. The grape grows best in cooler, damper climatic conditions and tends to be lighter in color and tannins than cabernet sauvignon and therefore matures earlier in the bottle; these wines have a deep purple color with a herbaceous aroma.

GEWÜRZTRAMINER   The gewürztraminer grape produces white wines with a strong floral aroma and lychee nut–like flavor. Slightly sweet yet spicy, it's somewhat similar in style to the Johannisberg Riesling, and is occasionally used to make late-harvest dessert-style wine. The grape grows well in the cooler coastal regions of California, particularly Mendocino County.

PETITE SIRAH   Widely grown throughout the warmer regions of California, petite sirah's origins remain a mystery. The grape, which produces rich red wines high in tannins, serves mainly as the backbone for Central Valley "jug" wines. Very old vines still exist in cooler northern regions, where the grapes are often made into a robust and well-balanced red wine of considerable popularity.

PINOT BLANC   A mutation of the pinot-gris vine, the pinot-blanc grape is generally grown in France's Alsace region to make dry, crisp white wines. In California, pinot blanc is used to make a fruity wine similar to the simpler versions of chardonnay. It's also blended with champagne-style sparkling wines thanks to its acid content and clean flavor.

3

Planning a Trip to the Wine Country

*I*n the pages that follow, we've compiled everything you need to know to plan your trip—how to get there, the best times to go, how much you can expect to spend, strategies for touring the region, and more. If you're visiting from outside the United States, be sure to check out the "For Foreign Visitors" section for entry requirements and other pertinent information.

1 Visitor Information

There's so much to see and do in the Wine Country that it's best to familiarize yourself with what's available before you start your trip. Both Napa and Sonoma offer very informative visitor guides that provide information on everything each valley has to offer.

The slick, comprehensive *Napa Valley Guide* includes listings and photos of hotels, restaurants, and hundreds of wineries, as well as hours of operation, tasting fees, and picnicking information. The **Napa Valley Conference and Visitors Bureau,** 1310 Town Center Mall, Napa, CA 94559 (☎ **707/226-7459**), offers a $10 package that includes the guide plus a bunch of brochures, a map, a *Four Perfect Days in The Wine Country Itinerary,* and hot-air balloon discount coupons. If you want less to recycle, call **Vintage Publications,** 760 Adobe Dr., Santa Rosa, CA 95404 (☎ **800/651-8953**), to mail-order just the guide ($6, plus $3 for shipping within the U.S.). If you don't want to pay the bucks for the official publications, point your browser to **www.napavalley.com/nvcvb.html**, the NVCVB's official site, which has lots of the same information for free.

Like the town itself, the *Sonoma Valley Visitors Guide* is far less fancy—no glossy photos, and far less information. But the free pocket-size booklet does offer important lodging, winery, and restaurant details; contact the **Sonoma Valley Visitors Bureau,**

10 E. Spain St., Sonoma, CA 95476 (☎ **707/996-1090**), to order one, or check out their website at **www.sonomavalley.com**.

2 When to Go

THE SEASONS   The beauty of the valley is striking at any time of the year, but it's most memorable in **September** and **October,** when the grapes are being pressed and the wineries are in full production. Another great time to come is **spring,** when the mustard flowers are in full bloom and the tourist season is just starting; you'll find less traffic, fewer crowds at the wineries and restaurants, and better deals on hotel rooms. While **winter** promises the best budget rates and few crowds, it often comes with chilly days and the threat of rain; the valleys, while still lovely, temporarily lose some of their picturesqueness as miles of bare vines lay dormant over the cold months. **Summer?** Say hello to hot weather and lots of traffic.

THE CLIMATE   While the valleys claim a year-round average temperature of 70°F, if you come with a suitcase packed with T-shirts and shorts during the holiday season, you're likely to shiver your way to the nearest department store to stock up on winter clothes. In summer, rent a car without air-conditioning, and you're liable to want to make a pit-stop at every hotel swimming pool you pass. And don't let that morning fog and those early cool temperatures fool you; on most days, come noon, that big o' ball of flames in the sky sends down plenty of rays to bless the vineyards and your picnic spot. For the most comfortable experience no matter what time of year, dress in layers and keep in mind that the temperature can drop dramatically at night.

Seasonal Temperatures

	Spring (Mar–May)	Summer (June–Aug)	Fall (Sept–Nov)	Winter (Dec–Feb)
Average Highs (in °F)	78	92	85	72
Average Lows (in °F)	64	81	74	61

Packing Tip

If you're visiting the Wine Country between December and March, be sure to pack an umbrella and a pair of durable walking shoes. The rainy season isn't usually fierce, but it is wet—and you won't want to trudge the unpaved winery pathways in your new Ferragamos.

Festivities to Plan Your Trip Around: The Wine Country's Best Annual Events

A few years back, February and March were considered the slow season in Napa. So, to drum up interest in visiting the valley, the **Napa Valley Mustard Festival** was born. The idea was to celebrate the blossom of the mustard flowers that coat the valley and mountains with their rich yellow petals—and, of course, to generate a few dollars along the way. The result is 6 weeks' worth of events ranging from a kick-off gourmet gala featuring more than a dozen local restaurants at the CIA Greystone to a wine auction, golf benefit, recipe and photography competition, and plenty of food and wine celebrations. For information or a schedule of events, call ☎ **707/259-9020,** point your browser to **www.winery.com/ mustardfest**, or write to P.O. Box 3603, Yountville, CA 94599.

The **Napa Valley Wine Auction,** held each June, is the area's most renowned event. The annual charity affair brings close to 2,000 deep-pocketed wine aficionados to the Napa area. The schedule includes a weekend of culinary events, barrel tastings, a live auction, and a vintners' ball. But don't pack your bags yet: tickets to the event are $1,500 per couple—and they sell out every year. For information, call ☎ **707/942-9783.**

One of our favorite festivals in the Sonoma Valley is the **Heart of the Valley Barrel Tasting,** held in late March. This event, born 8 years ago to give the public a glimpse of Sonoma Valley's finest

3 Money Matters

WHAT THINGS COST IN THE WINE COUNTRY

North America's recent economic prosperity has made wine drinkers and high-lifers feel like celebrating again—and northern California's Wine Country is one of their favorite places to do it. Unfortunately, the region's ever-growing popularity has resulted in its well-founded reputation as one of the most expensive vacation destinations in the state. Nowadays, because hotels are booked almost year-round, innkeepers have the confidence to charge an average of $180 a night in Napa Valley, and things aren't much cheaper in the less touristy towns of Sonoma. It's gotten to the point where a charmless motel or a basic B&B can easily get $150 a night for a room.

And that's just the beginning. If you want to eat in any of the more renowned dining spots, you can pretty much count on

future releases, has since turned into a 2-day-long fiesta of barbecues, food parings, demonstrations, and all the world-class wine
you can drink—all for only $25 a ticket. For details and this year's
schedule, call the St. Francis Winery at ☎ 707/833-4666.

Sonoma Valley's other major celebration is the **Vintage Festival,** held the last weekend in September at Sonoma's central plaza.
This is a real blowout of a party, complete with live music, danc-
ing, parades, arts-and-crafts shows, and—of course—copious
amounts of wine tasting. Earlier in summer, Gundlach-Bundschu
Winery presents its annual **Shakespeare Festival,** held Friday
through Sunday from Memorial Day through Labor Day. You're
encouraged to bring a blanket and picnic basket to the winery's
outdoor amphitheater, which is set in a beautiful wooded area
surrounded by vineyards; call the winery at ☎ 707/938-5277 for
this year's schedule.

For more information on these and other Sonoma Valley events,
contact the **Sonoma Valley Visitors Bureau** at ☎ 707/996-1090,
or check out their website at **www.sonomavalley.com**. If you want
to find out what's going on in the Napa Valley when you're in
town, contact the **Napa Valley Conference and Visitors Bureau**
at ☎ 707/226-7459, or point your browser to **www.napavalley.
com/nvcvb.html**.

throwing down at least $30 per person just for food—not includ-
ing even one glass of wine. And don't even think of stepping foot
in a high-end haunt like the French Laundry without at least $70
per person to burn—and we're just talking lunch.

Is that cash register ringing in your head yet? Well, keep the tab
open, 'cuz there's more. While some wineries offer free wine tastings,
many—particularly in the Napa Valley—charge between $2 and $6;
Niebaum-Coppola charges a whopping $7.50 per person. Stop by
three or four in a day and—cha-ching!—they start to add up. Of
course, you'll also want to buy a few bottles of your favorite vino.
Cha-ching, cha-ching, cha-ching—it just keeps going. We're not
telling you this to try to scare you away from the Wine Country; we
just want you to know what to expect.

MONEY-SAVING TIPS   If you're starting to think that you just
can't afford a Wine Country visit, don't despair yet: There are a few

things you can do to keep your costs down and still enjoy the region to its fullest.

If you're on a budget, be sure to reserve your accommodations months in advance to secure the cheapest room; don't expect much more than a clean room and bed, and you won't be disappointed—but you're not planning to hang out in your room anyway, right? Other money-saving tips:

- Travel between December and March, when accommodations rates are at their lowest. Stay at a place whose rates include breakfast and afternoon hors d'oeuvres, which will save you big bucks on dining out.

- Visit wineries that don't charge to taste; plenty of wineries are happy to get you drunk without asking you for even one hard-earned cent.

- If you want to dine at one of the Wine Country's more expensive restaurants, have a late lunch there and make it the day's biggest meal. The lunch menu is often served until mid-afternoon, and main courses usually cost several dollars less than the same dishes do at dinner.

- There's no better place to picnic than the Wine Country. Stop at a grocery or gourmet shop—each valley has lots of wonderful ones, which we've recommended in the chapters that follow—and pick up the picnic fixings for breakfast, lunch, or dinner. Head to one of the fabulous picnic spots we recommend, pop the cork on a bottle you've picked up in your travels, and you've got the perfect alfresco feast—for a fraction of what it would cost you to eat in a restaurant.

- Buy wines not from the wineries, but from local wineshops. Believe it or not, prices in the shops are better, and they're likely to have that extrabuttery chardonnay or that perfectly balanced merlot that you fell in love with earlier in the day in stock. In Sonoma, your best bet is the **Wine Exchange,** on the plaza at 452 First St. E. (☎ **707/938-1794**), which boasts more than 700 domestic wines and a remarkably savvy staff. In Napa, head to St. Helena, where both **Dean & DeLuca,** 607 S. Main St. (☎ **707/967-9980**), and **Safeway,** 1026 Hunt Ave. (☎ **707/ 963-3850**), have enormous wine selections; Safeway tends to offer some of the best deals around.

LIVING THE HIGH LIFE   If you're not on a budget, we recommend you go for broke. Reserve a room at one of Napa's or

Sonoma's fabulous luxury resorts, such as St. Helena's Auberge du Soleil or the Kenwood Inn & Spa, and schedule massages twice a day; gorge yourself in gourmet fashion at the French Laundry, Pinot Blanc, and Tra Vigne; and drink yourself silly. The Wine Country may be hyped, but not without justification—there may be no place in the country that's more conducive to luxurious living.

PAYING YOUR WAY

Banks throughout the Napa and Sonoma valleys have automated teller machines **(ATMs)**, which accept cards connected to networks like Cirrus and Plus. For specific ATM locations, call ☎ **800/424-7787** for the Cirrus network, ☎ **800/843-7587** for the Plus system. You also can locate Cirrus ATMs on the Web at **www.mastercard.com**, and Plus ATMs at **www.visa.com**.

Of course, U.S.-dollar **traveler's checks** are still the safest way to carry currency—Visa and American Express are the kinds most widely accepted. Wine Country businesses are pretty good about taking traveler's checks, but you're better off cashing them in at a bank (in small amounts, of course) and paying in cash. *Remember:* You'll need identification, such a driver's license or passport, to change a traveler's check. And be sure to record the numbers of the checks, and keep that information separate from your checks in the unlikely event that they get lost or stolen. Note that there are no American Express offices in either valley.

Rather than fussing with traveler's checks, it's easier to just use **credit cards**—most notably American Express, MasterCard, and Visa—which are almost as good as cash and are accepted in most Wine Country establishments. Also, ATMs will make cash advances against MasterCard and Visa cards; make sure you have your PIN (personal identification number) with you.

4 Getting There

BY PLANE

Commercial planes don't fly into Napa's private airport, so unless you're traveling by corporate jet, your best bet is to fly into either **San Francisco International Airport (SFO)**, which is 60 minutes away by car, or **Oakland International Airport (OAK)**, which is 45 miles south of Napa. It's pretty much the same deal for Sonoma; though **United Express** (☎ **800/241-6522**) accesses the Santa Rosa Airport (a few miles north of Sonoma) via San Francisco, you don't save time—or money—by taking the additional flight.

Both SFO and OAK airports are serviced by the following major domestic airlines:

Airline	Phone number	Web address
Alaska Airlines	☎ 800/426-0333	www.alaskaair.com
American Airlines	☎ 800/433-7300	www.americanair.com
America West Airlines	☎ 800/235-9292	www.americawest.com
Continental Airlines	☎ 800/525-0280	www.flycontinental.com
Delta Air Lines	☎ 800/221-1212	www.delta-air.com
Northwest Airlines	☎ 800/225-2525	www.nwa.com
Southwest Airlines	☎ 800/435-9792	iflyswa.com
TWA	☎ 800/221-2000	www2.twa.com
United Airlines	☎ 800/241-6522	www.ual.com
US Airways	☎ 800/428-4322	www.usair.com

Regardless of which airport you fly into, you should rent a car and drive to the Wine Country (see "By Car", below, for driving directions). Although for $15 you can hitch a ride to Napa Valley from SFO with **Evans Airport Service** (☎ **707/255-1559**), and the **Sonoma Airporter** (☎ **707/938-4246**) offers door-to-door service six times daily from SFO to hotels and inns in most areas of Sonoma, there's no public transportation in either valley, which makes it almost impossible to explore the region without wheels.

RENTING A CAR   All the major companies have desks at the airports. Currently, you can get a compact car for about $170 a week, including all taxes and other charges (but remember that rates are always subject to change). Some of the national car-rental companies operating in San Francisco include:

Airline	Phone number	Web address
Alamo	☎ 800/327-9633	www.goalamo.com
Avis	☎ 800/331-1212	www.avis.com
Budget	☎ 800/527-0700	www.budgetrentacar.com
Dollar	☎ 800/800-4000	www.dollarcar.com
Enterprise	☎ 800/325-8007	www.pickenterprise.com
Hertz	☎ 800/654-3131	www.hertz.com
National	☎ 800/227-7368	www.nationalcar.com
Thrifty	☎ 800/367-2277	www.thrifty.com

The San Francisco Bay Area

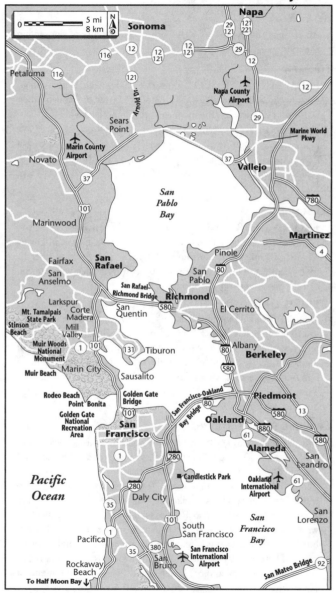

BY CAR

All of these routes are very well marked, with plenty of signs along the way.

TO NAPA

FROM SAN FRANCISCO   Cross the Golden Gate Bridge and go north on U.S. 101; turn east on Highway 37 (toward Vallejo), then north on Highway 29, the main road through Napa Valley.

FROM OAKLAND   Head eastbound on I-80 toward Sacramento; a few miles past the city of Vallejo (and after paying a $2 toll fee to cross the Carquinez Bridge), exit on Highway 12, which, after a few miles, intersects with Highway 29 and leads directly into Napa.

TO SONOMA

FROM SAN FRANCISCO   From San Francisco, cross the Golden Gate Bridge and stay on U.S. 101 north. Exit at Highway 37; after 10 miles, turn north onto Highway 121. After another 10 miles, turn north onto Highway 12 (Broadway), which will take you directly into the town of Sonoma.

FROM OAKLAND   Head eastbound on I-80 toward Sacramento. A few miles past the city of Vallejo (and after paying a $2 toll to cross the Carquinez Bridge), exit on Highway 12, which, after a few miles, intersects with Highway 29 at the southern foot of Napa Valley. Just before entering the city of Napa, you'll come to a major intersection, where Highway 29 meets Highway 12/121. Turn left onto Highway 12/121, which will take you directly to the Sonoma Valley.

CROSSING FROM VALLEY TO VALLEY

The easiest way to get from Napa to Sonoma and vice versa is to head to the southern end of either valley (the Carneros District) and cross over along the Sonoma Highway (Calif. 12/121). From Napa to Sonoma, the trip will take about 20 minutes, assuming there's no traffic. Another option is to take the Oakville Grade (a.k.a. Trinity Road) over the Mayacamas Range, which links Oakville in Napa with Glen Ellen in Sonoma. It's an extremely steep and windy road, but a real time-saver if you're headed to the northern end of either valley. There is a way to cross from Calistoga to the Sonoma Highway along Calistoga and St. Helena roads (at the northern end of Napa and Sonoma valleys), but the circuitous route takes so long that it isn't worth the effort.

5   For Foreign Visitors

BASIC ENTRY REQUIREMENTS

DOCUMENTS   The U.S. State Department has a **Visa Waiver Pilot Program** allowing citizens of certain countries to enter the United States without a visa for stays of up to 90 days. At press time, these included Andorra, Austria, Belgium, Brunei, Denmark, Finland, France, Germany, Iceland, Ireland, Italy, Japan, Liechtenstein, Luxembourg, Monaco, the Netherlands, New Zealand, Norway, San Marino, Spain, Sweden, Switzerland, and the United Kingdom. Citizens of these countries need only a valid passport and a round-trip air or cruise ticket in their possession upon arrival in the United States. Further information is available from any U.S. embassy or consulate. **Canadian citizens** may enter the United States without visas; they need only proof of residence.

Citizens of all other countries—including **Australia**—must have: 1) a **valid passport** with an expiration date at least 6 months later than the scheduled end of their visit to the United States; and 2) a **tourist visa,** which may be obtained without charge from the nearest U.S. consulate. To obtain a visa, you must submit a completed application form (either in person or by mail) with a $1^{1}/_{2}$-inch-square photo, and demonstrate binding ties to a residence abroad. Usually you can obtain a visa at once or within 24 hours, but it may take longer during the summer rush from June through August. If you cannot go in person, contact the nearest U.S. embassy or consulate for directions on applying by mail. Your travel agent or airline office also might be able to provide you with visa applications and instructions. The U.S. consulate or embassy that issues your visa will determine the terms of your visa, including any restrictions regarding the length of your stay.

U.K. citizens can obtain up-to-date passport and visa information by calling the **U.S. Embassy Visa Information Line** at ☎ **0891/200-290** or the **London Passport Office** at ☎ **0990/ 210-410** (for recorded information).

Foreign driver's licenses are recognized in California, although you might want to get an international driver's license if your home license is not written in English.

CUSTOMS   Every visitor over 21 years of age may bring in, free of duty, the following: (1) 1 liter of wine or hard liquor; (2) 200 cigarettes, 100 cigars (but not from Cuba), or 3 pounds of smoking tobacco; and (3) $100 worth of gifts. These exemptions are offered to travelers who spend at least 72 hours in the United States and who have not claimed them within the preceding 6 months. It is altogether forbidden to bring into the country foodstuffs (particularly fruit, cooked meats, and canned goods) and plants (vegetables, seeds, tropical plants, and the like). Foreign tourists may bring in or take out up to $10,000 in U.S. or foreign currency with no formalities; larger sums must be declared to U.S. Customs on entering or leaving, which includes filing form CM 4790. For more specific information regarding U.S. Customs, call the customs office at the **San Francisco International Airport** at ☎ **415/876-2816.**

MONEY

The U.S. monetary system is painfully simple: The most common bills (all ugly, all green) are the $1 (colloquially, a "buck"), $5, $10, and $20 denominations. There are also $2 bills (seldom encountered), $50 bills, and $100 bills (the last two are usually not welcome when paying for small purchases). Note that a newly redesigned $100 bill was introduced in mid-1996; despite rumors to the contrary, the old-style bill is still legal tender.

There are six denominations of coins: 1¢ (1 cent, or a penny); 5¢ (5 cents, or a nickel); 10¢ (10 cents, or a dime); 25¢ (25 cents, or a quarter); 50¢ (50 cents, or a half dollar); and, prized by collectors, the rare $1 piece (both an older, large silver dollar and the newer, small Susan B. Anthony coin).

Though traveler's checks are widely accepted, make sure that they are denominated in U.S. dollars, as foreign-currency checks are often difficult to exchange. The three most widely recognized traveler's checks—and least likely to be denied—are **Visa, American Express,** and **Thomas Cook.** For more on traveler's-check protocol, see section 3, "Money Matters," above.

GETTING TO THE U.S.

International carriers that fly into San Francisco International include:

Airline	Phone number
Aer Lingus	☎ 01/844-4747 in Dublin 061/415-556 in Shannon 800/223-6537 in the U.S.
Air Canada	☎ 888/247-2262 in Canada 800/776-3000 in the U.S.

British Airways	☎ 0345/222-111 in London
	800/247-9297 in the U.S.
Japan Air Lines	☎ 03/5489-1111 in Tokyo
	800/525-3663 in the U.S.
Qantas	☎ 008/177-767 in Australia
	800/227-4500 in the U.S.
Air New Zealand	☎ 0800/737-000 in Auckland
	64-3/379-5200 in Christchurch
	800/926-7255 in the U.S.
Virgin Atlantic	☎ 0293/747-747 in London
	800/862-8621 in the U.S.

In addition, many U.S. carriers offer international service to the United States. If they do not have direct flights to San Francisco, they can book you straight through on a connecting flight. You can make reservations by calling the following numbers in London:

Airline	Phone number
American	☎ 0181/572-5555
Continental	☎ 4412/9377-6464
Delta	☎ 0800/414-767
United	☎ 0181/990-9900

If possible, try to book a direct flight. Airlines that offer direct flights from London include **British Airways, United,** and **Virgin. Air Canada** offers direct service from Toronto, Montreal, Calgary, and Vancouver to San Francisco.

6 Getting Around

With hundreds of wineries scattered amidst Napa's 34,000 acres and Sonoma's 12,000 acres of vineyards, it's virtually impossible to explore the Wine Country without wheels. If you're arriving by air from another part of the country or abroad, see "Getting There," earlier in this chapter, for details on renting a car.

DRIVING AROUND THE WINE COUNTRY You might be wondering: Does that mean visitors are drinking and driving up here? And how. The catch is, most of the year there's so much traffic, a major high-speed collision is virtually out of the question. Meanwhile, getting totally trashed while wine tasting is the exception and the valley has somehow avoided having a major problem with drunk-driving accidents.

Napa Valley Traffic Tip

Travel the Silverado Trail as often as possible to avoid Highway 29's traffic. Avoid passing through Main Street in St. Helena during high season. While a wintertime cruise from Napa to Calistoga can take 20 minutes, in summer you can expect the trek to take you closer to 50 minutes.

Of course, we're not condoning driving under the influence. But since there's no decent public transportation, our best recommendation is that you take it slow, monitor the amount of wine you drink, or bring along a designated driver.

Driving Rules   California law requires both drivers and passengers to wear seat belts. Children under 4 years or 40 pounds must be secured in approved child-safety seats. Motorcyclists must wear helmets. Auto insurance is mandatory; the car's registration and proof of insurance must be carried in the car.

You can turn right at a red light, unless otherwise indicated—but be sure to come to a complete stop first. Pedestrians *always* have the right-of-way.

TAXIS   You can avoid the driving issue altogether by calling either of Napa's two main taxi services: **Valley Cab** (☎ 707/257-6444) or **Yellow Cab** (☎ 707/226-3731). Sonoma is serviced by **Valley Cab** (☎ 707/996-6733).

GUIDED TOURS   You won't have the same freedom that comes with driving yourself around, but a guided tour will allow you to meet other tourists, drink wine without worrying about getting behind the wheel, and kick back while your driver deals with the traffic. Napa has a handful of good options, including the famous **Napa Valley Wine Train** and **Napa Valley Holidays,** which offers wine-tasting tours of the valley in 29-passenger minibuses; see pages 59 and 60 for details. If you're an active traveler, you might want to tour Sonoma's wineries by bike with the **Goodtime Bicycle Company;** see page 136 for information.

7 Strategies for Touring the Wine Country

The best vacations are usually those that are loosely structured; that is, you form a game plan before you depart, but agree to deviate when favorable circumstances suggest otherwise. And so it goes for planning a trip to the Wine Country—we strongly suggest that you devise an itinerary before you arrive, because there's no possible way

Wine Country Orientation

you could visit all of Napa's and Sonoma's 350-plus wineries in one visit (at least not without a few free weeks on your hands, and a mid-vacation layover at the Betty Ford clinic).

Tour smarter, not harder, is the mantra you need to chant to yourself as you pour over this book in the process of planning your trip—because the less time you spend driving in circles means more time spent sticking your schnozzle in wineglasses and saying silly things like "full bodied, yet corky."

Of course, since we don't know how long you'll be touring the Wine Country or what your level of wine knowledge is, it's impossible for us to provide you with the touring strategy that will best suit your intentions and wishes. So instead, we'll supply you a few nuggets of Wine Country wisdom, gleaned both from experience and from picking the minds of tourist-savvy locals, and let you decide what's right for you.

NAPA VS. SONOMA: WHICH VALLEY IS RIGHT FOR YOU?

When it comes to comparing the two valleys, the most obvious distinction is size: Napa Valley dwarfs Sonoma Valley both in population, number of wineries, and sheer volume of tourism (and traffic). Napa is definitely the more commercial of the two; Sonoma still manages to maintain a backcountry ambiance thanks to its far lower density of wineries, restaurants, and hotels. Small, family-owned wineries are Sonoma's mainstay; tastings are low-key, and they come with plenty of friendly banter with the wine makers (who often will be doing the pouring themselves). But even though Sonoma lives in the shadow of far more famous Napa, its wines have actually won more awards than Napa's for the last 7 years running; don't let that "aw, shucks" attitude fool you—Sonomans know their stuff.

If it's serious R&R you're after, and you aren't too concerned with shopping outlets or visiting more than a handful of wineries each day, you'll probably be happier staying at one of Sonoma Valley's secluded inns and perhaps touring the valley by bicycle since most wineries are located down quiet, gently winding, woodsy roads. If, however, you're intent on really learning something about the wonderful world of wine making, Napa Valley may be the place for you. World-class wineries such as Sterling and Robert Mondavi offer the most interesting and edifying wine tours in North America, if not the world (though Sonoma's Benziger Winery gives them a run for their money). Compared to little brother Sonoma, Napa also has more big-name wineries, many more spas (at far cheaper rates) to choose from, and a far superior selection of fine restaurants, hotels, and quintessential Wine Country activities like hot-air ballooning. As Gertrude Stein might say, there's more of "there" there.

Indeed, perhaps the most important distinction between Napa and Sonoma is that the Napa Valley is the undisputed cornerstone of the Wine Country. If your intention is to immerse yourself in the culture of the Wine Country, then there's no better place to start than by cruising down Napa Valley's Highway 29, the Sunset Boulevard of the Wine Country. It's along this high-rent route that all the big players in the California wine industry—Beringer, Beaulieu, Charles Krug, Niebaum-Coppola, Clos Pegase—dazzle you with their multimillion-dollar estates and pricey art collections; this is where top-notch restaurants like the French Laundry and Tra Vigne serve world-class cuisine to casually clad diners while fresh-faced Silicon Valley millionaires play croquet at the exclusive resorts just up the hill.

As you might expect, humbleness isn't one of Napa's strongest attributes; humility does not go hand-in-hand with a position as top dog in the domestic-wine world. So don't be surprised if you encounter a bit of snobbishness at some Napa wineries, as well as a pricey tasting fee or two. On the other side of the hill, good ol' Sonomans pride themselves on their rural roots, laid-back attitude, and fee-free tasting rooms.

Is there a friendly feud between the two valleys? You betcha, which makes touring the entire Wine Country all the more interesting. If you have the leisure of time, don't just pick one: tour them both so you can compare and contrast these two very different—and very wonderful—worlds of wine making.

THE GOLDEN RULE OF WINE TASTING: LESS IS MORE

Yes, we know—they all sound great. Unfortunately, it's almost impossible to hit every winery. Actually, your best plan of action is to take it slow: **Pick three or four wineries** for a single day's outing, and really get to know not only the wines but also the story behind each winery: its history, the types of wines they make and where they're grown, and the colorful people who make them. You can *taste* California wines just about anywhere in the world, but only by visiting the Wine Country can you learn about the painstaking, delicate, and very personal processes and the years of collective experience that go into each and every bottle. Like a fine glass of wine, the Wine Country should not be rushed, but savored.

When planning your trip through the Wine Country, consider the following: Is there a specific wine you want to taste? A specific tour you'd like to take? Maybe it's the adjoining restaurant, picnic setting, or art collection that piques your interest most. Whatever your intentions may be, the best advice we can give you about visiting your chosen wineries is to **arrive early:** Most tasting rooms open at 10am, and even on the busiest of weekends, most are empty that early in the morning. "What? Start drinking at 10am?" Absolutely. First of all, you're not drinking, you're tasting and learning. Second, the staff pouring the wines will have considerably more time to pontificate about their product. Come one or two in the afternoon, the tasting room will probably be packed, and other visitors will be waiting in line simply to get a sample—while you're relaxing under an oak tree, finished with your wine-tasting rounds, enjoying a picnic lunch and seriously contemplating an afternoon nap. Afterwards, why not spend your time doing a little window-shopping or visiting Old Faithful while the late-birds duke it out over a sip of chardonnay?

Another consideration when wine tasting is money. It used to be that none of the wineries charged for sampling their wares, but when the popularity of the Wine Country began to soar (along with a growing intolerance for drinking and driving), wineries—particularly those in Napa—began requesting **tasting fees.** It wasn't to make additional profit, but to discourage what the winery staffs usually refer to as "recreational drinkers": visitors who, whether they're aware of it or not, prefer quantity over quality. Nowadays, the norm at Napa Valley wineries is to charge anywhere between $2 and $6 per tasting, which usually includes the tasting glass (etched with the winery's logo) and/or a refund toward purchase. If money is a concern, consider visiting during the week: Many wineries, such as Grgich Hills, only charge a fee on the weekend.

The wineries in Sonoma, however, rarely charge for tasting wines. The exceptions are wineries offering samples of their reserve wines (usually at a separate tasting area) and champagne houses, which usually charge a few dollars for a glass of sparkling wine.

DEALING WITH THE CROWDS

Anyone who's visited the Wine Country on a sunny August weekend knows how absurd the traffic can be. The Napa Valley's roads simply weren't designed to handle such an influx of traffic, which can turn a 30-minute drive along Highway 29 from Napa to Calistoga into 2 hours of maddening gridlock. It's ironic, of course:

Wine Buying Tip

Just because you're buying wine at the source—directly from the people that made it—doesn't mean that you'll save money by purchasing bottles in the tasting room. In fact, it's usually the other way around: You'll probably end up spending a bit more at a winery than you would at superstores that buy cases in bulk and pass the per-bottle savings on to the customer (such as **Safeway** in St. Helena, which locals tell us is the best place to buy wine in Napa Valley).

If you want to save money, the smart approach is to make a list of your favorite wines as you taste at the wineries, then make your purchases when you return from your vacation. You'll not only save money on the wine, you'll save a bundle on packaging and shipping fees—but be sure to ask the winery if the release you're interested in is available in your state, and where you can purchase it. If the selection of California wines is limited where you live, head to Safeway or one of the wine shops we've recommended in the following chapters, buy the wine you want, and take it to one of the shippers we've recommend (see pages 54 and 55) who can pack it up and ship it for you. Some wine shops, such as the **Wine Exchange** in Sonoma, will even do the shipping for you (and you might be able to sidestep the red tape that may accompany shipping wine to your home state; see "The Ins & Outs of Shipping Wine Home," below).

Exceptions to this strategy are wineries that offer big discounts on cases of wine, or wineries such as **Peju Province** that only sell their wines directly (that is, they have no distribution). Note: If you're able to ship your wine directly from the winery, you'll avoid having to pay sales tax; for the ins and outs of that, see "The Ins & Outs of Shipping Wine Home," below.

People arrive for a vacation in the countryside, only to be stuck in traffic for hours.

If you want to avoid the masses altogether, the solution is simple: Either **come during the off-season** (Nov through May) **or midweek.** Though the optimum time to plan your trip is during the "crush"—the grape harvest season starting in late August and continuing through October when the grapes are harvested, sorted, crushed, and fermented—this is also the Wine Country's peak tourist season. This is a good time to schedule a midweek visit, if possible.

But even if your only option is to arrive on a high-season weekend, there are still ways to avoid the Napa Valley cattle drive. The smartest option is to **avoid the big wineries** such as Mondavi and Beringer and opt for the smaller family-run places recessed into the hillsides such as Prager and Heitz. Even the wineries along the Silverado Trail, which parallels the main highway through Napa Valley, receive significantly less traffic; locals use it as their main thoroughfare during high season.

Another high-season option is to avoid Napa altogether and stick to the **Sonoma Valley.** Although it, too, suffers from traffic congestion, Sonoma usually gets far less saturated with visitors.

A FEW MORE WORDS OF WINE-COUNTRY WISDOM

Here are a few final tips that should help make your visit a more pleasant experience:

- **Chart your winery tours** on a map before venturing into the countryside. It'll save you time and traffic frustration, as well as a lot of unnecessary backtracking.
- **Plan a lunchtime picnic** at the last winery you're going to visit for the day (let's face it—you'll probably be too pooped to drink more wine late in the day). Many wineries offer free picnic facilities, and though few provide food, many wonderful gourmet shops in both Napa and Sonoma specialize in picnic items; see pages 131 and 176 for recommendations.
- Most wineries are open from 10am to 4:30 or 5pm and are closed on major holidays such as Thanksgiving, Christmas, and New Year's Day. Many also have restricted hours during the off-season, so **call ahead** if there's a winery you don't want to miss.
- Fine wine is a temperamental beast that hates to be mistreated. If you let that $60 bottle of merlot cook in the back seat of your car all day, you'll probably be surprised at the new taste it has acquired. Buy a cheap Styrofoam cooler and a couple of blue ice packs, place them in the trunk of your car, and voilà!—you have a **portable wine cellar.**
- Anyone who's ever lived in a one-road town knows that you can't avoid the law for long. In our last three trips to the Wine Country, we've been bathed in a radar gun's rays twice. So there you have it: Don't speed, and for gawds sake, **don't drive while intoxicated.**

8 The Ins & Outs of Shipping Wine Home

Perhaps the only thing more complex than that $400 case of cabernet you just purchased are the rules and regulations regarding

shipping it home. Due to absurd and forever fluctuating "reciprocity laws"—which are supposedly created to protect the business of
the country's wine distributors—wine shipping is limited by state
regulations that vary in each of the 50 states. Shipping rules also vary
from winery to winery—not to mention that, to make matters more
confusing, according to at least one shipping company the list of
reciprocal states (those that have agreements with California that
make it no problem to ship wine there) changes almost daily! Hence,
depending on which state you live in, sending even a single bottle
of wine can be a truly Kafkaesque experience—and, aside from sum-
mertime traffic, one of the most frustrating aspects of a Wine Country vacation.

Sound confusing? Believe us, it is. The fact is, no one can give us
the straight scoop on shipping. We've spoken to a number of agen-
cies and each one tells us a different story. While we can't exactly
outline a foolproof way to send your wine home, the following best
explains what we do know about it and offers tips to help you cut
through the red tape as painlessly as possible. (Note that this information was current at press time. Unfortunately, because the laws
and shipping companies' procedures are ever-changing, we can't
guarantee you an absolute solution; you'll have to check and see
what the current situation is pertaining to your particular home state
as you tour the Wine Country.)

If you happen to live in a reciprocal state and the winery you're
buying from offers shipping, you're in luck. You buy, pay the post-
age, and the winery sends your purchase for you. It's as simple as
that. If that winery doesn't ship, they will most likely be able to give
you an easy shipping solution.

If you live in a nonreciprocal state, the winery may still have shipping advice for you, so definitely ask! But there's a good reason most
wineries don't offer shipping to nonreciprocal states: One winery
was fined big bucks (around $35,000) for breaking the law and ship-
ping directly to Maryland, a nonreciprocal state. As this book goes
to press, if you're a New York (another nonreciprocal state) resident,
the odds of having your wine shipped home varies from winery to
winery: Some refuse to ship at all, while others are more than accommodating ("New York has bigger fish to fry," we've been told). Do
be cautious of wineries that tell you they can ship to nonreciprocal
states, and make sure you get a firm commitment: When one of our
New York–based editors visited Napa, a winery promised her they
could, in fact, ship her purchase; but when she got home they

reneged, leaving her with no way to get the wine and no potable memories of the trip.

It's possible that you'll face the challenge of finding a shipping company yourself. If that's the case, bear in mind the following:

According to the U.S. Postal Service, shipping alcoholic beverages is against the law. Of course, it's hard to imagine that anyone's getting arrested for sending a congratulatory bottle of bubbly to Aunt Myrna in Delaware, but if you tote a case labeled "pinot noir" into the post office, the postal clerk isn't likely to be exactly helpful. (While we're not recommending that you break the law, if you did appear with a well-packed box, they would ship it, but you'd have to declare you were shipping something other than wine—and then, of course, you'd be fibbing. Not to mention it's questionable to insure your supposed case of olive oil for $500.)

When we asked UPS about shipping, they, too, told us it was against the law. But one shipping company in the valley told us they can currently ship by either FedEx or UPS (or both, in some cases) within California and to Colorado, Idaho, Illinois, Louisiana, Maine, Minnesota, Missouri, Nebraska, New Mexico, Oregon, Virginia, Washington, and Wisconsin. (Again, don't forget the list is in constant flux.) While Airborne was lenient with shipping at one time, they seem to be buckling down after getting fined for shipping to a nonreciprocal state.

All we can really tell you about shipping is to do your homework before you buy. Talk with wineries and, if necessary, shipping companies. We've listed a few below, but you also should ask the winery from which you're buying about shipping companies; because the winery wants you to buy, they've probably done more than their fair share of shipping research and resolutions, and they should be up on the latest.

Do keep in mind that it's illegal to box your own wine and send it to a nonreciprocal state; the shippers could lose their license and you could lose your wine. However, if you do get stuck shipping illegally (not that we're recommending you do that), you might want to head to a post office, UPS, or other shipping company outside of the Wine Country area; it's far less obvious that you're shipping wine from, say, Vallejo or San Francisco than from Napa Valley.

NAPA VALLEY SHIPPING COMPANIES

Aero Packing, 1733 Trancas St. (at Highway 29), Napa (☎ 707/255-8025), will pack and ship to reciprocal states and insures the first $100 (it's 50¢ extra per hundred beyond the first). Ground shipping of one case to Los Angeles is $19 and Florida is $41. They currently do not ship to a handful of states, including New York and Massachusetts.

The **St. Helena Mailing Center,** 1241 Adams St. (at Highway 29), St. Helena (☎ **707/963-2686**), tells us that they will pack and ship anywhere in the United States, with rates around $17 per case for ground delivery to Los Angeles and $33 to New York. While those who live in reciprocal states insure their package for up to $100 (it costs extra beyond the first $100), the Mailing Center does not insure packages shipped to nonreciprocal states. However, it's no big deal; each bottle is well-packed in Styrofoam and should make it home without a problem.

SONOMA VALLEY SHIPPING COMPANIES

Mail Boxes, Etc., 19229 Sonoma Hwy. (at Verano Street), Sonoma (☎ **707/935-3438**), which has a lot of experience with shipping wine, claims it will ship your wine to any state, either via UPS (which as of now only ships to a dozen states) or Federal Express. Prices vary from $14 to L.A. via UPS to as much as $78 to the East Coast via FedEx.

The **Wine Exchange of Sonoma,** 452 First St. E. (between East Napa and East Spain streets), Sonoma (☎ **707/938-1794**), will ship your wine, but there's a catch: You must purchase an equal amount of the same wine at their store (which they assured us would be in stock, and probably at a better rate). Shipping rates range from $15 to L.A., $36 to the East Coast.

FAST FACTS: The Wine Country

For valley-specific information, also see the "Fast Facts" sections in chapters 4 and 5.

Area Code   Both Napa and Sonoma counties use the **707** area code.

Banks   Most banks are open Monday through Friday from 9am to 3pm; several stay open until about 5pm at least 1 day a week and offer limited hours on Saturday. **Bank of America** has several branches throughout the area, including locations at 1700 First St. in Napa (☎ 707/257-9111), 1001 Adams St. in St. Helena (☎ 707/963-6807), and 35 W. Napa St. in Sonoma (☎ 707/935-1604); for a complete listing, call ☎ **800/348-5202.** You'll also find **Wells Fargo** throughout the region, including branches in Napa at 955 Franklin St. (☎ 707/258-0191) and at 217 Soscol Ave., inside Raleys supermarket (☎ 707/254-8690). The Sonoma Wells Fargo is located at 480 W. Napa St. (☎ 707/996-2360). For a complete listing, call ☎ **800/869-3557.** You'll find ATMs throughout both valleys, though not as many as you'd find in a big city. For information on how to locate the nearest ATM, see "Money Matters" earlier in this chapter.

Car Rentals   See "Getting Around," earlier in this chapter.

Emergencies   Dial ☎ **911** for police, ambulance, or the fire department. No coins are needed from a working public phone.

Liquor Laws   Liquor and grocery stores, as well as some drugstores, can sell packaged alcoholic beverages between 6am and 2am. Most restaurants, nightclubs, and bars are licensed to serve alcoholic beverages during the same hours. The legal age for purchase and consumption is 21; proof of age is required.

Safety   Considering the Napa Valley's 5.1 million and Sonoma's 2.4 million annual visitors, the Wine Country still has a remarkably safe, sleepy-town atmosphere. The only safety consideration you will need to heed is your own basic common sense.

Taxes   An 7.25% sales tax is added at the register for all goods and services purchased in the Napa Valley; it's 7.5% in Sonoma. (Note that you won't have to pay sales tax if you have your purchases shipped directly from the store out of state.) Napa hotel taxes range from 10% to 12%; in Sonoma, hotel tax is 9% to 10%.

Time   The Wine Country is in the Pacific standard time zone, which is 8 hours behind Greenwich mean time and 3 hours behind eastern standard time. For the local time, call ☎ **707/ 767-8900.**

Weather   Though a general weather recording does not exist, there's an emergency number, which is only in operation during very wet weather. For information on flood conditions, contact the **Travel Advisory** at ☎ **888/854-NAPA.**

4

The Napa Valley

*C*ompared to its sister valley, Sonoma, Napa is a bit farther from San Francisco, is home to hundreds more wineries, and has more of an overall touristy, big-business feel to it. You'll still find plenty of rolling, mustard flower–covered hills and vast stretches of vineyards, but they come hand in hand with large, upscale restaurants; designer discount outlets; rows of hotels; and, in summer, plenty of traffic. But even with hordes of visitors year-round, Napa Valley is still pretty sleepy, with a focus on daytime attractions—wine tasting, outdoor activities, and spas—and fabulous food. Nightlife is very limited, but after indulging all day, most visitors are ready to turn in early anyway.

1 Orientation & Getting Around

Napa Valley is relatively compact. Just 25 miles long, it claims 34,000 acres of vineyards, making Napa the most densely planted wine-growing region in the U.S. It's an easy venture from one end to the other; you can drive it in less than half an hour (although expect it to be closer to 50 minutes during high season).

Conveniently, most of the large wineries—as well as most of the hotels, shops, and restaurants—are located along a single road, **Calif. 29,** which starts at the mouth of the Napa River, near the north end of San Francisco Bay, and continues north to Calistoga and the top of the growing region. All of the Napa Valley coverage in this chapter—every town, winery, hotel, and restaurant—is organized below from south to north, beginning in the village of Napa, and can be reached from this main thoroughfare.

ALONG HIGHWAY 29: NAPA'S TOWNS IN BRIEF

While it's virtually impossible to tell when you cross from one town into the next, each does have its own distinct personality. The **village of Napa** serves as the commercial center of the Wine Country and the gateway to Napa Valley—hence the high-speed freeway that whips you right past it and on to the "tourist" towns of St. Helena and Calistoga. However, if you do veer off the highway, you'll be surprised to discover a small but burgeoning community of 63,000 residents with the most cosmopolitan (if you can call it that) atmosphere in the county—and some of the most affordable accommodations in the valley. Unfortunately, any charm Napa may exude is all but squelched by the used-car lots and warehouse superstores surrounding the quaint neighborhoods.

Heading north on either Highway 29 or the Silverado Trail leads you to Napa's wineries and the more idyllic pastoral towns beyond.

Yountville, population 3,500, was founded by the first white American to settle in the valley, George Calvert Yount. While it lacks the small-town charm of neighboring St. Helena and Calistoga—primarily because it has no rambunctious main street—it does serve as a good base for exploring the valley, and it's home to a handful of excellent wineries, inns, and restaurants, including James Beard's 1997 top dining spot in the nation, the French Laundry.

Driving farther north on the St. Helena Highway (Calif. 29) brings you to **Oakville,** most easily recognized by Oakville Cross Road and the Oakville Grocery Café (see p. 117), one of our favorite new restaurants and one of the only indications that you've reached the small town. If you so much as blink after Oakville, you're likely to overlook **Rutherford,** the next small town that borders on St. Helena. Still, each has their share of spectacular wineries, but you won't see most of them while driving along Highway 29.

Next comes **St. Helena,** located 17 miles north of Napa on Calif. 29. St. Helena is a former Seventh Day Adventist village that manages to maintain a pseudo–Old West feel while simultaneously catering to upscale shoppers with deep pockets, as well as its resident population of 6,000. This quiet, attractive little town is home to a slew of beautiful old houses, as well as great restaurants, first-rate accommodations, and many exceptional wineries.

Calistoga, the last tourist town in Napa Valley, was named by Sam Brannan, entrepreneur extraordinaire and California's first millionaire. After making a bundle supplying miners during the gold rush, he went on to take advantage of the natural geothermal springs at the north end of the Napa Valley by building a hotel and spa here in 1859. Flubbing up a speech in which he compared this natural California wonder to New York State's Saratoga Springs resort, he serendipitously coined the name "Calistoga," and it stuck. Today, this small, simple resort town with 4,400 residents and an old-time main street (no building along the 6-block stretch is more than two stories high) is popular with city folk who come here to unwind.

Calistoga is a great place to relax and indulge in mineral waters, mud baths, Jacuzzis, massages, and, of course, wine. The vibe is more casual—and a little more groovy—than you'll find in neighboring towns to the south.

VISITOR INFORMATION

Even if you plan to skip over the town of Napa, you may want to stop at the **Napa Valley Conference and Visitors Bureau,** 1310 Town Center Mall (off First Street), Napa, CA 94559 (☎ **707/ 226-7459**), to pick up a variety of local information and money-saving coupons.

All over Napa and Sonoma you can pick up a very informative, free weekly called the *Wine Country Review,* which provides the most up-to-date information on the area's wineries and related events.

WINE-TASTING TOURS

Let's say you've had your fill of driving from winery to winery. Or you already know that family dynamics get a little stressed when that certain back-seat driver tries to navigate through traffic. Or the whole point of this vacation is to drink too much, eat too much, and avoid exercising your brain whatsoever. If any of these scenarios ring true for you, you may want to consider letting someone else figure out all the details of your Wine Country tour; below are a few companies who'll be happy to do it for you.

RIDING THE NAPA VALLEY WINE TRAIN   You don't have to worry about drinking and driving if you tour the Wine Country aboard the **Napa Valley Wine Train,** a rolling restaurant that makes a leisurely 3-hour, 36-mile journey through the vineyards of Napa, Yountville, Oakville, Rutherford, and St. Helena. You'll love riding in the vintage-style cars, each finished with polished Honduran mahogany paneling and etched-glass partitions.

During the trip, optional gourmet meals are served by an attentive staff, complete with all the finery—damask linen, bone china, silver flatware, and etched crystal. The fixed menus consist of three to five courses, which might include a salmon dish or Black Angus filet mignon served with a cabernet and Roquefort sauce. In addition to the dining rooms, the train pulls a Wine Tasting Car, a Deli Car, and four 50-passenger lounges. A recent addition to the daytime rides is an optional stop in Yountville and at the Grgich Winery in Rutherford for a tour of the barreling, bottling, and wine-making process, followed by a tasting.

The train departs from the McKinstry Street Depot, 1275 McKinstry St. (near First Street and Soscol Avenue), Napa (☎ 800/427-4124 or 707/253-2111). Train fare without meals is $25 for daytime rides and evening rides in the Deli Car; fare with meals is $56.50 for brunch, $63 for lunch, and $74.50 for dinner. The Wine Train's latest addition, the more modern 1950s Vista Dome Car, offers only upstairs seating and has a glass top; it can only be ridden if you opt for the pricier lunch or dinner served within it. Including train fare, lunch is $75 for a four-course French affair; dinner, $82.50. Departures are Monday through Friday at 11:30am; Saturday, Sunday, and holidays at 8:30am and noon; Tuesday through Friday and holidays at 6pm; and Saturday and Sunday at 5:30pm. (The schedule is reduced in Jan and Feb.) *Tip:* Sit on the west side for the best views. *Fair Warning:* As passengers board, a professional photographer snaps photos, available for purchase after the trip—so if you want this captured moment on film, be prepared.

BICYCLING AROUND THE WINE COUNTRY Getaway Adventures, 620 Washington St., Suite 206, Petaluma, CA 94954 (☎ 800/499-2453 or 707/763-3040; **www.getawayadventures. com**), the Wine Country's only full-time operator dedicated to bicycling and adventure tours, offers a unique way to explore Napa and Sonoma. Sign up for a weekend or 6-day package and everything's taken care of—lodging, continental breakfasts, gourmet picnic lunches (served with linens, glassware, and silverware), dinner at local restaurants, wine tours and tastings, and an unforgettable ride through the majestic valley via Cannondale bicycle (helmet and drinking water included). On weekdays they'll even deliver bikes to you. One-day tours, which include lunch and a visit to three to five wineries, cost $89; the $49 half-day downhill is a better choice for people who hate to pedal. Two-day tours start at $589 per person; a 6-day trip goes for around $1,500.

LETTING SOMEONE ELSE DO THE DRIVING At about 4pm on any given day in the valley, there's gotta be more *legally* drunk drivers on the road per capita than in any other location on earth. And while traffic makes it impossible for any high-speed collisions, being stuck behind a never-ending chain of cars can definitely ruin a good buzz. That's why **Napa Valley Holidays,** 1525 Andrea Circle, Napa, CA 94558 (☎ **707/255-1050; www.charterbus.com/ napavalley.html**), has found a good niche for themselves. Its regularly scheduled winery tours, which utilize 29-passenger, air-conditioned minibuses, start with pickups from two Napa locations. Passengers visit three or five wineries over 4 hours; all tasting fees are included. Tours run daily from April through November and start at $30 per individual; prices vary depending on the size of the group and the departure point.

FAST FACTS: The Napa Valley

Hospitals   **Queen of the Valley Hospital,** 100 Trancas St., Napa (☎ **707/257-4008**), offers minor emergency care from 9am to 9pm. For after-hours emergencies, head to **St. Helena Hospital,** about 5 minutes from the town of St. Helena at 650 Sanitarium Rd., Deer Park (☎ **707/963-3611**), or call ☎ **911.**

Information   See "Visitor Information," above.

Newspapers/Magazines   The *Napa Valley Register* covers the entire Napa Valley; it's available at newspaper racks on the main streets in towns throughout the county. Other local town weeklies include the *Weekly Calistogan* and the *St. Helena Star,* which are both free. Essential for all visitors is the *Napa Valley Guide,* an annual, glossy 124-page magazine packed with valuable tourist information; it's sold in most shops and hotels and is also available at the **Napa Valley Conference and Visitors Bureau,** 1310 Napa Town Center Mall, off First Street (☎ **707/226-7459**).

Pharmacies   **Smith's St. Helena Pharmacy,** 1390 Railroad Ave. (at Adams Street), St. Helena (☎ **707/963-2794**), is open Monday through Friday from 9am to 6pm, Saturday from 9am to 5pm, and Sunday from 10am to 3pm. **Vasconi Drug Store,** 1381 Main St., St. Helena (☎ **707/963-1447**), is open Monday through Friday from 9am to 7pm, but their pharmacist is part-time.

Police   Call ☎ **707/967-2741** or, in an emergency, ☎ **911.**

Post Offices   Each town has its own post office. **Napa Central,** 1625 Trancas, at Claremont (☎ **707/255-1621**), is open Monday through Friday from 8:30am to 5pm. **Napa Downtown,** 1352 Second St., between Franklin and Randolf streets (☎ **707/ 255-1268**), is open Monday through Friday from 8am to 4pm. You'll find local branches in **Yountville** at 96514 Washington St., at Mulberry (☎ **707/944-2123**), open Monday through Friday from 8am to 4pm, Saturday from 9:30am to noon; in **Oakville** at 1856 St. Helena Hwy., at Oakville Cross Road (☎ **707/ 944-2600**), open Monday through Friday from 8am to 4pm, Saturday from 8am to noon; and in **Rutherford** at 1190 Rutherford

Rd., at Highway 29 (☎ **707/963-7488**), operating Monday through Friday from 8am to 1pm and 2 to 4pm, Saturday from 8am to noon. The **St. Helena Post Office,** 1461 Main St., between Adams and Pine streets (☎ **707/963-2668**), is open Monday through Friday from 8:30am to 5pm and Saturday from 10am to 1pm. In **Calistoga,** head to 1013 Washington St., at Lincoln (☎ **707/942-6661**), open Monday through Friday from 9am to 4pm.

Shipping Companies   Aero Packing, 1733 Trancas St., at Highway 29, Napa (☎ **707/255-8025**), will pack and ship wine to reciprocal states. The **St. Helena Mailing Center,** 1241 Adams St., at Highway 29, St. Helena (☎ **707/963-2686**), will (at press time, anyway) pack and ship wine to anywhere in the United States. For more on the reciprocity laws associated with shipping wine out of California, see "The Ins & Outs of Shipping Wine Home" in chapter 3.

2 Touring the Wineries

Touring Napa Valley takes a little planning. With more than 250 wineries each offering distinct wines, atmosphere, and experience, the best thing you can do is decide what you're most interested in and chart your path from there. (For more on this, see "Strategies for Touring the Wine Country" in chapter 3.)

The towns and wineries listed below are organized geographically, from Napa village in the south to Calistoga in the north. Bear in mind that because some wineries are on Highway 29 while others are on the Silverado Trail (which parallels Calif. 29), the order in which they're listed is not necessarily the best path to follow. To save time, plan your wine tour to avoid zigzagging between the two parallel roads (see the "The Napa Valley Wineries" map on p. 63 to get your bearings).

We've featured only our favorite Napa Valley wineries below; this portable guide would grow into a tome if we included reviews of *every* valley winery. For a complete list of local wineries, be sure to pick up one of the free guides to the valley (see "Visitor Information" and "Fast Facts," above).

While you're exploring, keep in mind that some of the most memorable Wine Country experiences aren't made on tours or in formal tasting halls, but at the mom-and-pop wineries that dot the region. These are the places where you'll discover bottles that are

The Napa Valley Wineries

Beaulieu Vineyard ⑭
Beringer Vineyards ㉜
Cakebread Cellars ⑪
Carneros Alambic Distillery ①
Charles Krug Winery ㉝
Chateau Montelena ㊸
Clos Du Val ⑤
Clos Pegase ㊷
Cuvaison ㊴
Domaine Chandon ⑦
Domaine Charbay Winery
    & Distillery ㊱
Flora Springs Wine Co. ㉖
Freemark Abbey ㊲
Frog's Leap Winery ㉒
Girard Winery ⑲
Grgich Hills Cellar ⑮
Groth Vineyards & Winery ⑰
Heitz Wine Cellars ㉘
The Hess Collection ②
Joseph Phelps Vineyards ㉔
Kornell Champagne Cellars ㊳
Louis M. Martini ㉙
Mumm ㉑
Newlan Vineyards ③
Niebaum-Coppola ⑯
Opus One ⑩
Peju Province Winery ⑬
PlumpJack Winery ⑱
Prager Winery & Port Works ㉛
Raymond Vineyard & Cellar ㉕
Robert Keenan Winery ㉞
Robert Mondavi Winery ⑨
Rutherford Hill Winery ㉓
St. Clement Vineyards ㉟
St. Supéry Winery ⑫
Schramsberg ㊶
Silver Oak Wine Cellars ⑧
Stag's Leap Wine Cellars ⑥
Sterling Vineyards ㊵
Sutter Home Winery ㉚
Trefethen Vineyards ④
V. Sattui Winery ㉗
ZD Wines ⑳

only sold from the proprietor's front room, and get to talk one-on-one with the colorful people who made the wine you're buying with their own hands. Of course, the big-name wineries are not to be missed—but don't pass up the other, more personal side of the Napa Valley experience either.

NAPA

Newlan Vineyards. 5225 Solano Ave., Napa. ☎ **707/257-2399.** Daily 10am–5pm. Tours by appointment only. From Calif. 29, take Oak Knoll Ave. west to Solano Ave., turn right, and head north 1 mile.

This small, family-owned winery produces only about 10,000 cases a year. Varieties include cabernet sauvignon, pinot noir, chardonnay, zinfandel, and late harvest Johannisberg Riesling. Wine tasting, which is offered any time during open hours, costs $3 and includes a take-home wineglass. The 20-minute tour includes a peek at the vineyards and a tasting.

✪ **The Hess Collection.** 441 Redwood Rd., Napa. ☎ **707/255-1144.** Daily 10am–4pm. From Calif. 29 north, exit Redwood Rd. west, and follow Redwood Rd. for $6^1/_2$ miles.

No place in the valley brings together art and wine better than this combination winery/art gallery on the side of Mount Veeder. While others strive to pair wine with food, Swiss art collector Donald Hess went a different route: After acquiring the old Christian Brothers winery in 1978, he continued to produce wine while funding a huge restoration and expansion project that would honor both wine and the fine arts. The result is a working winery interspersed with gloriously lit rooms that exhibit his truly stunning art collection; the free self-guided tour takes you through these galleries as it introduces you to the wine-making process.

For a $3 fee, you can sample the winery's current cabernet and chardonnay as well as one other featured wine. If you want to take some with you, by-the-bottle prices start at $9.95 for the second-label Hess select brand, while most other selections range from $15 to $35.

Trefethen Vineyards. 1160 Oak Knoll Ave. (east of Calif. 29), Napa. ☎ **707/ 255-7700.** Daily 10am–4:30pm. Tours by appointment only.

Listed on the National Register of Historic Places, the vineyard's main building was built in 1886 and remains Napa's only wooden, gravity-flow winery. Although Trefethen is one of the valley's oldest wineries, it didn't produce its first chardonnay until 1973—but thank goodness it did. Their whites and reds are both award-

---

House of the Spirits

When you've had it with wine tasting for the day and you can no longer tell your oaky cabs from your fruity pinots, it's time to pay a visit to the **Carneros Alambic Distillery,** 1250 Cuttings Wharf Rd. (1 mile south of Highway 12/121), Napa (☎ **707/253-9055**). This replica of the brandy houses of France's Cognac region is the oldest alambic distillery in the United States, and a great place to learn about brandy.

Even if you're not a fan of brandy, you'll love this tour. It starts with a slick presentation of a miniature-scale model of the distillery (to give you an overview of the brandy-making process), then continues to the Still House, which contains eight beautiful French-built copper stills. Next you're led to the Barrel House, an enormous building that houses nearly 4,000 barrels of aging brandy. The vapors emanating from the barrels—called the "Angel's Share"—are enough to make you heady, and the Gregorian chants piped through the sound system add to the intoxicating experience. The tour ends with not a tasting (which is illegal under U.S. law unless you buy the bottle), but rather a sniffing: Several grades of brandy are passed around as the tour guide describes the vapors of each distinct variety.

This is a truly fascinating and educational $3 tour that we guarantee you'll enjoy. Half-hour tours are offered roughly every 45 minutes, daily from 10:30am to 5pm in summer, to 4:30pm in winter. No reservations are necessary. Sorry, no picnic facilities are available.

---

winners and a pleasure to the palate. Tastings are free, but if you want to sample a reserve wine, it'll cost you $5.

Clos Du Val. 5330 Silverado Trail (north of Oak Knoll Ave.), Napa. ☎ **707/259-2200.** Daily 10am–5pm. Tours by appointment only.

If you're starting your tour in Napa along the Silverado Trail, this is a good place to stop: It has all the elements a winery should have. The beautiful ivy-covered building and well-manicured rose garden set the scene for a romantic wine-tasting experience before you even step foot in the door; once inside, the French-accented employees authenticate the mood.

While the French have been known to make a great bottle of wine or two, here in the valley it's the exception, not the rule, when a winery is run by a Frenchman. In this case it's Bordeaux-born wine maker Bernard Portet who's responsible for the cabernet (which makes up 45% of the winery's production), chardonnay, zinfandel, pinot noir, and merlot. You can try them all in the rather matter-of-fact tasting room, which is refreshingly free of merchandise. There's a $3 tasting charge (refunded with purchase) for around four wines, which may include the new release chardonnay ($16 a bottle), cab ($24), merlot ($28), and perhaps a library selection or two.

Lovely picnic facilities offer respite in grassy nooks along the grounds. An added bonus is the friendly, helpful staff, who happily offer directions to other wineries, along with a small map.

Stag's Leap Wine Cellars. 5766 Silverado Trail, Napa. ☎ **707/944-2020.** Daily 10am–4pm. Tours by appointment only. From Calif. 29, go east on Trancas St. or Oak Knoll Ave., then north to the cellars.

Founded in 1972, Stag's Leap shocked the oenological world in 1976 when its 1973 cabernet won first place over French wines in a Parisian blind tasting. For $5 per person, you can be the judge of the winery's current releases, or you can fork over another fiver for one of Stag's Leaps's best-known wines, Cabernet Sauvignon Cask 23. The 1-hour tour runs through everything from the vineyard to production facilities and ends with a tasting; by the end of 1998, it could also include their new caves, which are currently under construction.

YOUNTVILLE

✪ **Domaine Chandon.** 1 California Dr. (at Calif. 29), Yountville. ☎ **707/944-2280.** Nov–Apr Wed–Sun 10am–6pm; May–Oct daily 10am–6pm. Free tours every hour on the hour from 11am to 5pm; no reservations necessary.

The valley's most renowned sparkling winery was founded in 1973 by French champagne house Moët et Chandon. The grounds suit Domaine Chandon's reputation perfectly—this is the kind of place where the world's wealthy might stroll the beautifully manicured gardens under the shade of a delicate parasol, stop at the outdoor patio for sips of the famous sparkling wine, then glide into the dining room for a world-class luncheon.

If you can pull yourself away from the bubbly (sold by the glass for $3.50 to $6.25 and served with complimentary bread and spread), the comprehensive tour of the facilities is worth the time. In addition to a shop, there's a small gallery housing artifacts from Moët et Chandon depicting the history of champagnes. The Domaine Chandon restaurant is one of the best in the valley (see "Where to Dine," below, for details).

OAKVILLE

♻ **Robert Mondavi Winery.** 7801 St. Helena Hwy. (Calif. 29), Oakville. ☎ **800/MONDAVI** or 707/226-1395. May–Oct daily 9:30am–5:30pm; Nov–Apr daily 9:30am–4:30pm. Reservations recommended for the guided tour (book 1 week in advance, especially for weekend tours).

If you continue on Calif. 29 up to Oakville, you'll arrive at the ultimate high-tech Napa Valley winery, housed in a magnificent mission-style facility. At Mondavi, almost every variable in the wine-making process is controlled by computer—it's absolutely fascinating to watch. After the tour, you can taste the results of all this attention to detail in selected current wines (free of charge). You also can taste without taking the tour, but it will cost you: The Rose Garden (an outdoor tasting area open in summer) offers an etched Reidel glass and three wines for $10; tastings in the ToKalon Room go from $3 for a 3-ounce taste to $15 for a rare library wine.

Fridays feature an "Art of Wine and Food" program, which includes a slide presentation on the history of wine, a tour of the winery, and a three-course luncheon with wine pairing; the cost is around $55 and you must reserve in advance. Though there's no picnicking on the grounds, Mondavi does offer gourmet picnic lunches from time to time. The Vineyard Room usually features an art show, and you'll find some exceptional antiques in the reception hall. In summer, the winery also hosts some great outdoor jazz concerts. Call to learn about upcoming events.

Opus One. 7900 St. Helena Hwy. (Calif. 29), Oakville. ☎ **707/944-9442.** Daily 10:30am–3:30pm. Tours by appointment only (in high season, book 3 weeks in advance).

Unlike most other vineyard experiences, a visit to Opus One is a serious and stately affair that takes after its wine and its owners: Robert Mondavi and Baroness Phillipe de Rothschild, who, after years of discussion, embarked on this state-of-the-art collaboration. Architecture buffs in particular will appreciate the tour, which takes in both the impressive Greco-Roman-meets-20th-century building and the no-holds-barred ultra-high-tech production and aging facilities.

This entire facility caters to one ultrapremium wine, which is offered here for a whopping $15 per 4-ounce taste (and a painful $90 per bottle). But wine lovers should happily fork over the cash: It's likely to be one of the most memorable reds you'll ever sample. Grab your glass and head to the redwood rooftop deck to enjoy the view.

RUTHERFORD

Silver Oak Wine Cellars. 915 Oakville Cross Rd. (at Money Rd.), Oakville. ☎ **707/944-8808.** Tasting room Mon–Sat 9am–4pm. Tours Mon–Thurs at 1:30pm, by appointment only.

Twenty-five years ago, an oil man from Colorado, Ray Duncan, and a former Christian Brothers monk, Justin Meyer, formed a partnership and a mission to create the finest cabernet sauvignon in the world. "We still haven't produced the best bottle of cabernet sauvignon of which Silver Oak is capable," admits Meyer, but this small winery is still the Wine Country's undisputed king of cabernet.

A narrow tree-lined road leads to the handsome Mediterranean-style winery, where roughly 44,000 cases of 100% varietal cab are produced annually. The elegant tasting room is refreshingly quiet and soothing, adorned with redwood panels stripped from old wine tanks and warmed by a wood fire. Tastings and tours are $5, which includes a beautiful German-made burgundy glass. At press time, only two wines were released: a 1993 Alexander Valley and a 1993 Napa Valley. If the $40-per-bottle price tag is a bit much, for half the price you can take home one of the winery's first noncab releases in 25 years—a velvety Meyer Family Port. No picnic facilities are available.

✪ PlumpJack Winery. 620 Oakville Cross Rd. (just west of the Silverado Trail), Oakville. ☎ **707/945-1220.** Daily 10am–4pm.

If most wineries are like a traditional and refined Brooks Brothers suit, PlumpJack stands out as the Todd Oldham of wine tasting: chic, colorful, a little wild, and popular with a young, hip crowd. Like the franchise's PlumpJack restaurant and wine shop in San Francisco and their resort in Tahoe, this playfully medieval winery is a welcome diversion from the same old, same old. But with Getty bucks behind what was once Villa Mt. Eden winery, the budget covers far more than just atmosphere: There's some serious wine making going on here, too, and for $5 you can sample the cabernet, petite sirah, Riesling, and chardonnay—each an impressive product from a winery that's only been open to the public since mid-1997. The few vintages for sale currently range from $15 to $30, and average around $20 per bottle. There are no tours or picnic spots, but this refreshingly stylized and friendly facility will make you want to hang out for a while nonetheless.

Groth Vineyards & Winery. 750 Oakville Cross Rd. (off Calif. 29 or the Silverado Trail), Oakville. ☎ **707/944-0290.** Mon–Sat 10am–4pm. Tours and tastings by appointment only.

Dennis Groth first made it big as Atari's CFO; his contemporaries must have thought he was nuts when he declared "Game Over" and went into the wine business. But when his 1985 Cabernet Sauvignon Reserve received a perfect score of 100 from wine critic Robert Parker—who had never before given an American wine such high marks—his name was back up among the highest-scoring players.

Recognition may be reward enough, but Groth's latest trophy is his stunning mission-style building, a big salmon palace surrounded by 121 acres of vineyards. The formal setting is the kind of place where for some reason you're inclined to whisper. You must make an appointment to visit, and then fork over $3 to taste his $27-a-bottle cab (which is still one of the most revered in the state), $18 chardonnay, and $11 sauvignon blanc. (Tasting fees are refunded with purchase.) Unfortunately, no picnicking is allowed, but you can enjoy your wine out on the terrace or in the charming garden on sunny days, or in front of the fireplace during winter. Production tours, which end with a tasting, are given by appointment only on weekdays at 11am and 2pm and Saturday at 11am.

Girard Winery. On the Silverado Trail at Oakville Cross Rd., Oakville. ☎ **707/ 944-8577.** Daily 11am–4pm.

While the tasting room staff is welcoming, there's no denying that this serious winery will appeal most to serious wine drinkers. For 15 years straight, Girard's cabernet has consistently received 90 points (out of 100) or better by the country's top wine aficionados. And despite all the hoopla, the winery has intentionally kept its production down to around 15,000 per year and continues to use only estate-grown grapes; the combination guarantees better quality control and also explains why most bottles go for $25 or more. Since Dean & DeLuca's owner, Mr. Leslie Rudd, purchased the winery in 1996, a brand new tasting room has been added. Samples are free, but swigs of older wines cost $3 for two or three varieties. Picnic facilities and tours are not currently offered.

Cakebread Cellars. 8300 St. Helena Hwy. (Calif. 29), Rutherford. ☎ **800/ 588-0298** or 707/963-5221. Daily 10am–4:30pm. Tours by appointment only.

This winery's moniker is actually the owners' surname, but it suits the wines produced here, where the focus is on making wine that pairs well with food. They've done such a good job that 85% of their 65,000 annual cases go directly to restaurants, which means only a select few wine drinkers get to take home a bottle. Even if you've found their label in local wine store, your choice has been limited: Just three varieties are distributed nationally. Here you can sample the sauvignon blanc, chardonnay, cabernet, merlot, zinfandel, pinot noir, the Rubaiyat-blend wine, and their dry rose Vin de Porche, which are all made from Napa Valley grapes. Prices range from an affordable $14 for a bottle of the 1996 sauvignon blanc to a pricey $53 for the 1994 reserve cab, but the average bottle sells for just a little more than $20. In the tasting room, a large barnlike space, the hospitable hosts pour either a $3 or $6 sampling; both include a keepsake wineglass.

✪ **St. Supéry Winery.** 8440 St. Helena Hwy. (Calif. 29), Rutherford. ☎ **800/ 942-0809** or 707/963-4507. Daily 9:30am–4:30pm.

The outside may look like a modern corporate office building, but inside you'll find a functional and welcoming winery that encourages first-time wine tasters to learn more about oenology. On the self-guided tour, you can wander through the demonstration vineyard where you'll learn about growing techniques. Inside, kids gravitate toward "SmellaVision," an interactive display that teaches you how to identify different wine ingredients. Adjoining is the Atkinson House, which chronicles more than 100 years of wine-making history. For $3 you'll get lifetime tasting privileges, and though they probably won't be pouring their ever-popular Moscato dessert wine, the sauvignon blanc and chardonnay flow freely. Even the prices make visitors feel at home: Many bottles go for around $8, although their 1994 Meritage cabernet will set you back $40.

Peju Province Winery. 8466 St. Helena Hwy. (between Oakville Cross and Rutherford Cross rds.), Rutherford. ☎ **707/963-3600.** Daily 10am–6pm.

Although Peju Province Winery is a relative newcomer to the Napa Valley, the Peju family has been making award-winning wines since the early 1980s. This small winery produces fewer than 10,000 cases a year, all of which are sold from the winery only (which probably explains why you haven't seen the label on many wine lists). It's a pretty, unassuming place, adorned with modern sculptures, well-tended gardens, and large windows that bathe the high-ceilinged tasting room in copious amounts of sunshine.

Prices range from $9.50 for a bottle of the 1996 Carnival French Colombard to $55 for Peju's pride and joy: their Gold Award–winning 1994 cabernet sauvignon from HB Vineyard. Markedly less expensive—and almost as good—is their 1994 cabernet franc, another Gold Award winner priced at a reasonable $25. The tasting fee is $3, which is refunded with wine purchase. No picnic facilities or tours are available.

Niebaum-Coppola. 1991 St. Helena Hwy. (Calif. 29), Rutherford. ☎ **707/ 963-9099.** Daily 10am–5pm. Tours offered daily.

In March 1995, Hollywood met Napa Valley when Francis Ford Coppola bought historic Inglenook Vineyards. Although the renowned film director has been dabbling in wine production for years (he's had a home in the valley for almost 25 years), Niebaum-Coppola (pronounced *Nee*-bomb *Coh*-pa-la) is his biggest endeavor yet. He plunked down millions to renovate the beautiful 1880s ivy-draped stone winery and restore the surrounding property to its historic dimensions, gilding it with the glitz and glamour you'd expect from Tinseltown in the process. On display are Academy awards and memorabilia from such Coppola films as *The Godfather* and *Bram Stoker's Dracula;* the Centennial Museum chronicles the history of the estate and its wine making as well as Coppola's filmmaking.

In spite of all the Hollywood hullabaloo, wine is not forgotten. Available for tasting are a Rubicon (a blend of estate-grown cabernet, cabernet franc, and merlot, aged for more than 5 years), cabernet franc, merlot, chardonnay, zinfandel, and others, all made from organically grown grapes and ranging from around $10 to more than $50. There's also a wide variety of both expensive and affordable gift items. Speaking of expensive, the steep $7.50-per-person tasting fee might make you wonder whether a movie is included in the price— it's not (but you'll at least get to keep the souvenir glass). And at $20 a pop for the château and garden tour, you've gotta wonder whether you're *funding* his next film. But the grounds are indeed spectacular, and the 1 1/2-hour journey includes private tasting and glass.

Don't let the prices deter you; if nothing else, at least visit the grounds—they're absolutely stunning and it costs nothing to stroll. You can also perk yourself up at the cappuccino bar, where you'll get *Godfather*-like atmosphere with your latte. You're welcome to picnic at any of the designated garden sites.

Beaulieu Vineyard. 1960 S. St. Helena Hwy. (Calif. 29), Rutherford. ☎ **707/ 963-2411.** Daily 10am–5pm. Tours daily 11am–4pm; in summer, roughly every half hour; call for winter schedule.

Bordeaux native Georges de Latour founded the third-oldest continuously operating winery in Napa Valley in 1900—and, with the help of legendary oenologist André Tchelistcheff, produced world-class, award-winning wines that have been served by every president of the United States since Franklin D. Roosevelt. The brick-and-redwood tasting room isn't much to look at, but with Beaulieu's (pronounced *Bowl*-you) stellar reputation, they have no need to visually impress. They do, however, offer a complimentary glass of chardonnay the minute you walk through the door as well as a variety of bottles under $15. The Private Reserve Tasting Room offers a "flight" of reserve wines to taste for $12.50–but if you want to take a bottle to go, it may cost as much as $50. A free tour explains the wine-making process and the vineyard's history. No reservation is necessary.

Grgich Hills Cellar. 1829 St. Helena Hwy. (Calif. 29, north of Rutherford Cross Rd.), Rutherford. ☎ **707/963-2784.** Daily 9:30am–4:30pm. Free tours by appointment only, Mon–Fri 11am and 2pm, Sat–Sun 11am and 1:30pm.

Yugoslavian émigré Miljenko (Mike) Grgich made his presence known to the world when his Château Montelena chardonnay bested the top French white burgundies at the famous 1976 Paris tasting. Since then, this master vintner has teamed up with Austin Hills (of the Hills Brothers coffee fortune) and started this extremely successful and respected winery in Rutherford.

The ivy-covered stucco building isn't much to behold, and the tasting room is even less appealing, but people don't come here for the scenery: As you might expect, Grgich's (pronounced *Grr*-gitch) chardonnays are legendary—and priced accordingly. The smart buys, however, are Grgich's outstanding zinfandel and cabernet sauvignon, which are very reasonably priced at around $18 and $25, respectively. The winery also produces a fantastic fumé blanc for as little as $15 a bottle. Before you leave, be sure to poke your head into the barrel-aging room and inhale the divine aroma. Tastings cost $3 on weekends, which includes the glass, and are free on weekdays. No picnic facilities are available.

ZD Wines. 8383 Silverado Trail (between Oakville Cross and Rutherford Cross rds.), Rutherford. ☎ **707/963-5188.** Daily 10am–4:30pm. Tours offered daily 10:30am–4:30pm, by appointment only.

What started as little more than a hobby in 1968 by two former aerospace engineers, Norman de Leuze and Gino Zepponi, has become a serious (and successful) family operation, as its fancy new digs along the Silverado Trail attest. Now owned and operated by the de Leuze family, ZD's wines have garnered more than 340 awards of excellence in prestigious competitions around the world. ZD is well known among the wine world's cognoscenti for their barrel-fermented chardonnay, intense pinot noir, and fruity cabernet sauvignon. They recently added a fourth wine to the family: a ZD merlot from the mountainous Atlas Peak area of the Napa Valley. These are carefully crafted wines in limited supply, so expect to pay at least $20 to $25 for their most recent labels (the 1994 cabernet is outstanding). Tastings are $5, which is credited toward your wine purchase. The moniker ZD, by the way, stands for both the original founders' initials, as well as an engineering term for Zero Defects—a fitting mantra for their wine-making process. No picnic facilities are available.

Mumm. 8445 Silverado Trail (just south of Rutherford Cross Rd.), Rutherford. ☎ **800/686-6272** or 707/942-3434. Apr–Oct daily 10:30am–6pm; Nov–Mar daily 10am–5pm. Tours offered every hour daily 11am–4pm in summer, 11am–3pm in winter.

At first glance, Mumm, housed in a big redwood barn, looks almost humble. But once you're in the front door, you'll know that they mean business—big business. Just beyond the extensive gift shop (filled with all sorts of namesake mementos) is the tasting room, where you can purchase sparkling wine by the glass (ranging from $3.50 to $6) or the bottle ($14 to $40, with most closer to $15), and take in the breathtaking vineyard and mountain views. Unfortunately, there's no food or picnicking here, but during warm weather, out on the open patio with a glass of champagne in hand, you'll forget all about nibbling. Mumm also offers a 45-minute educational tour and an art gallery with exhibits of Ansel Adams photographs of the Wine Country.

Frog's Leap Winery. 8815 Conn Creek Rd. (west of the Silverado Trail), Rutherford. ☎ **800/959-4704** or 707/963-4704. E-mail: Ribbitt@ frogsleap.com. Mon–Sat 10am–4pm; closed weekends during winter. Tastings and tours by appointment only. From Calif. 29, take Rutherford Cross Rd. and turn left at the fork.

One of the valley's leaders in organic farming, Frog's Leap is known for its kick-ass zinfandels (not to mention the sauvignon blancs, merlots, cabernets, and chardonnays). The entrance is confusing, so bear in mind that the beautifully restored 1884 big red barn is where the action takes place; the small gift shop behind the barn on the left is the best place to locate an employee if you don't find someone immediately. It's here that you'll find gifts featuring the winery's motto—"Time's fun when you're having flies"—and where you'll start your tour. The 45-minute expedition gives "a scintillating history" of how Frog's Leap began, a tour of the barn, and wine tasting, which may even be poured directly from the tanks. If there's action on the vines, you may get to pick and eat fresh grapes.

Considering that Frog's Leap is a favorite on restaurant wine lists and has a small annual production of 55,000 cases, the wine is well priced: The 1995 zin goes for $16 a bottle; the 1996 sauvignon blanc, $13. The only current releases topping $20 are the cab ($24) and merlot ($22).

Rutherford Hill Winery. 200 Rutherford Hill Rd. (off the Silverado Trail), Rutherford. ☎ **800/MERLOT-1** or 707/963-7194. Daily 10am–5pm. Tours daily at 11:30am, 1:30, and 3:30pm (Sat–Sun also at 12:30 and 2:30pm).

Though Rutherford Hill Winery offers a wide array of wines—chardonnay, cabernet, zinfandel port, sangiovese, cabernet sauvignon—it's best known for its merlot. In fact, Rutherford Hill is Napa Valley's leading producer of premium merlots, committing 75% of its entire wine production to this popular fruity varietal. Using massive drilling machinery imported from England, nearly a mile has been carved into the limestone slopes behind the winery, where more than 8,000 barrels of wine are stored in a naturally temperature-controlled environment. Half-hour tours include a trip through the caves (including a rare barrel tasting) and take you into the bowels of the immense wooden structure that houses the fermentation tanks and tasting room ($4, including wineglass).

Perched high above the valley, Rutherford Hill is also the Wine Country's premier picnicking site, offering the same superb views of the valley that guests of Auberge du Soleil (see "Where to Stay," below) pay big bucks for. Prices for current wines range from $13.50 for their 1995 sauvignon blanc to $44 for the exceptional 1992 zinfandel port, sold exclusively at the winery.

ST. HELENA

Raymond Vineyard & Cellar. 849 Zinfandel Lane (off Calif. 29 or the Silverado Trail), St. Helena. ☎ **800/525-2659** or 707/963-3141. Daily 10am–4pm. Tours by appointment only.

As fourth-generation vintners from Napa Valley and relations of the Beringers, brothers Walter and Roy Raymond have had plenty of time to develop terrific wines—and an excellent wine-tasting experience. The short drive through vineyards to reach Raymond's friendly, unintimidating cellar is case in point: Passing the heavy-hanging grapes makes you feel you're really in the thick of things before you even get in the door. Then comes the spacious, warm room, complete with dining table and chairs—a perfect setting for sampling the four tiers of wines, most of which are free for the tasting and well priced to appeal to all levels of wine drinkers: The Amber Hill label starts at $9 a bottle for the chardonnay and $13 for the cab; the reserves are priced in the midteens, while the "Generations" cab costs $35.

Along with the overall experience, we also liked the great gift selection, which includes barbecue sauces, mustard, a chocolate wine syrup, and a gooey hazelnut merlot fudge sauce. Private reserve tastings cost $2.50. Sorry, there are no picnic facilities.

✪ **V. Sattui Winery.** 1111 White Lane (at Calif. 29), St. Helena. ☎ **707/ 963-7774.** Winter daily 9am–5pm; summer daily 9am–6pm.

One of our friends has always wanted to write a guidebook on the best places for free food tastings in northern California; if that book ever comes to be, V. Sattui (pronounced Vee Sa-*too*-ee) will be one of the highlights. At this combination winery and enormous gourmet deli, you can fill up on wine, pâté, and cheese samples without ever reaching for your pocketbook. The gourmet store stocks more than 200 cheeses, sandwich meats, pâtés, breads, exotic salads, and delicious desserts such as a white-chocolate cheesecake. It would be an easy place to graze were it not for the continuous mob scene at the counter.

The long wine bar in the back offers everything from chardonnay, sauvignon blanc, Riesling, cabernet, and zinfandel to a tasty Madeira and a muscat dessert wine. Their wines aren't distributed, so if you taste something you simply must have, buy it. (If you buy a case, ask to talk with a manager, who'll give you access to the less crowded, more exclusive private tasting room.) Wine prices start around $9, with many in the $13 range; reserves top out at around $75.

V. Sattui's expansive and grassy picnic facilities make this a favorite for families. This is one of the most popular stops along Highway 29, so prepare for an enormous picnic party and you won't be disappointed. *Note:* To use the facilities, food and wine must be purchased here.

Flora Springs Wine Co. 677 St. Helena Hwy. S. (across from V. Sattui), St. Helena. ☎ **707/967-8032.** Winter daily 10am–5pm; summer daily 10am–6pm. Tours by appointment only.

While Flora Springs used to conduct tastings at their handsome stone winery, as of 1998 they're pouring their sauvignon blanc, cabernet, and other varieties at their new tasting room, flanked by a lovely mural. The label, which first appeared in 1978, is well known for its barrel-fermented chardonnay, a cabernet sauvignon, and Trilogy, a Bordeaux-style blend. Tasting costs $3 and includes a souvenir glass, which will forever be refilled if you bring it with you each time you visit. While there are many bottles available for around $10 (like the sauvignon blanc), the cab goes for $25.

Heitz Wine Cellars. 436 St. Helena Hwy. (Calif. 29), St. Helena. ☎ **707/ 963-2047.** Daily 11am–4pm. Tours by appointment only; call ☎ 707/963-3542.

If you're looking for a big wine-tasting hullabaloo, don't come here. At Heitz's tiny, modest tasting room, the point is the wine and the wine alone. Joe Heitz launched his winery in 1961, when there were fewer than 20 wineries in the valley. Today, he oversees the production of 40,000 cases per year, and although his reputation was built on cabernets (such as the Martha's Vineyard cab, which will set you back 80 big ones per bottle), he's also produced a highly-coveted 1990 chardonnay as well as less costly cabs, zins, and more unusual offerings such as the Grignolino rose (just $6.50). Tastings are complimentary, but if you want to take home the fruits of Heitz's labors, count on spending upwards of $20 per bottle.

Louis M. Martini. 254 S. St. Helena Hwy. (across the street from Sutter Home), St. Helena. ☎ **800/321-WINE.** Daily 10am–4:30pm. Tours available daily; call ahead for reservations and/or schedule.

Louis M. Martini is a comfortable stop for first-time as well as more refined wine tasters. Founded in 1922, this winery is as integral a part of the Wine Country as the Carneros region, which the Martini family developed. In fact, they actually initiated development of that area's vineyards and its production of chardonnays and pinot noirs. Their large tasting room is known for its friendly atmosphere, no-charge tastings, and free-flowing chardonnay, cabernet, merlot, and plenty more. (You can sample the reserve list for $6 and take home the large keepsake cabernet glass.)

Per-bottle prices "are the best in the valley," claims one employee, who also pointed out that while they range from $6 to $20, most are closer to $10. Another bonus: the great array of gourmet gift items, including the very fun and informative Food First Tasting Kit, which helps explain the art of pairing food and wine and discusses how food affects the flavor of wine more than wine affects the flavor of food.

✪ **Joseph Phelps Vineyards.** Taplin Rd. (off the Silverado Trail), P.O. Box 1031, St. Helena. ☎ **800/707-5789.** Mon–Sat 9am–5pm, Sun 9am–4pm. Tours and tastings by appointment only.

Visitors interested in intimate, comprehensive tours and looking for a knockout tasting should schedule a tour at this stellar winery. A quick and discreet turn off the Silverado Trail in Spring Valley (there's no sign, so watch for Taplin Road or you'll blast right by it), Joseph Phelps was founded in 1973 and has since become a major player in both the region and the worldwide wine market. Phelps himself is attributed with a long list of valley firsts, including launching the syrah varietal in the valley and extending the 1970s Berkeley food revolution (led by Alice Waters) up to the Wine Country via his store, the Oakville Grocery (see p. 131).

Joseph Phelps is a favorite stop for serious wine lovers. The modern, state-of-the-art winery and big-city vibe are proof that Phelps's annual 100,000 cases prove fruitful in more ways than one. When you pass through the wisteria-covered trellis to the entrance of the redwood building, you'll encounter an air of seriousness that hangs heavier than harvest grapes. Fortunately, the mood lightens as the well-educated tour guide explains the details of what you're tasting while pouring samples of five to six wines, which may include Riesling, sauvignon blanc, gewürztraminer, syrah, merlot, zin, and cab. (Unfortunately, some wines are so popular that they sell out quickly; come late in the season and you may not be able to taste or buy them.) The three excellently located picnic tables, on the terrace overlooking the valley, are available by reservation.

Sutter Home Winery. 277 St. Helena Hwy. (at Thomann Lane), St. Helena. ☎ **707/963-3104.** Winter daily 9:30am–4:30pm; summer daily 9am–5:30pm.

This winery's been around since 1874, but its widespread reputation stems from the early 1980s, when their introduction of white zinfandel to the mass market made pink the prominent color in America's wineglasses. While trends have changed and the popularity of white zin has waned, Sutter Home's department store–like tasting room is fair indication that this winery is still pouring for the people. In the friendly, bustling room, visitors surround the enormous U-shaped bar to sample a slew of wines, with chardonnay, cabernet, zin, and other varieties topping out at $7 a bottle. (Alcohol-free wines are as low as $4; the reserve cab is $12.) Along the periphery of the room is an endless selection of food products, ranging from mustard and barbecue to pasta and chocolate sauces, as well as a complete Sutter Home wardrobe line, featuring everything from boxers to baseball-style jackets.

Tasting is free, but for $10 you can participate in a unique new interactive process that allows you to blend your own wine, bottle it, and custom sign the label. No tours are offered, but you're invited to take a self-guided walk through the surrounding Victorian Gardens.

✪ **Prager Winery & Port Works.** 1281 Lewelling Lane (just west of Calif. 29, behind Sutter Home), St. Helena. ☎ **800/969-PORT** or 707/963-7678. Daily 10:30am–4:30pm.

If you want a real down-home, off-the-beaten-track experience, Prager's can't be beat. Turn the corner from Sutter Home and roll into the small gravel parking lot; you're on the right track—but when you pull open the creaky old wooden door to this shack of a wine-tasting room, you'll begin to wonder. By all means, don't turn back! Pass the oak barrels and you'll quickly come upon the clapboard tasting room, made homey with a big Oriental rug, a cat, and, during winter, a small space heater. Most days, your host will be Jim Prager himself, who's undeniably a sort of modern Santa Claus in both looks and demeanor. But you won't have to sit on his lap for your wish to come true: Just fork over $5 (refundable with purchase) and he'll pour you samples of his delicious $25 Madeline dessert wine, a late-harvest Johannisberg Riesling, the recently released 10-year-old port (which costs close to $50 per bottle), and a few other yummy selections like chardonnay and cab, which retail in the mid-30s. Also available is "Prager Chocolate Drizzle," a chocolate liqueur that tops ice creams and other desserts.

We recommend tasting here even if you can't afford to purchase; if you do want to buy, this is the only place to do it, as Prager doesn't distribute. If you're looking for a special gift, Jim's daughter custom etches bottles for around $100 in the design of your choice, plus the cost of the wine.

Robert Keenan Winery. 3660 Spring Mountain Rd. (off Calif. 29), St. Helena. ☎ **707/963-9177.** Daily 10am–4pm. Tours and tastings by appointment only, except Mar–Sept, when you can simply drop by on any Sat.

It's a winding, uphill drive to reach secluded Robert Keenan, but a diversion this far off the tourist track guarantees you more elbow room at the tasting bar and a quieter, less commercial experience. When you drive through the gate and pass a few modest homes with kids' toys out front, you'll ask yourself whether one of the buildings is the family winery. It's not. Keep driving (slowly—kids and dogs at play) and you'll know when you get to the main building and its redwood tasting room.

The 10,000 cases produced here per year are the result of yet another fast-paced professional who left his business behind and headed for the hills. In this case, it's native San Franciscan Robert Keenan, who ran his own insurance agency for 20 years. When he merged with another firm and was bought out in 1981, he had already purchased his "retirement property," the winery's 176 acres, and soon turned his fascination with wine making into a second career. The renovated stone building has a much older history, dating back to the old Conradi Winery, which was founded in 1890.

Today Robert Keenan Winery is known for its big, full-bodied reds, such as the Mountain cab, merlot, chardonnay, and cabernet franc, all ranging from $17 to $25 per bottle. Older vintages, which you won't find elsewhere, are for sale here as well. Take the tour to learn about their vineyards, production facilities, and wine making in general. Those looking for a pastoral picnic spot should consider spreading their blankets out here. The four tables, situated right outside the winery and surrounded by vineyards, offer stunning views.

✪ **Domaine Charbay Winery & Distillery.** 4001 Spring Mountain Rd. (5 miles west of Calif. 29), St. Helena. ☎ **800/MDISTILL** (800/634-7845) or 707/963-9327. Daily (except holidays) by appointment only.

After you finally reach this mountaintop hideaway affectionately called "the Still on the Hill," you immediately get the sense that something special is going on here. Owner Miles Karakasevic considers himself more of a perfume maker than the 12th-generation master distiller he is, and it's easy to see why: This is truly a family-owned and -operated passion. The tiny distillery is crammed with bottles of his latest fragrant projects-in-the-making, such as tequila, anise liqueur (he'll name it after his wife, Susan) and habanero pepper-infused spirits. Other elixirs he's quietly becoming famous in the Valley for: black walnut liqueur, apple brandy, a line of ports, several red wines, and their charter product—Charbay (pronounced shar-BAY)—a brandy liqueur blended with chardonnay. The tour centers around a small, 25-gallon copper alambic still; you'll be lovingly guided through an explanation fo the distilling process by either Miles, his gregarious son (and apprentice) Marko, or Susan. It's all very low-key and laughter-filled at Domaine Charbay, one of the most unique and interesting places to visit in Wine Country. It's $10 to taste their various releases (what you'll get to taste depends on their mood, we suspect), which is credited toward purchases. No picnic facilities.

Beringer Vineyards. 2000 Main St. (Calif. 29), St. Helena. ☎ **707/ 963-7115.** Off-season daily 9:30am–5pm (last tour 4pm, last tasting 4:30pm); summer 9:30am–6pm (last tour 5pm, last tasting 5:30pm). Free 45-min. tours offered every hour between 9:30am–4pm; no reservations necessary.

Follow the line of cars just north of St. Helena's business district to Beringer Vineyards, where everyone stops at the remarkable Rhine

House to taste wine and view the hand-dug tunnels carved out of the mountainside. Founded in 1876 by brothers Jacob and Frederick, this is the oldest continuously operating winery in the Napa Valley—it was open even during Prohibition, when Beringer kept afloat by making "sacramental" wines. While their white zinfandel is still the winery's most popular nationwide seller, the 1994 chardonnay is the choice for more discerning palates: It won *Wine Spectator*'s 1996 Wine of the Year award. Free tastings of current vintages are conducted in the upstairs gift shop, where there's also a large selection of bottles for less than $20. Reserve wines are available in the Rhine House for a fee of $2 to $6 per taste.

Charles Krug Winery. 2800 St. Helena Hwy. (just north of the tunnel of trees at the northern end of St. Helena), St. Helena. ☎ **707/963-5057.** Daily 10:30am–5:30pm. Tours daily at 11:30am, 1:30, and 3:30pm.

Founded in 1861, Krug was the first winery built in the valley, and is today owned by the family of Peter Mondavi (yes, Robert is his brother). It's worth paying your respects here with a $3 tour, which takes just under an hour and encompasses a walk through the historical redwood Italianate wine cellar, built in 1874, as well as the vineyards, where you'll learn more about grapes and varietals. The tour ends with a tasting in the retail center. But you don't have to tour to taste: Just stop by and fork over $3 to sip current releases, $5 to sample reserves; you'll also get a souvenir glass. On the grounds are picnic facilities with umbrella-shaded tables overlooking vineyards or the historic wine cellar.

St. Clement Vineyards. 2867 St. Helena Hwy. N., St. Helena. ☎ **800/331-8266** or 707/967-3033. Daily 10am–4pm. Guided tours daily 10am and 2pm; reservations required for weekend 10am tours and all 2pm tours.

Perched on a knoll above Highway 29, St. Clement's tasting room is a contradictory combination of homey and corporate, comfortable and cramped. The building itself is a charming Gothic Victorian, but step inside for a sampling and you'll notice that the decor is rather businesslike. On the flip side, the staff is casual and friendly, making this a good stopover for folks who are intimidated by more stuffy scenarios. The bar has room for only three or so guests—but that's the perfect excuse to tote a glass of merlot out onto the charming landscaped terrace.

Tours feature a walk through the cellar and/or winery plus complimentary barrel, fresh grape juice (depending on the time of year), and wine tastings. If you come just to imbibe, there's a $2 fee, which is refundable with any wine purchase (most bottles run about $25) and includes some wines that you can't get elsewhere. The picnic tables are pleasant, but the sound of Highway 29's traffic keeps the site from being entirely splendorous.

Freemark Abbey. Hwy. 29 at Lodi Lane, St. Helena. ☎ **800/963-9698.** Daily 10am–4pm. Tour daily at 2pm.

Set in a low-key shopping mall, Freemark Abbey's friendly tasting room has a hunting-lodge feel. The huge space features open-beamed ceilings, a roaring fire (in winter), and comfy couches. The town's only politically correct moose head on a plaque hangs above the tasting bar—check it out for yourself to see what we mean. There's a $4 charge for tasting and a keepsake wineglass, which may be filled with a sampling of the $10 1996 Riesling, plus chardonnay, cabernet, and merlot, which are priced closer to $20. During summer you can take your taste out onto the lovely outdoor terrace. While they probably won't be pouring the 1986 cabernet, you can buy a bottle for $57. The half-hour guided tour covers the history, viticulture, and wine cellars. No picnic facilities are available.

CALISTOGA

✪ **Kornell Champagne Cellars.** 1091 Larkmead Lane (just off the Silverado Trail), Calistoga. ☎ **707/942-0859.** Daily 10am–4:30pm.

You've gotta love this place, which used to be the Larkmead Winery. Kornell's wine dudes—Dennis, Bob, Chris, and Rich—will do practically anything to maintain their self-proclaimed reputation as the "friendliest winery in the valley." They'll serve you all the bubbly you want (four to six varieties: Brut, blanc de blanc, blanc de noir, and extra-dry reserve, all ranging from $15 to $20 a bottle). They guarantee that you'll never wait more than 10 minutes to take the 20-minute tour of the oldest champagne cellar in the region, and even offer up a great story about Marie Antoinette's champagne-glass design.

Considering that the winery is owned by former Disney president Richard Frank, it's not surprising that, as one employee pointed out, the unpretentious place is a "celebrity stopover." But that's nothing new: It was once the summer home of San Francisco's renowned Lillie Hitchcock Coit (as in Coit Tower), and Marilyn used to hang out here when she was married to DiMaggio.

While the tasting room is so casual you may find yourself kicking back on a case of wine, the stone cellar (listed on the National Register of Historic Places) captures the essence of the Wine Country's history. Be sure to meander into the Back Room, where chardonnay, zinfandel, and cabernet are poured. Kornell makes fewer than 500 cases of still wines a year, which means if you don't try (and buy) 'em here, you may never get another chance; the same goes for their motto T-shirt: "Kiss French, Drink California." Behind the tasting room is a choice picnic area, situated under the oaks and overlooking the vineyards.

✪ **Schramsberg.** 1400 Schramsberg Rd. (off Calif. 29), Calistoga. ☎ **707/ 942-4558.** Daily 10am–4pm. Tours and tastings by appointment only.

This 200-acre champagne estate, a landmark once frequented by Robert Louis Stevenson, has a wonderful old-world feel and is one of our all-time favorite places to explore. Schramsberg is the label that presidents serve when toasting dignitaries from around the globe, and there's plenty of historic memorabilia in the front room to prove it. But the real mystique begins when you enter the champagne caves, which wind $2^1/2$ miles (the longest in North America, they say) and were partly hand-carved by Chinese laborers in the 1800s. The caves have an authentic Tom Sawyer ambiance, complete with dangling cobwebs and seemingly endless passageways; you can't help but feel you're on an adventure. The comprehensive, unintimidating tour ends in a charming tasting room, where you'll sit around a big table and sample several surprisingly varied selections of bubbly. Tasting prices are a bit dear at $7.50 per person, but it's money well spent. Note, however, that tastings are only offered to those who take the free tour, and you must reserve a spot in advance.

✪ **Clos Pegase.** 1060 Dunaweal Lane (off Calif. 29 or the Silverado Trail), Calistoga. ☎ **707/942-4981.** Daily 10:30am–5pm. Tours daily at 11am and 2pm.

What happens when a man falls in love with art and wine making, purchases more than 450 acres of prime growing property, and sponsors a competition commissioned by the San Francisco Museum of Modern Art to create a "temple to wine"? You'll find out when you visit this magnificent winery. Renowned architect Michael Graves designed this incredible oasis, which integrates art, 20,000 square feet of aging caves, and a luxurious hilltop private home. Viewing the art here is as much the point as tasting the wines— which, by the way, don't come cheap: Prices range from $18.50 for the 1995 Mitsuko's chardonnay to as much as $50 for the 1994 Hommage Artist Series Reserve, an extremely limited blend of the winery's finest lots of cabernet sauvignon and merlot. Tasting all the current releases will cost $2.50, and reserves are $2 each. The grounds at Clos Pegase (pronounced Clo Pay-*goss*) feature an impressive sculpture garden as well as scenic picnic spots.

⟡ **Sterling Vineyards.** 1111 Dunaweal Lane (off Calif. 29, just south of Calistoga), Calistoga. ☎ **707/942-3300.** Daily 10:30am–4:30pm.

No, you don't need climbing shoes to reach this dazzling white Mediterranean-style winery, perched 300 feet up on a rocky knoll. Just fork over $6 and you'll arrive via aerial tram, which offers dazzling bucolic views along the way. Once on land, follow the self-guided tour (the most comprehensive in the entire Wine Country) of the entire wine-making process. Currently owned by the Seagram company, the winery produces more than 200,000 cases per year. Samples at the panoramic tasting room are included in the tram fare. Expect to pay anywhere from $8 to $50 for a souvenir bottle ($16 is the average), and if you can find a bottle of their 1995 Napa Valley chardonnay (currently going for about $14), buy it—it's already garnered a septuplet of awards.

Cuvaison. 4550 Silverado Trail (just south of Dunaweal Lane), Calistoga. ☎ **707/942-6266.** Daily 10am–5pm. Tours at 10:30am daily with 24-hour notice or by appointment.

In 1969, Silicon Valley engineers Thomas Cottrell and Thomas Parkhill began Cuvaison (pronounced Koo-vay-*sawn,* a French term for the fermentation of wine on the skins) with a 27-acre vineyard of cabernet, just south of Calistoga. Today that same vineyard has expanded to 400 acres, producing 63,000 cases of premium wines every year. Known mainly for their chardonnays, wine maker John Thacher also produces a limited amount of merlot, pinot noir, cabernet sauvignon, and zinfandel within the handsome Spanish mission–style structure. If you're curious what an exceptional chardonnay tastes like, beg for a sample of the award-winning 1995 Napa Valley/Carneros chardonnay, which embodies a green apple–citrus character typical of grapes from the Carneros region.

Tastings are $3, which includes a glass. Wine prices range from $13 for a 1996 Rose pinot noir to as much as $50 for a 1994 merlot, though the bottle to take home is their award-winning 1995 Carneros chardonnay or pinot noir, both currently priced just under $20. *Insider Tip:* Bring back the same glass on your next visit, and the wine's free. Beautiful picnic grounds are situated amidst 350-year-old moss-covered oak trees.

Chateau Montelena. 1429 Tubbs Lane (off Calif. 29, just past the Old Faithful Geyser), Calistoga. ☎ **707/942-5105.** Daily 10am–4pm. Guided tours by appointment only at 11am and 2pm.

You've probably heard of the California chardonnay that revolutionized the world of wine when it won the legendary Paris tasting test of 1976, beating out France's top white burgundies. That wine was a Chateau Montelena 1973 chardonnay, the product of Mike Grgich's (who now owns his own winery, Grgich Hills) second vintage as wine maker for Chateau Montelena. Though the tasting room is rather plain, the winery itself—housed in a replica of the great châteaux of Bordeaux—is a feast for the eyes, as are the Chinese-inspired lake and gardens behind the château. Tastings are $5, which is credited toward wine purchase; bottle prices are also on the steep side, ranging from $15 for a Riesling to $45 for the 1993 Montelena Estate cabernet sauvignon. After sampling the winery's superb chardonnay, cabernet, and Calistoga Cuvee (a blend of cabernet sauvignon, cabernet franc, and merlot), wander around back to marvel at this classic French castle and picturesque grounds replete with wild fowl, lush foliage, and romantic walkways. Unfortunately, picnicking is no longer an option.

3 More to See & Do

We're not going to humor you: If days filled with wine tasting, dining on fancy food, and just lounging around in the country is about as exciting to you as a trip to the DMV, you should buy a *TV Guide* and make yourself real cozy—'cause it's going to be one helluva long stay.

However, there are a few daytime attractions—such as golf, spectacular spas, a few wonderful shops, and museums—that will perk up anyone who simply can't take one more glass of wine; we've discussed them below.

Don't think we just forgot to mention nightlife. With few exceptions, there's more action in a 1-block ghost town than there is in Napa Valley after dark. So what do you do when it's 8pm, you've already had dinner, and thumb-twiddling already has your fingers cramped? Beats us—but if you figure it out, let us know.

NAPA

If you have plenty of time and a penchant for Victorian architecture, the **Napa Valley Conference and Visitors Bureau,** 1310 Napa Town Center Mall, off First Street (☎ **707/226-7459; www.napavalley.com**), offers self-guided walking tours of the town's historic buildings.

Anyone with an appreciation for art absolutely must visit the ✪ **di Rosa Preserve,** which until recently was closed to the public.

Up, Up & Away . . .

Admit it: floating across lush green pastures in a hot-air balloon is something you've always dreamed of but never got around to actually doing. Well, here's your best chance, because believe it or not, Napa Valley is the busiest hot-air balloon "flight corridor" in the *world*. Northern California's temperate weather allows for ballooning year-round, and on summer weekends in the valley, it's a rare day when you don't see at least one of the colorful airships floating above the vineyards.

Trips usually depart early in the morning, when the air is cooler and the balloons have better lift. Flight paths vary with the direction and speed of the changing breezes, so "chase" crews on the ground must follow the balloons to their undetermined destinations. Most flights last about an hour and end with a traditional champagne celebration and breakfast. Reservations are required and should be made as far in advance as possible. Prices range from $165 to $195 per person for the basic package (which includes shuttle service from your hotel); wedding, wine-tasting, picnic, and lodging packages are also available. For more information or reservations, call Napa's **Bonaventura Balloon Company** (☎ 800/ FLY-NAPA), a highly reputable organization owned and operated by master pilot Joyce Bowen. Another good choice is **Adventures Aloft** (☎ 800/944-4408 or 707/944-4408; **www.nvaloft.com**), Napa Valley's oldest hot-air-balloon company.

Rene and Veronica di Rosa, who have been collecting contemporary American art for more than 40 years, converted their 88 acres of prime Wine Country property into a monument to northern California's regional art and nature. Their world-renowned collection features 1,500 works in all media by more than 600 greater Bay Area artists. Their treasures are displayed practically everywhere, from along the shores of their 30-acre lake to each nook and cranny of their 110-year-old winery-turned-residence, adjoining building, two new galleries, and gardens. With hundreds of surrounding acres of rolling hills protected under the Napa County Land Trust, this place is truly a must-see for both art and nature lovers. It's located at 5200 Sonoma Hwy. (Highway 121/12)—look for the blue-colored gate. Visits are by appointment only, when a maximum of 25 guests are guided through the preserve. Each tour lasts 2 to 2$^{1}/_{2}$

hours and costs $10 per person. Call ☎ **707/226-5991** to make reservations.

SHOPPING   If you're looking for a trinket but don't quite know what you want, plan to spend at least an hour strolling **Red Hen's** co-op collection of antiques. You'll find everything from baseball cards to living-room sets, and prices are remarkably affordable. You can't miss this enormous red barn-style building at 5091 St. Helena Hwy., on Calif. 29 at Oak Knoll Avenue West (☎ **707/257-0822**). It's open daily from 10am to 5:30pm. Its sister property in central Napa is the **Riverfront Antique Center,** 705 Soscol Ave., at Third Street (☎ **707/253-1966**). Here, 70 antique-art dealers exhibit their collections in stalls throughout a mazelike warehouse. During winter, bring a scarf and mittens—there's no indoor heating here. Hours are daily from 10am to 5pm.

HITTING THE LINKS   South of downtown Napa, 1.3 miles east of Calif. 29 on Calif. 12, is the **Chardonnay Club** (☎ **707/257-8950**), a challenging 36-hole land-links golf complex with first-class service. You pay just one fee, which makes you a member for the day. Privileges include the use of a golf cart, the practice range (including a bucket of balls), and services usually found only at a private club (the day we played, a snack cart came by on the course with a full selection of sandwiches and soft drinks—and at the end of the round our clubs were cleaned). The course ambles through and around 325 acres of vineyards, hills, creeks, canyons, and rock ridges. There are three nines of similar challenge, all starting at the clubhouse so that you can play the 18 of your choice. Five sets of tees provide you with a course measuring from 5,300 yards to a healthy 7,100. Starting times can be reserved up to 2 weeks in advance. Greens fees (including mandatory cart and practice balls) from March 16 through November are $60 on weekdays (with a 2pm twilight for $45) and $80 on weekends (with a 2pm twilight for $55). Rates are discounted in winter.

RUTHERFORD

Want to bring home an unusual and beautiful handcrafted decoration for your home or yard? Seek out **Napa Valley Grapevine Wreath Company,** P.O. Box 67, Rutherford, CA 94573 (☎ **707/963-8893**), which weaves big and small indoor or outdoor sculptures made out of little more than cabernet grapevines. Options range from a basic wreath to a star or full-scale reindeer; all are priced competitively. Call for directions—this tiny shack of a shop is hidden on a side road among Rutherford's vineyards. Hours vary during winter, but are generally Wednesday through Monday from 10:30am to 5:30pm.

ST. HELENA

Literary buffs and other romantics will want to visit the **Silverado Museum,** 1490 Library Lane (☎ 707/963-3757), which is devoted to the life and works of Robert Louis Stevenson, who honeymooned here in 1880 in an abandoned Silverado Mine bunkhouse. The collection of more than 8,000 items includes original manuscripts, letters, photographs, and portraits, plus the desk he used in Samoa. Hours are Tuesday through Sunday from noon to 4pm; admission is free.

SPAS   If the Wine Country's slow pace and tranquil vistas aren't soothing enough for you, St. Helena's diverse selection of spas can massage, bathe, wrap, and steam you into an overly-pampered pulp. Should you choose to indulge, we recommend you do so toward the end of your stay—when you've wined and dined yourself to the point where you have only enough energy left to make it to and from the spa.

Unlike the cosmopolitan-chic day spas of Sonoma Mission Inn (Sonoma) and Health Spa Napa Valley (St. Helena), ✪ **White Sulphur Springs Retreat & Spa,** 3100 White Sulphur Springs Rd. (☎ 707/963-4361), offers a more spiritual day of cleansing and pampering. Yes, you will encounter massages, aromatherapy treatments, seaweed or mineral mud wraps, and a pool and Jacuzzi for guests' use. But the most blissful benefits are not the product of some well-known architect or fancy new massage oil. Mother Nature takes the credit for the magic here: acres of redwoods, streams, grassy fields, wooded groves, and hiking trails galore. The spa treatments only make the experience that much more relaxing. The resident spotted owls, woodpeckers, raccoon, deer, and fox don't take advantage of the natural outdoor hot sulphur spring, pool, Jacuzzi, or sauna (free for spa-goers), but you might catch a glimpse of them as you bathe. Massages are given in the homey spa building or outside amidst the redwoods ($55 to $65 per hour). A day of peaceful pampering doesn't come any cheaper, but take note: This is a casual place. Five-star fanatics should stick with Sonoma Mission Inn & Spa (see chapter 5) or Health Spa Napa Valley, which covers the other end of the spa spectrum.

If you're a fitness freak, ✪ **Health Spa Napa Valley,** 1030 Main St. (Highway 29; ☎ 707/967-8800), is a mandatory stop after a few days of inevitable overindulgence. Sure, you can hike, bike, run the roads, or convince yourself that flexing your biceps as you raise your wineglass is enough. But if your preferred way to work off last night's umpteenth vacation dessert is to treadmill or Stairmaster yourself silly, you'll want to get a temporary membership here. Along with the usual cardio machines, you can work off that second helping of crème brûlée with a spin class, yoga, or a few laps in the outdoor pool. Then reward yourself with spa treatments: Immerse yourself in Wine Country ways with a grape-seed mud wrap ($75) or go all out with a Pancha Karma treatment—two massage therapists get out the knots with synchronized motion ($135). These are the newest facilities around and the local favorite for fitness. Memberships are $15 per day Monday through Thursday, $20 per day Friday through Sunday, and free for guests of the Inn at Southbridge.

SHOPPING   St. Helena's Main Street is the best place to go if you're suffering serious retail withdrawal. Though you'll find only a few blocks of stores that are credit-card worthy, trust us, a lot of damage can still be done. Take, for example, ✪ **Vanderbilt and Company,** 1429 Main St., between Adams and Pine streets (☎ **707/963-1010**), which offers the crème de la crème of cookware, hand-painted Italian dishware, and everything else you could possibly convince yourself you need for your gourmet kitchen and dining room. They're the largest seller of Vietry Italian cookware in the United States. We did almost all our holiday shopping here last year. Open daily from 9:30am to 5:30pm.

Another excellent find is **fideaux,** 1400 Oak Ave. (☎ **707/967-9935**), a charming boutique known as the Eddie Bauer for dogs and cats. Hand-painted feeders, beautiful ceramic water bowls, custom-designed scratching posts, silk-screened dog and cat pillows, rhinestone collars, unique toys, and gourmet dog treats are just a few pet must-haves you'll find here. The ultimate way to bring the Wine Country home to Spot? Try a wine-barrel doghouse. And if your trip is causing doggie withdrawal, you can always stop by and give a few pats to the shopkeepers' dogs: Melbourne, the yellow Lab, and Zoe, the black standard poodle. Hours are Monday through Friday from 8:30am to 5:30pm, and Saturday and Sunday from 9:30am to 5:30pm.

Shopaholics won't be able to avoid at least one sharp turn off Highway 29 for a stop at the **St. Helena Premium Outlets,** two miles north of downtown St. Helena (☎ **707/963-7282**). Featured designers include Donna Karan, Coach, Movado, London Fog, and more. The stores are open daily from 10am to 6pm.

Napa's best deals on wine are found not in the wineries, but in a couple of St. Helena stores. **Dean & DeLuca,** 607 S. Main St. (Calif. 29; ☎ **707/967-9980**), and—believe it or not—**Safeway,** 1026 Hunt Ave. (☎ **707/963-3850**), have enormous wine selections; Safeway tends to have some of the best deals around.

One last favorite stop: **Napa Valley Olive Oil Manufacturing Company,** 835 Charter Oak Rd., at the end of the road behind Tra Vigne restaurant (☎ **707/963-4173**), a tiny market that presses and bottles its own oils and sells them at a fraction of the price you'll pay elsewhere. They also have an extensive selection of Italian cooking ingredients, imported snacks, and the best deals on exotic mushrooms we've ever seen. You'll also love their age-old method for totaling the bill, which you simply must find out for yourself.

BICYCLING   The quieter northern end of the valley is an ideal place to rent a bicycle and ride the Silverado Trail. **St. Helena Cyclery,** 1156 Main St. (☎ **707/963-7736**), rents bikes for $7 per hour or $25 a day, including rear rack and picnic bag.

CALISTOGA

Calistoga Depot, 1458 Lincoln Ave. (on the site of Calistoga's original 1868 railroad station), now houses a variety of shops, some of which are housed in six restored passenger cars dating from 1916.

NATURAL WONDERS   **Old Faithful Geyser of California,** 1299 Tubbs Lane (☎ **707/942-6463**), is one of only three "old faithful" geysers in the world. It's been blowing off steam at regular intervals for as long as anyone can remember. The 350°F water spews out to a height of about 60 feet every 40 minutes, day and night (varying with natural influences such as barometric pressure, the moon, tides, and tectonic stresses). The performance lasts about a minute, and you can watch the show as many times as you want. Bring along a picnic lunch to munch on between spews. An exhibit hall, gift shop, and snack bar are open every day. Admission is $6 for adults, $5 for seniors, $2 for children 6 to 12, free for children under 6. Open daily from 9am to 6pm (to 5pm in winter). To get there, follow the signs from downtown Calistoga; it's between Calif. 29 and Calif. 128.

You won't see thousands of trees turned into stone, but you'll still find many interesting petrified specimens at the **Petrified Forest,** 4100 Petrified Forest Rd. (☎ **707/942-6667**). Volcanic ash blanketed this area after the eruption of Mount St. Helena three million years ago. As a result, you'll find redwoods that have turned to rock through the slow infiltration of silicas and other minerals, as well as petrified seashells, clams, and marine life indicating that water covered this area even before the redwood forest. Admission is $4 for adults, $3 for seniors and children 12 to 17, $1 for children 4 to 11, and free for children under 4. Open daily from 10am to 5:30pm (to 4:30pm in winter). Heading north from Calistoga on Calif. 128, turn left onto Petrified Forest Road, just past Lincoln Street.

BICYCLING   Cycling enthusiasts can rent bikes from **Getaway Adventures BHK** (Biking, Hiking, and Kayaking), 1117 Lincoln Ave. (☎ **800/499-BIKE** or 707/942-0332; **www.getawayadventures. com**). Full-day tours cost $89 and include lunch and a visit to four or five wineries; downhill cruises ($49) are available for people who hate to pedal. On weekdays they'll even deliver bikes to you.

GLIDER RIDES   Calistoga offers a unique way of seeing its vineyard-filled valleys—from a glider. These quiet "birds" leave from the **Calistoga Gliderport,** 1546 Lincoln Ave., Calistoga, CA 94515 (☎ **707/942-5000**). Twenty-minute rides are $79 for one, $129 for two (weight limits apply); 30-minute rides are also available.

HORSEBACK RIDES   If you like horses and venturing through cool, misty forests, then $40 will seem like a bargain for a 1¹/₂-hour ride with a friendly tour guide from **Napa Valley Trail Rides** (☎ **707/996-8566; www.thegridnet/trailrides/**). After you've been saddled and schooled in the basics of horse handling at the stable, you'll be led on a leisurely stroll (with the occasional trot thrown in for excitement) through beautiful Bothe–Napa Valley State Park, located off Highway 29 near Calistoga. Napa Valley Trail Rides also offers a Western Barbecue Ride, Sunset Ride, Full Moon Ride, and Gourmet Boxed Lunch Ride & Winery Tour. We've taken the trip ourselves and loved every minute of it—sore butts and all.

✪ MUD BATHS   The one thing you should do while you're in Calistoga is what people have been doing here for the last 150 years: Take a mud bath. The natural baths are composed of local volcanic ash, imported peat, and naturally boiling mineral hot-springs water, all mulled together to produce a thick mud that simmers at a temperature of about 104°F.

After you've overcome the hurdle of deciding how best to place your naked body into the mushy stone tub, the rest is pure relaxation—you'll soak with surprising buoyancy for about 10 to 12 minutes. A warm mineral-water shower, a mineral-water whirlpool bath, and a mineral-water steam-room visit follow. Afterward, a relaxing blanket wrap will slowly cool down your delighted body. All of this takes about 1¹/₂ hours and costs about $45; with a massage, add another half hour and $20 (we recommend a full hour). The outcome is a rejuvenated, revitalized, squeaky-clean you. *Note:* Mud baths aren't recommended for those who are pregnant or have high blood pressure.

The spas also offer a variety of other treatments, such as hand and foot massages, herbal wraps, acupressure face-lifts, skin rubs, and herbal facials. Prices range from $35 to $125, and appointments are necessary for all services; call at least a week in advance, and as far in advance as possible during the busy summer season.

Indulge yourself at any of these Calistoga spas:

Spa	Address	Telephone Number
Dr. Wilkinson's Hot Springs	1507 Lincoln Ave.	707/942-4102
Lincoln Avenue Spa	1339 Lincoln Ave.	707/942-5296
Golden Haven Hot Springs Spa	1713 Lake St.	707/942-6793
Calistoga Spa Hot Springs	1006 Washington St.	707/942-6269
Calistoga Village Inn & Spa	1880 Lincoln Ave.	707/942-0991
Eurospa & Inn	1202 Pine St	707/942-6829
Indian Springs Resort	1712 Lincoln Ave.	707/942-4913
Lavender Hill Spa	1015 Foothill Blvd.	800/528-4772
Mount View Spa	1457 Lincoln Ave.	707/942-5789
Nance's Hot Springs	1614 Lincoln Ave.	707/942-6211
Roman Spa Motel	1300 Washington St.	707/942-4441

4 Where to Stay

With more than 2,500 hotel rooms available throughout the county, you'd think it'd be a snap to secure a room. Unfortunately, choosing and reserving accommodations—especially from April through November—can be a challenge, and to add to the frustration is that ever-burdening 2-night minimum.

Because the Napa Valley is so small, it really doesn't much matter which town you base yourself in; everything's within a half-hour or 45-minute drive from everything else. There are, however, a number of other things you should think about when deciding where to stay. Consider whether you want to be in a modern hotel with all the expected conveniences or a quaint turn-of-the-century B&B; surrounded by acres of vineyards or closer to the highway; in the company of the more conservative wealthy or those leading alternative lifestyles. Accommodations here run the gamut—from motels and B&Bs to world-class luxury retreats—and all are easily accessible from the main highway. While we recommend shacking up in the more romantically pastoral areas such as St. Helena, there's no question you're going to find better deals in the towns of Napa or laid-back Calistoga. As always, the primary determining factor will come down to one question: how much are you willing to spend?

We've arranged the listings below first by area and then by price, using the following categories: **Very Expensive,** more than $250 per night; **Expensive,** $200 to $250 per night; **Moderate,** $150 to $200 per night; and **Inexpensive,** less than $150 per night (sorry—the reality is that anything less than $150 a night qualifies as inexpensive 'round these parts).

When planning your trip, keep in mind that during the high season—between June and November—most hotels charge peak rates and sell out completely on weekends; many have a 2-night minimum. Always ask about discounts. During the off-season, you have far better bargaining power and may be able to get a room at almost half the summer rate. Also note that while the valley is reasonably small and condensed, tourist traffic makes it beneficial to stay as close to the attractions you want to visit as possible.

HELPING HANDS: LOCAL RESERVATIONS SERVICES   A number of companies offer help with hotel and B&B reservations at no charge. **Accommodation Referral Bed & Breakfast Exchange** (☎ **800/240-8466,** 800/499-8466 in Calif., or 707/963-8466), which also represents hotels and inns, will ask you which dates you're traveling, your price range, and what kind of accommodation you're looking for before coming up with recommendations. **Bed & Breakfast Inns of Napa Valley** (☎ **707/944-4444**), an association of 26 Napa Valley B&Bs, provides inn descriptions and makes reservations. **Napa Valley Reservations Unlimited** (☎ **800/251-NAPA** or 707/252-1985) is also a source for everything from hot-air balloon and glider rides to wine-tasting tours by limousine.

NAPA

Wherever tourist dollars are to be had, you're sure to find big hotels with familiar names catering to independent vacationers, business travelers, and groups. **Embassy Suites,** 1075 California Blvd., Napa, CA 94559 (☎ **800/362-2779** or 707/253-9540), offers 205 of their usual two-room suites, which include a kitchenette, coffeemaker, modem capabilities, and two TVs; extras include a

Napa Valley Accommodations

93

complimentary cooked-to-order breakfast, indoor and outdoor pools, and restaurant; rates range from $144 to $250. The 191-room **Napa Valley Marriott,** 3425 Solano Ave., Napa, CA 94558 (☎ 800/228-9290 or 707/253-7433), offers lighted tennis courts, an exercise room, a heated outdoor pool and spa, and two restaurants; rates range from $109 to $180.

VERY EXPENSIVE

Silverado Country Club & Resort. 1600 Atlas Peak Rd., Napa, CA 94558. ☎ **800/532-0500** or 707/257-0200. Fax 707/257-2867. 280 suites. A/C MINIBAR TV TEL. $215 junior suite; $280 1-bedroom suite; $385–$485 2- or 3-bedroom suite. Golf and promotional packages available. AE, CB, DC, DISC, MC, V. Drive north on Calif. 29 to Trancas St.; turn east to Atlas Peak Rd.

If you long for the opulence of an East Coast country club, bring your racquet and golf clubs to this 1,200-acre resort in the Napa foothills, where the focus is on the sporting life. The spacious accommodations—which range from very large studios ("junior suites") with a king-size bed, kitchenette, and a roomy, well-appointed bathroom to one-, two-, or three-bedroom cottage suites—are up to par, and each comes with a wood-burning fireplace. Cottage suites are in private, low-rise groupings, each tucked away in shared courtyards along peaceful walkways. All rooms are individually decorated with country home–style furnishings, and manage to offer a sense of privacy despite the resort's size.

Dining/Diversions: There's a quintessential steak-and-seafood restaurant, as well as a garden-view restaurant serving superb California and Pacific Rim cuisine and a large indoor/outdoor bar and grill that serves breakfast, lunch, and cocktails.

Amenities: Limited room service, concierge, dry cleaning, laundry, baby-sitting, secretarial services, valet parking. Two cleverly designed golf courses by Robert Trent Jones, Jr.—the 6,500-yard South Course, with a dozen water crossings, and the 6,700-yard North Course, somewhat longer but a bit more forgiving; a staff of pros are on hand (greens fee $115 for 18 holes on either course, including a mandatory cart). Tennis courts, several swimming pools, tour desk, conference rooms, and business center.

EXPENSIVE

La Residence Country Inn. 4066 St. Helena Hwy., Napa, CA 94558. ☎ **707/253-0337.** Fax 707/253-0382. 20 units. A/C TEL. $175–$225 double; lower rates Dec–Apr. AE, DC, MC, V.

If you consider a B&B too homespun and a luxury hotel too impersonal, La Residence is a good bet for you. Set on 2 acres just off

Highway 29, the inn's 20 rooms are situated in either the late-18th-century-revival–style main house or the newer French-barn–style building. Rooms are individually decorated with wall-to-wall carpeting, period antiques, armoires, designer fabrics, fireplaces (in most), CD players, and patios or verandas. The pool-area spa is secluded and well manicured. A full breakfast is served in the attractive dining room, which is often warmed by a roaring fire on chilly mornings; in the afternoon, wine, cheese, and hors d'oeuvres are offered.

MODERATE

✪ **Cedar Gables Inn.** 486 Coombs St., Napa, CA 94559. ☎ **800/309-7969** or 707/224-7969. Fax 707/224-4838. www.CedarGablesInn.com. 6 units. $129–$189 double ($10 less in winter). Rates include breakfast. AE, DISC, MC, V. From Calif. 29 north, exit onto First St. and follow signs to downtown; turn right onto Coombs St.; the house is at the corner of Oak St.

Innkeepers Margaret and Craig Snasdell have developed quite a following with their cozy, romantic B&B in Old Town Napa. The Victorian was built in 1892, and rooms reflect the era with rich tapestries and stunning gilded antiques. Four rooms have fireplaces; four have whirlpool tubs; and all feature queen-size brass, wood, or iron beds. Guests meet each evening in front of the roaring fireplace in the family room for complimentary wine and cheese. At other times, it's a perfect place to cuddle up and watch the large-screen TV.

INEXPENSIVE

Best Western Inn Napa Valley. 100 Soscol Ave., Napa, CA 94559. ☎ **800/528-1234** or 707/257-1930. Fax 707/255-0709. 70 units. A/C TV TEL. Apr–Nov $130–$175 double, from $155 suite; Dec–Mar $98–$140 double, from $169 suite. AE, CB, DC, DISC, JCB, MC, V.

Let's face it, this motel and its location—at the industrial southern edge of Napa—are about as fashionable as jug wine. But when frilly B&Bs with smaller rooms and noisy neighbors are charging two or three times what you'll pay here, a view of the 24-hour Denny's downstairs starts looking pretty good. Many of the traditional motel-style rooms at this Best Western have small balconies, but not much in the way of views—so keep your gaze inward at the clean, spacious, and basic accommodations. The loftlike suites are perfect for families and come with amenities aplenty: two TVs, two phones, coffeemaker, fridge, and decent toiletries.

Chablis Inn. 3360 Solano Ave., Napa, CA 94558. ☎ **707/257-1944.** Fax 707/226-6862. 34 units. A/C TV TEL. Apr to mid-Nov $75–$125 double; mid-Nov to Mar $60–$95 double. AE, DC, DISC, MC, V.

There's no way around it. If you want to sleep cheaply in a town where the *average* room goes for upward of $200 per night in high season, you're going to have to motel it. But look on the bright side: Because your room is likely to be little more than a crashing pad after a day of eating and drinking, a clean bed and a remote control are all you'll really need anyway. But Chablis offers much more than that. Each of the superclean motel-style rooms has a refrigerator and coffeemaker; some even boast kitchenettes and/or whirlpool tubs. Guests have access to an outdoor heated pool and hot tub, plus a basic continental breakfast. Friendly owner Ken Patel is on hand most of the time and is constantly upgrading his tidy highway-side hostelry; his current project: replacing all mattresses in 1998.

Château Hotel. 4195 Solano Ave., Napa, CA 94558. ☎ **800/253-6272** in Calif. or 707/253-9300. Fax 707/253-0906. 121 units. A/C TV TEL. Apr–Oct $115–$120 double; Nov–Mar $95–$100 double; from $155 suite. Rates include buffet breakfast. AAA, government, corporate, senior-citizen, and other discounts available. AE, CB, DC, MC, V. From Calif. 29 north, turn left just past Trower Ave., at the entrance to the Napa Valley wine region.

This contemporary two-story motel complex tries to evoke the aura of a French country inn, but it isn't fooling anybody—a motel's a motel. But the rooms and bathrooms are spacious and have separate vanity/dressing areas; most units have refrigerators. Ten rooms are specially designed for guests with disabilities. If you're used to a daily swim, the Château also has a heated pool and spa, and all guests receive a $3-off coupon to the adjoining Wine Country Bistro. Bargain travelers: Be sure to ask about discounts; some special rates will knock the price down by $20.

The Hennessy House Bed & Breakfast Inn. 1727 Main St. (between Lincoln and First sts.), Napa, CA 94559. ☎ **707/226-3774.** Fax 707/226-2975. 10 units. A/C TEL. May–Nov $105–$190 double; Dec–Apr $85–$170 double. Rates include full breakfast, afternoon tea and cookies, and nightly wine-and-cheese hour. AE, DISC, MC, V.

This Eastlake-style Queen Anne Victorian may be old enough to be on the National Register of Historic Places, but its antiquity is contrasted by the fresh hospitality of new owners Alex and Gilda Feit. Since the couple took over the B&B in late 1997, they've been on a mission to satisfy each and every guest. Their genuine concern makes a stay here very personable. Rooms in the main house are quaint, with a combination of antique furnishings, queen-size bed, fireplace, and/or a claw-foot bathtub. Carriage-house accommodations, located just off the main house, are larger but less ornate and feature whirlpool tubs (a bummer to climb into if you're not agile); two have fireplaces. Because walls are thin throughout both structures, TVs are out of the question (except for one room), and if your neighbor's a snorer, you'll know it firsthand. But it'll make for fun conversation over breakfast, when guests meet in the dining room for an impressive full meal which might include crepes or quiche and fresh baked muffins, juice, gourmet coffee, breads, and cereal. The adjoining living room allows TV junkies to stay tuned. The small garden is a nice spot for a bit of morning sun and is also the access point for the sauna.

Napa Valley Budget Inn. 3380 Solano Ave., Napa, CA 94558. ☎ **707/ 257-6111.** Fax 707/252-2702. 58 units, all with bathroom (shower only). A/C TV TEL. Apr to mid-Nov from $90 double; mid-Nov to Mar $60–$105 double. Rates include continental breakfast. AE, DC, DISC, MC, V. From Calif. 29 north, turn left onto the Redwood Rd. turnoff and go 1 block to Solano Ave.; then turn left and go a half block to the motel.

This no-frills lodging offers excellent location—close to Calif. 29— and simple, clean, and comfortable rooms. Local calls are free, and guests can enjoy the complimentary coffee in the lobby and the small pool on the premises (heated in summer only).

Napa Valley Travelodge. 853 Coombs St., Napa, CA 94559. ☎ **800/ 578-7878** or 707/226-1871. Fax 707/226-1707. 45 units. A/C TV TEL. $54– $189 double. CB, DC, DISC, JCB, MC, V.

Rarely does so much come so cheaply. This Travelodge has been around for a while, but even if you've stayed here before you won't recognize it. In early 1998 the owners gutted the entire place with the intent of turning it into a "New Orleans–style" motel (including a cobblestone center courtyard/parking area). And while there are no wild partiers hanging over the balconies throwing beads, there's still plenty to celebrate. Every room has a VCR, 36-inch TV, coffee, ironing board, and hair dryer; some feature a Jacuzzi tub. Guests have access to coin-operated laundry facilities, a pool, video library, and for a nominal fee, a fitness center 2 blocks away. If you're lucky enough to secure a room—especially when they're going for under $100 per night—you will have struck one of the best deals around.

Tall Timbers Chalets. 1012 Darms Lane, Napa, CA 94558. ☎ **707/ 252-7810.** Fax 707/252-1055. 8 cottages. A/C MINIBAR TV. Mar–Oct Sun– Thurs $105 double, Fri–Sat and holidays $125–$150 double; Nov–Feb Sun–Thurs $75 double, Fri–Sat and holidays $90–$150 double. Extra person $20. AE, MC, V. Free parking. From Calif. 29 north, turn left onto Darms Lane before you reach Yountville.

While many hotels' prices skyrocket during the high season, Tall Timbers—a group of eight whitewashed, roomy cottages surrounded by pines and eucalyptus—remains a cute, centrally located, and affordable option. Each cottage is nicely decorated and includes a toaster oven and coffeemaker, as well as a basket of fresh fruit waiting for you upon your arrival. Other sweet touches include a basic breakfast of muffins and fruit drinks in the refrigerator and a complimentary bottle of champagne. Each cottage sleeps up to four (there's a bedroom plus a queen-size sofa bed in the living room) and two have sundecks (though you cannot be guaranteed one).

Mary, who runs the place, requires a check in advance to reserve a room, and when the valley is booked, she may even rent out her own room adjoining the office. If you come expecting some of the cheapest simple lodgings in the area rather than the Ritz, you'll be pleased with your stay. There are no phones in the cottages, but you can use the one in the main office. Tall Timbers isn't particularly difficult to find, but to be on the safe side, ask for specific directions. Smoking is not allowed.

Wine Valley Lodge. 200 S. Coombs St. (between First and Imola sts.), Napa, CA 94558. ☎ **707/224-7911.** 53 units. A/C TV TEL. $57–$94 double; $77–$154 suite. AE, DISC, MC, V.

Dollar for dollar, the Wine Valley Lodge offers the most for the least in all of Wine Country. Located at the south end of town in a quiet residential neighborhood, the mission-style motel is extremely well kept and accessible, just a short drive from Calif. 29 and the wineries to the north. Soft pastels dominate the color scheme, featured prominently in the matching quilted bedspreads, furniture, and objets d'art. Its decor is reminiscent of Grandma's house, to be sure, but at these prices, who cares? The clincher on the whole deal is a fetching little oasis in the center courtyard, consisting of a sundeck, barbecue, and pool flanked by a cadre of odd tea cup–shaped hedges.

YOUNTVILLE
EXPENSIVE

Vintage Inn. 6541 Washington St. (between Humboldt St. and Webber Ave.), Yountville, CA 94599. ☎ **800/351-1133** or 707/944-1112. Fax 707/944-1617. 80 units. A/C TV TEL. $175–$250 double; $250–$300 minisuites and villas. Additional person $25 extra. Rates include continental breakfast and afternoon tea. AE, CB, DC, DISC, MC, V. Free parking. From Calif. 29 north, take the Yountville exit and turn left onto Washington St.

This contemporary, French-country luxury inn is situated on an old 23-acre winery estate in the heart of up-and-coming Yountville.

Rooms are bright and cozy; each has a fireplace or private veranda, oversize beds, and a coffeemaker, plus a Jacuzzi tub and plush bathrobes. If you're looking for a workout, you may rent a bike, reserve one of the two tennis courts, or take a dip in the 60-foot swimming pool or outdoor whirlpool, both heated year-round. A continental champagne breakfast (cereals, yogurt, pastries, egg salad, and fruit) and afternoon tea are served daily in the Vintage Club. Services include concierge and laundry/valet.

MODERATE

✪ **Maison Fleurie.** 6529 Yount St. (between Finnel Rd. and Humboldt St.), Yountville, CA 94599. ☎ **800/788-0369** or 707/944-2056. 13 units. A/C TV TEL. $110–$230 double. Rates include full breakfast and afternoon hors d'oeuvres. AE, DC, MC, V.

Maison Fleurie is one of the prettiest hotels in the Wine Country, a trio of beautiful 1873 brick-and-fieldstone buildings overlaid with ivy. Seven rooms are located in the main house—a charming Provençal replica complete with thick brick walls, terra-cotta tile, and paned windows—while the remaining rooms are split between the old bakery building and the carriage house. All have private baths, and some feature private balconies, patios, sitting areas, Jacuzzi tubs, and fireplaces. Breakfast is served in the quaint little dining room; afterwards, you're welcome to wander the landscaped grounds, use the pool or outdoor spa, or borrow a mountain bike (free of charge) to ride around town, returning in time for afternoon hors d'oeuvres. It's truly impossible not to enjoy your stay at Maison Fleurie.

✪ **Napa Valley Lodge.** 2230 Madison St., Yountville, CA 94599. ☎ **800/ 368-2468** or 707/944-2468. Fax 707/944-9362. 55 units. A/C MINIBAR TV TEL. $172–$320 double. Rates include champagne breakfast buffet. MC, V.

Many frequent visitors compare this contemporary hotel to the Vintage Inn, noting that its even more personable and accommodating. The lodge is just off Highway 29, though they do a good job of disguising it. Facilities include a pool, redwood sauna, and small exercise room; the newly upgraded guest rooms are large, ultraclean, and better appointed than many in the area. Many have vaulted ceilings and 33 have fireplaces. All come with a king- or queen-size bed, wicker furnishings, coffeemaker, robes, and either a private balcony or a patio. In 1997 all the bathrooms were also upgraded to include a vanity area and nice tile work. The cheapest rooms are at ground level; these are smaller and get less sunlight than those on the second floor. Extras include concierge, on-demand video, afternoon tea and cookies in the lobby, Friday-evening wine tasting in the library, and a full champagne breakfast—with all this, it's no wonder AAA gave the Napa Valley Lodge the four-diamond award for excellence. Ask about winter discounts—they can be as high as 30%.

INEXPENSIVE

Bordeaux House. 6600 Washington St., Yountville, CA 94599. ☎ **707/ 944-2855.** Fax 707/944-2855. 7 units. A/C TV. Sun–Thurs $115 double, Fri– Sat $145 double. Additional person $25 extra. 2-night minimum during high season. Rates include expanded continental breakfast. MC, V.

Considering the name, we were expecting this centrally located hotel on a quiet Yountville street to be some kind of romantic, antique- French-style structure. We were way off. How far? Try 1970s two- story brick. Nonetheless, there are seven ultratidy rooms here, each renting for what in this neck of the woods is considered a very rea- sonable price. Each has a private entrance, six have fireplaces, and four have private patios. While someone took a stab at attractive in- terior design, whoever it was didn't have the best aim (although the grass cloth walls are pretty cool). Added bonuses include port and sherry, which are available in the common area, where breakfast is also served.

Burgundy House Country Inn. 6711 Washington St. (P.O. Box 3175), Yountville, CA 94599. ☎ **707/944-0889.** 5 units, all with bathroom (shower only). A/C. $145–$165 double. Rates include breakfast. MC, V. From Calif. 29 north, take the Yountville exit and turn left onto Washington St.

This distinctly French country inn, built in the early 1890s as a brandy distillery of local fieldstone and river rock, is tiny but impres- sive. The interior still features thick stone walls and hand-hewn post and lintel beams, enhanced today by antique country furnishings. The five cozy guest rooms (all nonsmoking) have colorful quilted spreads and comfortable beds along with very small bathrooms. Delightful touches include fresh flowers in each of the rooms; a full breakfast that might include eggs, pastries, and a casserole; and com- plimentary port and sherry in the common area. The full breakfast can be taken inside or outdoors to the pretty garden.

Napa Valley Railway Inn. 6503 Washington St. (adjacent to the Vintage 1870 shopping complex), Yountville, CA 94599. ☎ **707/944-2000.** 9 units. A/C TV. $75–$130 double. AE, MC, V.

This is one of our favorite places to stay in the Wine Country. Why? Because it's inexpensive and it's cute as all get out. Looking hokey as heck from the outside, the Railway Inn consists of two rows of sun-bleached cabooses and railcars sitting on a stretch of Yountville's

Where to Stay 101

original track and connected by a covered wooden walkway. Things get considerably better, though, as you enter your private caboose or railcar, each sumptuously appointed with comfy love seats, queen-size brass beds, and tiled full baths. The coups de grâce are the bay windows and skylights, which let in plenty of California sunshine. The railcars are all suites, so if you're looking to save your pennies, opt for the cabooses. Adjacent to the inn is Yountville's main shopping complex, which includes wine tastings and some good low-priced restaurants.

OAKVILLE & RUTHERFORD
VERY EXPENSIVE

✪ **Auberge du Soleil.** 180 Rutherford Hill Rd., Rutherford, CA 94573. ☎ **707/963-1211.** Fax 707/963-8764. 50 units. A/C MINIBAR TV TEL. $350–$535 double; $700–$900 suite; $2,000 cottage suite. Rates discounted Dec–Mar. AE, DC, DISC, MC, V. From Rutherford, turn right on Calif. 128 and go 3 miles to the Silverado Trail; turn left and head north about 200 yd. to Rutherford Hill Rd.; turn right.

This spectacular Relais & Châteaux member is the kind of place you'd imagine movie stars frequenting for clandestine affairs or weekend retreats. Set high above the Napa Valley in a 33-acre olive grove, it's quiet, indulgent, and luxuriously romantic. The Mediterranean-style rooms are large enough to get lost in—and you might want to once you discover all the amenities. The bathtub alone—an enormous hot tub with a skylight overhead—will entice you to grab a glass of California red and settle in for a while. A wood-burning fireplace is surrounded by oversized, cushy furniture—the ideal place to relax and listen to CDs (the stereo comes with a few selections, and there's also a VCR). Fresh flowers, original art, terra-cotta floors, and natural-wood and leather furnishings whisk you out of the Wine Country and into the Southwest. Each sun-washed private deck has views of the valley that are nothing less than spectacular. Those with money to burn should opt for the $2,000-per-night cottage suite; the 1,800-square-foot hideaway's got two fireplaces, two full baths, a den, and a patio Jacuzzi. Now *that's* living. All guests have access to a celestial swimming pool and a tiny exercise room with one of the grandest views around, plus an array of spa services. All in all, this is one of the best places we've ever stayed.

Dining: Another ethereal experience. See "Where to Dine," below.

Amenities: Concierge, newspaper delivery, valet parking, 24-hour room service, twice-daily maid service, laundry/valet, complimentary shoe-shine. Outdoor pool with sundeck, massage rooms, three tennis courts, exercise room, beauty salon. Sculpture and nature trail with picnic areas that crisscrosses the property.

MODERATE

Rancho Caymus. 1140 Rutherford Rd. (P.O. Box 78), Rutherford, CA 94573. ☎ **800/845-1777** or 707/963-1777. Fax 707/963-5387. 26 suites. A/C MINIBAR TV TEL. $145–$175 double; from $245 Master Suite; $295 2-bedroom suite. Rates include continental breakfast. AE, DC, MC, V. From Calif. 29 north, turn right onto Rutherford Rd./Calif. 128 E.; the hotel is ahead on your left.

This Spanish-style hacienda, with two floors opening onto wisteria-covered balconies, was the creation of sculptor Mary Tilden Morton (of Morton Salt). Morton wanted each room in the hacienda to be a work of art, thus she hired the most skilled craftspeople of her day. She designed the adobe fireplaces herself, and wandered through Mexico and South America purchasing artifacts for the property.

Guest rooms are situated around a whimsical garden courtyard with an enormous outdoor fireplace. The mix-and-match interior decor is on the funky side, with overly varnished dark-wood furnishings and braided rugs. The inn is cozy, however, and rooms are decent-sized, split-level suites with queen beds. Other amenities include wet bars, sofa beds in the sitting areas, and small private patios. Most of the suites have fireplaces, and five have kitchenettes and whirlpool tubs. Breakfast, which includes fresh fruit, granola, orange juice, and breads, is served in the inn's dining room. There are plans to open a full-service restaurant in 1998.

ST. HELENA
VERY EXPENSIVE

Harvest Inn. 1 Main St., St. Helena, CA 94574. ☎ **800/950-8466** or 707/963-9463. Fax 707/963-4402. 54 units. A/C TV TEL. May–Nov $249–$289 double, $449–$499 suite; Dec–Apr $149–$189 double, $349–$399 suite. AE, DC, DISC, MC, V.

If you like your accommodations loaded with 20th-century luxuries yet reminiscent of Olde England, you'll like the Harvest Inn. Ornate brick walkways lead through beautifully landscaped grounds to this Tudor-style inn. Each of the immaculate rooms—with names like "The Earl of Ecstasy" and "Camelot"—is furnished in Tudor style with dark-oak beds and dressers, black leather chairs, and antique furnishings; most have brick fireplaces, wet bars, and refrigerators. Facilities include a wine bar, heated pools, and outdoor spas. *A word of caution:* This is a large, big-business hotel, and though it does its best to set a charming stage, you can't help but notice the corporate vibe and accoutrements permeating the place.

The Inn at Southbridge. 1020 Main St., St. Helena, CA 9457
520-6800 or 707/967-9400. Fax 707/967-9486. MINIBAR TV TEL.
Mid-June to Nov $245–$335 double; Nov–Mar $205–$295 double; Mar to mid-
June $235–$325 double. AE, CB, DC, JCB, MC, V.

Eschewing the lace-and-latticework theme that plagues most Wine
Country inns, the Inn at Southbridge takes an unswervingly modern, pragmatic approach to accommodating its guests. Instead of
stuffed teddy bears, you'll find terry-cloth robes, fireplaces, bathroom skylights, down comforters, private balconies, and a host of
other little luxuries. The decor is upscale Pottery Barn—trendy, and
for some a welcome departure from quaintly traditional hotel-style
stuff. Functional touches include voice mail and fax modems. One
notable bummer: The hotel is located along the highway, so it lacks
that reclusive feel many other upscale hotels offer.

Dining: On the premises is Tomatina, owned and run by the
owners of Tra Vigne, an Italian restaurant conveniently located next
door (see "Where to Dine," below).

Amenities: Concierge, limited room service, dry cleaning,
laundry, newspaper delivery, in-room massage, twice-daily maid service, baby-sitting, secretarial services, complimentary refreshments
in lobby. The spa offers access to an excellent gym (including
classes), steam room, sauna, outdoor heated pool, Jacuzzi, and spa
treatments.

✪ **Meadowood Napa Valley.** 900 Meadowood Lane, St. Helena, CA 94574.
☎ **800/458-8080** or 707/963-3646. Fax 707/963-3532. 85 units. A/C MINIBAR
TV TEL. $320–$465 double; 1-bedroom lodge from $540; 2-bedroom from
$850; 3-bedroom from $1,180; 4-bedroom from $1,575. Ask about promo-
tional offers and off-season rates. 2-night minimum on weekends. AE, DISC, DC,
MC, V.

This ultra-luxurious resort, tucked away on 256 acres of pristine
mountainside amidst a forest of madrone and oak trees, is quiet and
reclusive enough to make you forget that the busy wineries are just
10 minutes away. Meadowood was originally a private country club
for Napa's well-to-do families before being converted into one of
California's top-ranked resorts, a favorite retreat for celebrities and
corporate CEOs. Rooms are furnished with American country clas-
sics and have beamed ceilings, private patios, stone fireplaces, and
forested views; many are individual suite-lodges that are so far re-
moved from the common areas that you must drive to get to them
(lazier folks can opt for more centrally located accommodations).

The resort offers a wealth of activities: You can spend your days
playing Meadowood's challenging 9-hole golf course, any of the

seven championship tennis courts, or croquet (yes, croquet) on two international regulation lawns. Other options include private hiking trails, a health spa, and heated pools and a whirlpool. Those who might actually want to leave here (we certainly never did) to do some wine tasting can check in with John Thoreen, the hotel's wine tudor, whose sole purpose is to help guests better understand and enjoy Napa Valley wines.

Dining: See "Where to Dine," below.

Amenities: Concierge, room service, dry cleaning and laundry, full-service spa, newspaper delivery, secretarial service, baby-sitting. Nine-hole golf course, croquet lawns, two outdoor pools with sundeck, massage rooms, seven tennis courts, exercise room, hiking trails, and an executive conference center.

EXPENSIVE

Bartels Ranch & Country Inn. 1200 Conn Valley Rd., St. Helena, CA 94574. ☎ **707/963-4001.** Fax 707/963-5100. 4 units. A/C TV TEL. $165–$365 double. AE, DC, DISC, JCB, MC, V. From downtown St. Helena, turn east on Pope St., cross Silverado Trail, and continue onto Howell Mountain Rd.; bear right onto Conn Valley Rd.; the inn is 2 miles ahead on the left.

Perched on 60 acres of rolling meadows studded with fig trees, cypress, old oaks, and a recently planted vineyard, this palatial retreat is run by ebullient innkeeper Jami Bartels, who designed the 7,000-square-foot stone ranch house and has decorated it with her own collection of butterflies and other mementos. Her four individually decorated rooms provide every comfort—fireplaces, VCRs (with video library), CD players, balconies—plus conveniences like ironing boards, hair dryers, and private baths; a couple of the rooms even have their own Jacuzzis. Our personal favorites: the Niagara adjustable beds and blue heart-shaped Jacuzzi tub. There's a communal sundeck and pool, as well as a book-filled game room with pool and Ping-Pong tables. The bountiful breakfasts consist of fresh fruits, breads, and egg dishes; complimentary wine, fruit, and cheese are served each afternoon. Other treats include evening dessert, and coffee, tea, and cookies are always on hand. Forever aiming to please, Jami provides her guests with picnic supplies and bicycles, and will arrange as much or as little of your vacation as you wish; she's also the ultimate source regarding the valley. A bocce-ball court, croquet lawns, and access to horseback riding and tennis are other outdoor options.

MODERATE

Hotel St. Helena. 1309 Main St., St. Helena, CA 94574. ☎ **888/478-4355** or 707/963-4388. www.napavalley.com/napavalley/lodging/hotels/sthelena. 18

units, 14 with private bathroom. A/C TEL. $145 double without bathroom; $165–$195 double with bathroom; $275 suite. Rates discounted in winter. Rates include continental breakfast. AE, DC, MC, V.

This downtown hotel occupies a historic 1881 building, the oldest wooden structure in St. Helena. The hotel keepers celebrated the building's 100th birthday with a much-needed renovation; now it's more comfortable than ever. The hallways are cluttered with stuffed animals, wicker strollers, and other memorabilia. Most of the rooms have been similarly decorated, with brass beds, wall-to-wall burgundy carpeting, and oak or maple furnishings. There's a garden patio and wine bar, and TVs are available upon request. Smoking is discouraged.

Prager Winery & Port Works. 1281 Lewelling Lane, St. Helena, CA 94574. ☎ **707/963-3720.** Fax 707/963-7679. 2 units. A/C. $175 double. Additional person $25 extra. Rates include a full breakfast en suite and unlimited tastings in the downstairs tasting room. MC, V.

Up until now the two rentable suites at Prager Winery were one of the best-kept secrets in the valley. Its incognito location—on a residential side street behind Sutter Home—gives no indication of the affordable accommodations within. The smaller suite, which is still huge, is perched above one of our favorite tasting rooms (See "Touring the Wineries," above), up a seemingly precarious flight of stairs. It boasts a queen bed, fireplace, fridge, coffeemaker, and a lovely private sundeck. The garden cottage is also enormous and immaculate, and has a piano, fireplace, and private garden. Both have homey appeal, sleep up to four, and come with a full, delivered breakfast, unlimited wine tastings, and access to Jim and Imogene Prager, two of the most gracious hosts around. Note that neither has a TV or phone.

Sutter Home Inn. At the Sutter Home Winery, 277 St. Helena Hwy. S., P.O. Box 248, St. Helena, CA 94574. ☎ **707/963-3104,** ext. 4100 weekdays from 8am–4pm, ext. 4130 evenings and weekends. Fax 707/963-5397. 9 units. TV TEL. $160 double. Rates include full breakfast. AE, DISC, MC, V.

Yes, it's on the grounds of Sutter Home's wine-tasting and sales building, but don't expect to be surrounded by vineyards. The building that houses the nine guest rooms is flanked by a Victorian garden, but take a few steps further west and you'll be playing chicken on Highway 29. Still, considering its St. Helena location, handsome Victorian-style rooms (nonsmoking, impeccably clean, and containing queen bed and TV), and moderate price, Sutter Home offers a darn good deal. But there is a catch: Since the winery holds over half its rooms for wine-industry professionals, reservations are hard to come by. On the flip side, if they don't fill the reserved spaces and you're looking for last-minute accommodations, you might get lucky (especially during the off-season). Another plus: There's no 2-night minimum. A full breakfast is served in the winery's neighboring, masterfully maintained 1884 Victorian.

✪ **Wine Country Inn.** 1152 Lodi Lane, St. Helena, CA 94574. ☎ **707/963-7077.** Fax 707/963-9018. E-mail: romance@winecountryinn.com. 24 units, all with bathroom (12 with shower only). A/C TEL. $130–$258 double. Rates include breakfast. MC, V.

Just off the highway behind Freemark Abbey vineyard, this attractive wood-and-stone inn, complete with a French-style mansard roof and turret, overlooks a pastoral landscape of Napa Valley vineyards. The individually decorated rooms are furnished with iron or brass beds, antique furnishings, and handmade quilts; most have fireplaces and private terraces overlooking the valley, while others have private hot tubs. One of the inn's best features, besides the absence of TVs, is the outdoor pool (heated year-round), which is attractively landscaped into the hillside. Another favorite is the selection of suites, which come with stereos, plenty of space, and lots of privacy. The family that runs this place puts their personal touches everywhere and makes every guest feel welcome. Wine and plenty of appetizers are served nightly, along with a big dash of hotel-staff hospitality in the inviting living room. A full buffet breakfast is served there, too.

Zinfandel Inn Bed & Breakfast. 800 Zinfandel Lane (off Hwy. 29), St. Helena, CA 94574. ☎ **707/963-3512.** Fax 707/963-5310. 3 units. A/C TV TEL. Mar–Nov $150–$295 double; Dec–Feb $100–$250 double. Rates include full breakfast, plus champagne and truffles on arrival. MC, V.

Frilly romantics, get ready to break out your credit cards. Within the walls of this English Tudor are three rooms guaranteed to charm anyone into lace and old-world elegance. A rock-work fireplace, champagne, and truffles come with the price of the Chardonnay Room (along with an old TV and very soft mattress). The Zinfandel Suite is not red but blue, and very romantic with its huge private deck, enormous bathroom (with a window overlooking the deck), and double shower and sink. The Petit Sirah room, which is styled in French Victorian fashion, is appropriately named—it's hardly bigger than a shoe box. It does have a private bathroom, but you'll have to step out of your room to get to it.

Sun worshipers will appreciate the manicured, grassy, and secluded backyard—a peaceful and expansive spot with a large aviary, small pool, gazebo, and canopied hot tub. Rates also include a delicious, full-service breakfast with such eye-openers as caramelized French toast or jalapeño eggs, pastries, breads, fruit, coffee, and juice. *Note:* While this place is sweet, we also consider it a bit overpriced.

INEXPENSIVE

✪ **Deer Run Bed & Breakfast.** 3995 Spring Mountain Rd., P.O. Box 311, St. Helena, CA 94574. ☎ **800/843-3408** or 707/963-3794. Fax 707/963-9026. 4 units, all with bathroom (shower only). A/C TV. $130–$165 double. AE, MC, V.

Regardless of your budget, if romantic solitude is a big part of your vacation plan, Deer Run had better be on your itinerary. Situated 4¹/₂ miles (10 min. by car) from downtown St. Helena along a winding mountain road, this four-room B&B is the ultimate heavenly hideaway. Each of the wood-paneled rooms looks onto owners Tom and Carol Wilson's 4 acres of forest, and all feature gorgeous antiques, feather beds, a private entrance, deck, decanter of brandy, fridge, coffee and tea, robes, hair dryer, and access to hiking trails. One unit adjoins the cedar-shingled main house and boasts a king bed, Laura Ashley textiles, wood-burning fireplace, and an open-beam ceiling. The Carriage House Suite offers an antique queen bed, Spanish tile floors, gas stove, and huge bathroom. The Studio Bungalow is fashioned after Ralph Lauren, with more Spanish tile, a cathedral ceiling, and an overall whitewashed-cedar look. Deer meander by the Honeymoon Suite (the most secluded), a sweet split-level cottage with a separate bedroom and gas fireplace; its price includes breakfast delivered to your doorstep. The full breakfast served in the main house may include a frittata or apple crepes with chicken apple sausage. Outside you'll find Cody, the resident chocolate Lab, hanging out by the very small pool.

✪ **El Bonita Motel.** 195 Main St. (at El Bonita Ave.), St. Helena, CA 94574. ☎ **800/541-3284** or 707/963-3216. Fax 707/963-8838. 41 units. A/C MINIBAR TV TEL. June–Oct $95–$115 double; Apr–May and Nov $89–$115 double; Dec–Mar $75–$89 double. AE, CB, DC, DISC, MC, V.

This 1930s art-deco motel was built a bit too close to Calif. 29 for comfort, but the 2¹/₂ acres of beautifully landscaped gardens behind the hotel (away from the road) help even the score. The rooms, while small, are spotlessly clean and decorated with new furnishings; all have microwaves and coffeemakers, and some have kitchens or whirlpool baths. Families, attracted to the larger bungalows with kitchenettes, often consider El Bonita one of the best values in Napa

Valley—especially considering the heated outdoor pool, Jacuzzi, sauna, and new massage facility.

✪ White Sulphur Springs Retreat & Spa. 3100 White Sulphur Springs Rd., St. Helena, CA 94574. ☎ **707/963-8588.** Fax 707/963-2890. 28 units, 9 cottages. Carriage House (shared bathroom) $65–$115 double; The Inn $85–$125 double; small Creekside Cottages $105–$155; large Creekside Cottages $125–$185. Additional person $15 extra. Discounts available during off-season and midweek. Single-night stays accepted in Carriage House rooms, but cottages require a 2-night minimum weekends from Apr–Oct and all holidays.

If your idea of the ultimate vacation is a cozy cabin set among 330 acres of creeks, waterfalls, hot springs, hiking trails, and redwood, madrone, and fir trees, paradise is a short winding drive away from downtown St. Helena. Established in 1852, Sulphur Springs claims to be the oldest resort in California. It was purchased in 1983 by Seward "Buzz" and Betty Foote, who have been gradually and respectfully upgrading the property while retaining its natural rustic charm. Guests stay at the inn or in small and large creek-side cabins. Each is decorated with simple but homey furnishings; some have fireplaces or wood-burning stoves, and/or kitchenettes. The most luxurious are the newly renovated cabins, but the well-worn, wood-paneled ones seem appropriate considering the natural surroundings. Frankly, you can't help but feel at peace here—so much so that, if you're the nature-retreat type, you could never leave the property and your vacation would still be fulfilling. Venture off on a hike; take a dip in the natural hot sulphur spring; lounge by the pool; sit under a tree and watch for deer, fox, raccoon, spotted owl, or woodpecker; or schedule a day of massage, aromatherapy, and other spa treatments. Do whatever you want, but don't book a room here if you're the type who needs superluxury accommodations—this place will be too earthy for you. *Note:* No RVs are allowed without advance notice. Construction of a restaurant began in winter 1997, but is still in the works; ultimately, it will serve three meals, but is not expected to open until the end of 1998.

CALISTOGA
MODERATE

Brannan Cottage Inn. 109 Wapoo Ave., at Lincoln Ave. (P.O. Box 81), Calistoga, CA 94515. ☎ **707/942-4200.** 6 units. A/C. $140–$160 double. Rates include full buffet breakfast. MC, V.

At the east end of town on a quiet side street stands this cute little 1860 cottage, complete with requisite white picket fence. One of Sam Brannan's original resort cottages, the inn was restored through a community effort to salvage an important piece of Calistoga's heritage; it's now on the National Register of Historic Places. The six spacious, cozy rooms are decorated with country-style antiques, down comforters, and white lace curtains; each room also has air-conditioning, ceiling fan, private bathroom, and its own entrance. There's a comfortable parlor and a pleasant brick terrace furnished with umbrella tables. A full buffet-style breakfast is served in the outdoor garden, weather permitting.

Silver Rose Inn & Spa. 351 Rosedale Rd. (off the Silverado Trail), Calistoga, CA 94515. ☎ **800/995-9381** or 707/942-9581. 20 units. A/C TEL. $145–$240 double weekdays, $165–$260 double weekends. AE, DISC, MC, V.

If you like big, ranch-style spreads complete with a large wine-bottle–shaped pool, hot tub, tennis courts, and even a chipping and putting green, then you'll love the Silver Rose Inn & Spa. Situated on a small oak-covered knoll overlooking the upper Napa Valley, the inn offers so many amenities that you'll have a tough time searching for reasons to leave (other than to eat dinner, of course). Each spacious guest room is individually decorated, ranging from the peach-colored theme in the aptly named Peach Delight to the Oriental Room, complete with shoji screens and Oriental rugs. Several rooms come with fireplaces, whirlpool baths, and private balconies or terraces. Guests are offered exclusive on-site spa treatments—from massages to mud baths—as well as an afternoon "Hospitality Hour" and a tray of fresh fruit, breads, coffee, and juice served in your room.

✪ **Cottage Grove Inn.** 1711 Lincoln Ave., Calistoga, CA 94515. ☎ **800/799-2284** or 707/942-8400. Fax 707/942-2653. 16 cottages. A/C TV TEL. $195 double. Rates include continental breakfast and evening wine and cheese. AE, DC, MC, V.

Standing in two parallel rows at the end of the main strip in Calistoga are the perfect couples retreats—brand-spanking-new cottages that, though located on a residential street, seem well-removed from the action once you've stepped across the threshold. Each compact guest house comes complete with a wood-burning fireplace, homey furnishings (perfect for curling up in front of the fire), cozy quilts, and an enormous bathroom with a skylight and a deep, two-person Jacuzzi tub, plus such niceties as gourmet coffee, a stereo with CD player, VCR (a video library is on site), wet bar, and fridge. Smokers beware: It's not allowed inside, but you can puff all you want on the small front porch. Several major spas are within walking distance. This is our top pick if you want to do the Calistoga spa scene in comfort and style.

Mount View Hotel. 1457 Lincoln Ave. (on Calif. 29, near Fairway St.), Calistoga, CA 94515. ☎ **800/816-6877** or 707/942-6877. Fax 707/942-6904. 29 units, 3 cottages. A/C TV TEL. $110–$150 double; $155–$200 suite; $205 cottage. Packages available. 2-night minimum on high-season weekends. AE, DISC, MC, V.

Located on the main highway in the middle of Calistoga, this National Historical Landmark is one of the sweetest options in town. Rooms are decorated in the best of taste, in either Victorian or art-deco style, and trimmed with beautiful hand-painted accents. There are also three self-contained cottages—with queen-size bed, wet bar, private deck, and hot tub—and nine suites. Almost everything in town is within walking distance, although once you settle in, you might not want to leave the quiet, sunny swimming area with heated pool; also on the premises are a Jacuzzi and a highly rated European spa, offering massage, mud wraps, and facials.

The hotel delivers a continental breakfast to your room, and there are plenty of great cafes within walking distance. The hotel's restaurant, Catahoula, serves tasty Cajun/Creole cuisine for lunch and dinner Wednesday through Monday (see "Where to Dine," below).

INEXPENSIVE

✪ **Calistoga Country Lodge.** 2883 Foothill Blvd. (1 mile north of Lincoln Ave.), Calistoga, CA 94515. ☎ **707/942-5555.** Fax 707/942-4214. 6 units, 2 with shared bathroom. $105–$145 double. AE, MC, V.

This rustic, secluded inn in the western foothills of Calistoga is one of the best bargains in the Wine Country. Where else can you get a spacious, attractively furnished room with fireplace, sitting chairs, and verdant views for as little as $105 a night? Innkeeper Rae Ellen has transformed this 1915 farmhouse into a decidedly anti–Laura Ashley, Southwestern-style retreat, complete with cowhide rugs, bleached pine and lodgepole furniture, Indian artifacts, American antiques, and plenty of bovine accessories. It's all very tastefully—and humorously—done. In winter, the two rooms with fireplaces are the way to go (although these are the same two rooms that share a hallway bathroom). In summer, the private deck in the attic-level "Lookout Room" offers bucolic views of the surrounding century-old oak groves. Just in case you're still not convinced, Rae Ellen has recently added a pool and 24-hour hot tub to her humble estate. An extended continental breakfast is served from 7 to 10am, plus wine and cheese in the evening.

Calistoga Spa Hot Springs. 1006 Washington St. (at Gerrard St.), Calistoga, CA 94515. ☎ **707/942-6269.** 57 units, 1 family unit. A/C TV TEL. Winter $70 double, $95 family unit, $110 suite; summer $85 double, $110 family unit, $130 suite. MC, V.

Very few hotels in the Wine Country cater specifically to families with children, which is why we strongly recommend the Calistoga Spa Hot Springs. Even if you don't have kids in tow, it's still a great bargain, offering unpretentious yet clean and comfortable rooms with kitchenettes, as well as a plethora of spa facilities ranging from exercise rooms to four naturally heated outdoor mineral pools, aerobic facilities, volcanic-ash mud baths, mineral baths, steam baths, blanket wraps, massage sessions, and more. All of Calistoga's best shops and restaurants are within easy walking distance, and you can even whip up your own grub at the barbecues set up near the large pool and patio area.

Calistoga Inn. 1250 Lincoln Ave. (at Cedar St.), Calistoga, CA 94515. ☎ **707/942-4101.** 18 units, none with bathroom. $49–$65 double. AE, MC, V.

Would the fact that the Calistoga Inn has its own brewery influence our decision to recommend it? You betcha. Here's the deal: You're probably in town for the spa treatments, but unfortunately, the guest rooms at almost every spa are lacking in the personality and warmth department. A better bet for the budget traveler is to book a room at this homey turn-of-the-century inn, then walk a few blocks up the street for your mud bath and massage. You'll have to share the bathrooms, and the rooms above the inn's restaurant can be noisy, but otherwise you get a cozy little room with a double or queen bed, washbasin, and continental breakfast for only $65 on weekends (that's half the average room rate in these parts). What's more, no 2-night minimum is required, and the best beer in town is served downstairs. *Tip:* Request a room as far from the bar/restaurant as possible.

Dr. Wilkinson's Hot Springs. 1507 Lincoln Ave. (Calif. 29, between Fairway and Stevenson aves.), Calistoga, CA 94515. ☎ **707/942-4102.** 42 units. A/C TV TEL. Winter $69–$109 double; summer $95–$129 double. Weekly discounts and packages available. AE, MC, V.

This spa/resort was originally established by "Doc" Wilkinson, who arrived in Napa Valley just after World War II. The rooms range from Victorian-style accommodations with sundecks and garden patios to rather basic and functional motel-like units. All rooms have coffeemakers; some have refrigerators and/or kitchens. Facilities include three mineral-water pools (two outdoor and one indoor), Jacuzzi, steam room, and mud baths. Facials and all kinds of body treatments are available in the salon.

Eurospa and Inn. 1202 Pine St. (between Myrtle and Cedar sts.), Calistoga, CA 94515. ☎ **707/942-6829.** Fax 707/942-1138. 12 units. A/C TV. $75–$100 double. AE, DC, DISC, MC, V.

Situated in a quiet residential section of Calistoga, this small European-style inn and spa provides a level of solitude and privacy that few other spas can match. The horseshoe-shaped inn consists of a dozen stucco bungalows, a spa center, and an outdoor patio where a light breakfast and snacks are served. The rooms, though small, are pleasantly decorated with pine furnishings and soft pastels; a few come with kitchenettes. Spa treatments range from Fango Naturium mud baths to honey-almond body scrubs, seaweed body wraps, and de-stress massage. If you're worried about going over your budget, opt for the "Wellness Packages," which include lodging, mineral bath, an hour of spa treatments, continental breakfast, and dinner voucher, for $159 per person ($259 per couple) per night.

Nance's Hot Springs & Motel. 1614 Lincoln Ave. (between Fairway St. and Stevenson Ave.), Calistoga, CA 94515. ☎ **707/942-6211.** 24 units. A/C TV TEL. $75–$80 double ($20 less Sun–Thurs). AE, DISC, MC, V.

The average room rate in Napa Valley is $140, so don't be surprised by what $75 will get you in Calistoga. Okay, so the rooms at this Spanish-style whitewashed motel are painfully plain, but it's your body you came to pamper, not your eyes—so stop complaining and ooze your aching bones into Nance's mud bath, followed by a mineral whirlpool bath, mineral steam, blanket wrap, and half-hour massage, all for only $65 (heck, Sonoma Mission Inn charges more than that just for the massage). Nance's, which has been in business since 1923, has a loyal following of budget-minded, no-frills-needed clientele who know they're going to get their money's worth. It's in a great location, too, just a short walk from the shops and restaurants along Calistoga's main street.

5 Where to Dine

Recently Napa's restaurants have been drawing as much attention to the valley as its award-winning wineries. Within the past 3 years alone, Yountville's French Laundry chef/owner Thomas Keller snagged the 1997 James Beard Award for "Chef of the Nation"; L.A.'s celebrity chef Joachim Splichal launched his first northern-California outpost, Pinot Blanc; and the Culinary Institute of America opened its West Coast annex and an enormous restaurant.

Dining in the Napa Valley is a special experience on a number of levels. First off, there's the food: Nowhere else in the state are

Napa Valley Dining

Alexis Baking Company 1
Alex's 19
All Seasons Café 18
Auberge du Soleil 10
Bistro Don Giovanni 2
Bosko's 18
Brava Terrace 17
Brix 7
Café Sarafornia 19
The Cantinetta 12
Catahoula 19
The Diner 5
Domaine Chandon 4
Downtown Joe's 1
First Squeeze Deli
   & Juice Bar 1
The French Laundry 6
Gillwoods Cafe 14
Gordon's Cafe
   and Wine Bar 5
Green Valley Cafe
   & Trattoria 13
La Boucane 1
Mustards Grill 8
Napa Valley Coffee
   Roasting Co. 14
Napa Valley Grille 5
Oakville Grocery Café 9
Pacifico 19
Pairs Parkside Café 13
Piatti 5
Pinot Blanc 11
The Red Hen Cantina 3
Restaurant at Meadowood 15
Smokehouse Café 18
Terra 13
Tomatina 12
Tra Vigne Restaurant 12
Trilogy 12
Wappo Bar & Bistro 19
Wine Spectator
   Greystone Restaurant 16

kitchens as deft at mixing fresh seasonal, local, organic produce into edible magic, which means that menus change constantly to reflect the best available ingredients. Then there's the wine list: With many of the world's top growers living next door, no restaurant can get away with a mediocre selection, and most offer fantastic wines by the glass from local boutique wineries. And finally, the ambiance: The whole reason to come to Wine Country is to indulge, hence the valley's knockout dining rooms and stunning views that are second only to what's on your plate and in your glass.

The most important advice we can offer about Napa Valley's restaurants: *reserve*—especially for a seat in a more renowned room. The French Laundry, for example, takes reservations up to 2 months in advance and is almost always completely booked. While there's always a chance of getting in on a cancellation, there's nothing more infuriating than futilely begging someone to allow you the coveted opportunity to part with upwards of $100 in their establishment. Also bear in mind that the food is rich around here; we make a point of eating in only one restaurant a day.

Finally, if your budget can't afford the more expensive restaurants for dinner (we know, they're all expensive), have a late lunch. You might not have a heck of a lot to do after the sun goes down, but you'll be full and your wallet won't be empty.

The restaurants below are divided first by area, then by price category, using the following guide: **Expensive,** more than $45 per person; **Moderate,** $25 to $45 per person; and **Inexpensive,** less than $25 per person. These categories reflect the price of the majority of dinner menu items and include an appetizer, main course, coffee, dessert, tax, and tip.

NAPA
MODERATE

Bistro Don Giovanni. 4110 St. Helena Hwy. (on Calif. 29, just north of Salvador Ave.), Napa. ☎ **707/224-3300.** Reservations recommended Fri–Sat. Main courses $11–$17. AE, DC, MC, V. Mon–Thurs 11:30am–10pm, Fri–Sun 11:30am–11pm. NORTHERN ITALIAN.

Donna and Giovanni Scala—who also run the fantastic Scala's Bistro in San Francisco—serve refined Italian fare prepared with top-quality ingredients and California flair at this large, lively, Mediterranean-style restaurant. The menu features pastas, risottos, pizzas (baked in a wood-burning oven), and half a dozen other main courses such as braised lamb shank and Niman Schell bistro burgers. Less traditional appetizers include a grilled pear with a frisée-

and-arugula salad with bleu cheese, caramelized walnuts, and bacon. The matchstick zucchini sprinkled with Parmesan cheese has become a signature dish. Pasta lovers should go for the farfalle with asparagus, porcini, wild mushrooms, pecorino cheese, and truffle oil; the seared salmon with tomato, white wine, and chive sauce is another winner. Alfresco dining among the vineyards is available—and highly recommended on a warm, sunny day.

La Boucane. 1778 2nd St. (1 block east of Jefferson St.), Napa. ☎ **707/ 253-1177.** Reservations recommended. Main courses $14–$21. MC, V. Mon– Sat 5:30–10pm. COUNTRY FRENCH.

You'll be graciously welcomed into the domain of chef-owner Jacques Mokrani, who took this 1885 "Victorian lady" and refurbished her in traditional French style with antiques and lots of chintz. The dinner-only menu is also classically French, featuring such dishes as duck à l'orange, sole meunière, and tournedos forestière. Try the poulet sauté Boucane, prepared with cognac, shallots, mushrooms, and sherry. To start, there are escargots and prawns Provençale, and to finish, a traditional chocolate mousse and crème caramel. Granted, La Boucane isn't on the road to glory, but its tried-and-true French fare is better than most in the area.

INEXPENSIVE

✪ **Alexis Baking Company.** 1517 Third St. (between Main and Jefferson sts.), Napa. ☎ **707/258-1827.** Main courses: breakfast $3.25–$6.25; lunch $6–$8; dinner $6.75–$13. Mon–Fri 6:30am–3pm, Sat 7:30am–3pm, Sun 8am–2pm. BAKERY/CAFE.

Napa is a prime example of what happens when a charming turn-of-the-century town expands without conscientious planning: an opposing combination of small-town-meets-industrial-megamall. Ironically, when you go beyond the used car lots and 1970s motels and make your way into Old Town, the quaint spots become all the more special. Alexis (a.k.a. ABC) is just such a place—and residents know it. Show up on a weekend morning and the line is out the door. But once you order from the counter and find a seat in the sunny room, you can relax, enjoy the casual coffeehouse atmosphere, and start your day with spectacular pastries, coffee drinks, and breakfast goodies like pumpkin pancakes with sautéed pears. Lunch also bustles with locals who come for the daily specials like fusilli pasta with roasted pumpkin, white beans, ham, and Parmesan in a cream sauce; grilled-chicken Caesar salad; roast-lamb sandwich with minted mayo and roasted shallots on rosemary bread; and lentil bulgar orzo salad. Desserts run the gamut and include a moist and magical steamed persimmon pudding during the holiday season. This is a great stopover for vegetarians and sweet tooths.

Downtown Joe's. 902 Main St. (at Second St.), Napa. ☎ **707/258-2337.** Dinner main courses $8–$14. AE, DC, DISC, MC, V. Mon–Fri 8:30–11am (breakfast) and 11am–10pm, Sat–Sun 8:30am–2pm (brunch) and 3–10pm. AMERICAN BISTRO.

Don't let the name fool you: Downtown Joe's is anything but a greasy diner. Working from a proven formula—good food and lots of it at a fair price—Joe's has capitalized on a prime location in downtown Napa and created what's widely regarded as the best place in town to grub and groove. The menu is all over the place, offering everything from porterhouse steaks to oysters, omelets, pasta, and seafood specials. The beers, such as the tart Lickety Split Lager, are made in-house, as are the breads and desserts. If the sun's out, request a table on the outside patio adjacent to the park. Thursday through Sunday nights, rock, jazz, and blues bands draw in the locals.

Another great reason to visit Joe's is "Hoppy Hour," from 4 to 6pm Monday through Thursday, featuring $2.50 pints and free appetizers plus a drawing every half hour to win free stuff. Every Friday is TGIF, with a giveaway (appetizers, wine, etc.) every 15 minutes.

First Squeeze Deli and Juice Bar. 1149 First St. (at Coombs St.), Napa. ☎ **707/224-6762.** Deli items $3–$7. AE, DC, MC, V. Summer Mon–Fri 8am–6pm, Sat 10am–6pm, Sun 10am–4pm; off-season Mon–Fri 8am–4pm, Saturday 10am–4pm. DELI/JUICE.

After you fuel up on your requisite cup of java at the **Napa Valley Coffee Roasting Co.,** located down the block at 948 Main St. (at First Street), head over here to load up on picnic supplies for the day's journey among the vineyards. Spartan furnishings (and decor to match) beg for a "to go" order, which is just as well—after one sip of a protein-powder shake, you won't be able to hold still anyway. Wheat grass, spirulina, ginseng, bee pollen, brewer's yeast—it's a health nut's paradise. Our favorite is the Berry Bonds, a zingy combo of blackberry, strawberry, apple juice, and frozen yogurt. Also available are sandwiches of every ilk, made big and bulky.

The Red Hen Cantina. 5091 St. Helena Hwy., Napa. ☎ **707/255-8125.** Reservations recommended for large parties. Main courses $8–$14. AE, DC, MC, V. Summer Sun–Thurs 11am–10pm, Fri–Sat 11am–10:30pm; off-season Sun–Thurs 11am–9pm, Fri–Sat 11am–10pm. MEXICAN.

This popular taqueria serving moderately priced food looks like a Swiss chalet that got lost somewhere south of the border. Seafood dishes supplement the traditional burritos, tacos, and pollo Mexicano (chicken strips sautéed in white wine, onion, mushrooms, and tomatoes). What you get isn't bad, but it loses something in the translation this far north. Your best bet is to rest your weary bones at a patio table adorned with chips, salsa, and a cool margarita.

OAKVILLE & RUTHERFORD
EXPENSIVE

Auberge du Soleil. 180 Rutherford Hill Rd., Rutherford. ☎ **707/963-1211.** Reservations recommended. Main courses $25–$30. AE, DISC, MC, V. Daily 7–11am, 11:30am–2:30pm, and 6–9:30pm. WINE COUNTRY CUISINE.

Auberge du Soleil may be better known for its inn, but it was the restaurant that started all the fuss over this world-class resort. Alfresco dining is taken to an entirely new level here, particularly on warm summer nights when diners are rewarded with a gorgeous sunset view of the mountains. Inside, a magnificent fireplace, huge wood pillars, and fresh flowers create a warm, rustic ambiance. Chef Andrew Sutton characterizes his cooking as "Wine Country cuisine," a reflection of the region's produce and international influences: Pacific Rim, Southwestern, and Mediterranean styles predominate. Signature dishes include a tasting platter of truffled deviled quail egg, smoked sturgeon, Thai lobster salad, caviar, and more; and a grapevine smoked salmon with walnut-wheat croutons and roasted shallot-caper relish. Regardless of what you order, be sure to arrive before sunset and beg for terrace seating.

INEXPENSIVE

✪ **Oakville Grocery Café.** 7848 St. Helena Hwy. (Hwy. 29, at the Oakville Cross Rd.), Oakville. ☎ **707/944-0111.** Reservations available for parties of 8 or more. Breakfast $4–$7.50; lunch main courses $5.50–$9. AE, MC, V. Daily 7:30am–11am and 11am–4pm. CALIFORNIAN.

Aficionados have practically gotten into brawls with each other to get their hands on a bottle of Joseph Phelps's coveted 1994 Insignia Cab, but since late 1997, when the wine wizard opened this roadside cafe (which is nowhere near the winery), there's now a fervent group of foodies banging on Phelps's door as well. One bite of the melt-in-your-mouth salmon, watercress, and herb aioli sandwich ($8) or the sweetly satisfying apple fruit tart, and you'll join the locals in their daily stampede for a table. Soups, such as a hearty vegetable barley; salads (Niçoise, goat cheese with field greens and peach-chardonnay vinaigrette, and hearts of romaine); pizzas, such as wild mushroom or sun-dried tomato, Kalamata olive, mozzarella, and feta; and lasagna round out the ovation-worthy lunch menu.

Breakfast is celebrated with "Small Plates" such as granola ($3.75), toasted breads with house preserves ($2), and a breakfast fruit tart, and "Big Plates" of chicken hash ($7), eggs, omelets, and frittatas. Counter service keeps the prices down, thick windows keep traffic noise out, and an absolutely fab meal and sweet ambiance keep the local constituency coming back for more. Fact is, it's been years since we've enjoyed a new Wine Country spot this much. Our only complaint: They weren't open for dinner yet. (But as of March 1998, they are open a few nights a week; call for details.)

YOUNTVILLE
EXPENSIVE

Domaine Chandon. 1 California Dr., Yountville. ☎ **707/944-2892.** Reservations required. Main courses $24–$28; lunch $13–$17. AE, DC, MC, V. Summer daily 11:30am–2:30pm; Wed–Sun 6–9:30pm. Winter Wed–Sun 11:30am–2:30pm and 6–9pm. Closed first 3 weeks of Jan. From Calif. 29 north, take the Yountville exit; the restaurant is on the west side of the highway. CALIFORNIA/FRENCH.

This dining room was once the most elaborate, expensive, and formal in the region. But in the past 10 years, the competition's gotten stiff, and if Domaine wants to keep its reputation, they might want to re-think the restaurant's outdated decor. The fact remains, however, that the grounds are still fabulous—on warmer days, you can dine outdoors overlooking the vineyards—and though there's been a change of the guard in the kitchen, the food is still respectable.

As for the menu, since Robert Curry became chef de cuisine in 1994, light, contemporary dishes have replaced the heavier French fare. You aren't likely to find the once-celebrated starter of cream of tomato soup in puff pastry; instead, try the delicate squash and dumpling soup. Other offerings might include caramelized day-boat scallop and spinach salad; Chilean sea bass on roasted artichokes, fennel, pearl pasta, cured lemon, and black-olive jus; and roasted lamb sirloin with red peppers, zucchini, roasted garlic potato croquettes, and red-wine jus. And, of course, the only way to wash it all down is with at least a few glasses of house bubbly. There's no question Robert Curry is a cuisine contender, but for those who've become accustomed to ex-chef Phillipe Jeanty's fare here over the past 20 years, you may suffer a brief period of adjustment.

✪ **The French Laundry.** 6640 Washington St. (at Creek St.), Yountville. ☎ **707/944-2380.** Reservations required. Fixed-price lunch $44, 5-course dinner $65, 9-course dinner $80. AE, MC, V. Fri–Sun 11:30am–1:45pm; daily 5:30–9:30pm. CLASSIC AMERICAN/FRENCH.

If your restaurant has the chutzpah to post neither a sign nor an address, it had better be good. Fortunately, this Yountville institution *is* that good. Though it's been around since 1978, it wasn't until renowned chef/owner Thomas Keller bought the place a few years back that it caught the attention of epicureans worldwide (including the judges of the James Beard Awards, who dubbed him 1997's "Chef of the Nation"). Dinner is an all-night affair; when it's finally over, you'll be ready to sit down and do it all over again—it's truly that wonderful.

Technically, the prix-fixe menu offers a choice of five or nine courses (including a vegetarian menu), but after a slew of cameo appearances from the kitchen, everyone starts to lose count. Signature dishes include Keller's "tongue in cheek" (a marinated and braised round of sliced lamb tongue and tender beef cheeks) and "macaroni and cheese" (sweet butter-poached Maine lobster with creamy lobster broth and orzo with mascarpone cheese). Portions are small, but only because Keller wants his guests to taste as many different things as possible—nobody leaves hungry. The excellent staff is well acquainted with the wide selection of regional wines; the house charges a $20 corkage fee if you choose to bring your own bottle. On warm summer nights, request a table in the flower-filled garden.

MODERATE

Brix. 7377 St. Helena Hwy. (Calif. 29), Yountville. ☎ **707/944-2749.** Reservations recommended. Main courses $17–$24. AE, DC, DISC, MC, V. Sun–Thurs 11:30am–9:30pm, Fri–Sat 11:30am–10pm. ASIAN FUSION.

One of the largest new restaurants to open in the area in 1997, Brix is also one of the most popular. In winter, a table by the corner fireplace promises romantic dining; in summer, you can overlook the vineyards for a more pronounced Wine Country experience. Executive Chef Tod Michael Kawachi does a wonderful job integrating Asian flavors with California cuisine, and the result is a rich culinary adventure. While starters—such as a very tasty grilled-portobello-mushroom salad with bleu cheese and sherry walnut vinaigrette (ask them not to go too heavy on the dressing!)—are interesting, only the starved should indulge, as portions are large and very satisfying. We tried the Hawaiian ono with a rock-shrimp and shiitake coconut curry ragout, and a Thai pesto smoked rack of lamb with spicy peanut sate and zinfandel glaze. Both were very good, with knockout sauces, but what really impressed us was the Chinese-style whole crispy fish with cilantro black-bean sauce—an absolute must-have.

✪ **Gordon's Cafe and Wine Bar.** 6770 Washington St., Yountville. ☎ **707/ 944-8246.** Reservations necessary for Fri dinner. Breakfast $5–$7; lunch $3.75– $7; fixed-price dinner $29.50. AE, DC, DISC, MC, V. Tues–Thurs and Sat–Sun 7:30am–6pm, Fri 7:30am–9pm. WINE COUNTRY.

If you want to escape the town's highfalutin restaurants for an intimate brush with the locals, this is the place to do it. Gordon is not a he, but a she—as in Sally Gordon, who opened this adorable Yountville favorite in May 1996. Part country store, part deli, and part restaurant, one wall is lined with an intriguing collection of jams, mustards, olive oils, wines, and other gourmet goods for sale; another posts the chalkboard breakfast and lunch menu above a glass display case housing a cornucopia of deli items, fluffy pastries, salads, cheeses, olives, and desserts. The floor is scuffed hardwood—the kind you'd expect to see in a rustic turn-of-the-century store—and fewer than a dozen tables are spaciously dispersed throughout the airy room. Breakfast (oatmeal, omelets, homemade pastries, and smoothies), lunch (soup, salads—including an excellent salad tasting plate for those who can't choose just one—and gourmet sandwiches), and real homemade flavor come from the open kitchen. Dinner, served only on Friday nights, is a fixed-price feast. On our visit, we opted for a velvety smooth lobster bisque; an outstanding and hearty pan-seared breast of chicken with chanterelles, shiitake mushrooms, and baby leeks over a pearl barley risotto; and the most unforgettable dessert we've had in a long, long time—a spectacular "buttermilk pie" topped with blueberries. A fine selection of local wines is served by the glass, or you can pull a bottle from the retail shelves.

Mustards Grill. 7399 St. Helena Hwy. (Calif. 29), Yountville. ☎ **707/ 944-2424.** Reservations recommended. Main courses $11–$17. CB, DC, DISC, MC, V. Apr–Oct daily 11:30am–10pm; Nov–Mar daily 11:30am–9pm. CALIFORNIA.

It's always a pleasant surprise to find a serious restaurant with a strong sense of humor; Mustards is one of those places. Housed in a convivial, barn-style space, it offers an 11-page wine list and an ambitious chalkboard list of specials. We started out with a wonderfully light seared ahi tuna that melted in our mouths the way ahi should. Although the Hoisin quail with apricot sauce and bok choy and the lamb shank braised in syrah with fennel and onions were tempting, we opted for a moist, perfectly flavored grilled chicken breast with mashed potatoes and fresh herbs. The menu includes something for everyone, from gourmands and vegetarians to good old burger lovers.

Napa Valley Grille. 6795 Washington St. (on Calif. 29 at Madison St.), Yountville. ☎ **707/944-8686.** Reservations recommended. Main courses $12–$22; lunch $7–$14. AE, CB, DC, DISC, MC, V. Mon–Thurs 11:30am–9:30pm, Fri–Sat 11:30am–10pm, Sun 10:30am–9:30pm. CALIFORNIA/WINE COUNTRY.

In case you've forgotten that you're in the thick of the wine-growing region, the grape motif woven into this restaurant's decor will undoubtedly remind you. The menu features "Wine Country cuisine," which equates to fresh, local ingredients and an extensive wine list featuring—you guessed it—Napa Valley wines. On sunny afternoons, most opt for the umbrella-shaded patio, but inside you can watch the swirl of activity in the open kitchen. Choose from an array of dishes: smoked duck, grilled game hen, or a pasta such as black spaghetti with rock shrimp, scallops, calamari, enoki mushrooms, and a white-wine sauce. Lunches feature a long list of salads to cool you off from the summer heat, and brunch always offers myriad morning munchies, including a smoked-salmon omelet with roasted peppers and herbed cream, or Dungeness crab cakes with poached eggs and Cajun hollandaise. Though many locals adore this restaurant, on our last visit we were only mildly impressed.

✪ **Piatti.** 6480 Washington St. (between Mission and Oak sts.), Yountville. ☎ **707/944-2070.** Reservations recommended. Main courses $7–$16. AE, DC, MC, V. Mon–Thurs 11:30am–10pm, Fri–Sat 11:30am–11pm, Sun 11:30am–10pm. ITALIAN.

This local favorite—the first (and best) of a swiftly growing northern-California chain—is known for serving excellent, reasonably priced food in a rustic Italian-style setting. Chef Peter Hall, a seasoned Napa Valley cook who honed his culinary art at Tra Vigne and Mustards before taking over the helm here, performs to a mostly sold-out crowd nightly. For the perfect meal, start with a salad of morning-cut field greens mixed with white corn and Napa Valley strawberry crostini, accompanied by a bowl of the spaghetti squash and sweet-potato soup. Though Hall offers a wide array of superb pastas and pizzas, it's the wood-oven–roasted duck—basted with a sweet cherry sauce and served over a bed of citrus risotto—that brings back the regulars. There are far fancier and more intimate restaurants in the valley, but we can't think of any that can fill you up on such outstanding fare at these prices. *Note:* Piatti also offers patio dining year-round, weather permitting.

INEXPENSIVE

The Diner. 6476 Washington St., Yountville. ☎ **707/944-2626.** Reservations not accepted. Breakfast $4–$8; lunch $6–$10; dinner $8–$13.25. No credit cards. Tues–Sun 8am–3pm and 5:30–9pm. From Calif. 29 north, take the Yountville exit and turn left onto Washington St. AMERICAN/MEXICAN.

Funky California meets traditional roadside eatery at this popular diner, decorated with a collection of vintage diner water pitchers and a rotating art exhibit. The Diner's fare is far from that of a regular greasy spoon—the "home-style" menu is extensive, portions are huge, and the food is very good. Breakfasts feature good old-fashioned omelets, French toast, and German potato pancakes. Lunch and dinner dishes include a host of Mexican and American dishes such as chicken picatta with veggies and rice, grilled fresh fish, giant burritos, and thick sandwiches made with house-roasted meats and homemade bread.

ST. HELENA
EXPENSIVE

✪ **Restaurant at Meadowood.** At the Meadowood Napa Valley, 900 Meadowood Lane, St. Helena. ☎ **707/963-3646.** Reservations recommended. A la carte menu $21.50–$28; fixed-price $52, $80 with wine pairings; vegetarian prix-fixe $40, $64 with wine pairings. AE, DISC, DC, MC, V. Daily 6–10pm. CALIFORNIA WINE COUNTRY.

Chef Maria del Pilar Sanchez presides over one of Napa Valley's finest—and most expensive—restaurants, located in the gazebo-style clubhouse dining room of the ultraluxurious Meadowood Resort. Though à la carte selections are offered, most guests prefer to choose between the prix-fixe menus. When we last dined here, dinner started with a flavorful warm quail salad with smoky lentils and soy sauce, which was robust but not too heavy. Next came a crispy skinned salmon trout served with exotic mushrooms and truffle oil—superb. Caramelized banana with currants and vanilla ice cream finished the evening, thank goodness, because we couldn't eat another bite. Though we didn't have room to try it, the four-course vegetarian meal sounded just wonderful: couscous layered with zucchini flavored with anise seeds, accompanied by a crispy strudel of artichokes, onions, and wild mushrooms. A popular après-dinner pastime is to retire to the small, romantic lounge and nurse a snifter of brandy as you warm your bones in the glow of the large stone fireplace.

✪ **Trilogy.** 1234 Main St. (at Hunt Ave.), St. Helena. ☎ **707/963-5507.** Reservations required. 3-course fixed-price menu $33, $45 with wine pairing. MC, V. Dinner Tues–Sat 6–9pm; wine bar Tues–Fri noon–9pm, Sat 3–9pm. Closed 3 weeks in Dec and 2 weeks in June. CALIFORNIA/FRENCH.

With a wine list that's probably second to none in the valley, this small, low-key restaurant is a favorite among Wine Country moguls.

Diane Pariseau and her assistant do virtually everything themselves, turning out exceptionally fresh, well-prepared food. Wines can be sampled at the wine bar, but the real treat here is the $33 three-course fixed-price menu, with each course accompanied by the appropriate glass of superior-quality wine for an extra $12 ("The best deal around," says Pariseau). The menu changes daily, but expect such delectable starters as salmon-potato cakes with chili aioli or seared tuna with Japanese noodle salad and wasabi dressing. Other selections may include roasted pork tenderloin with shiitake-mushroom sauce (recommended with a hearty Ravenswood 1994 zinfandel) or a sautéed duck breast with sun-dried–cherry sauce (best accompanied by a glass of 1992 Hanzell pinot noir).

MODERATE

Brava Terrace. 3010 St. Helena Hwy. (Calif. 29), St. Helena. ☎ **707/963-9300.** Reservations recommended, especially for weekend lunch. Main courses $8–$21. AE, DC, DISC, MC, V. Nov–Apr Thurs–Tues noon–9pm; May–Oct daily noon–9pm. CALIFORNIA/MEDITERRANEAN.

Fred Halpert earned acclaim as the head chef at the Portman Hotel in San Francisco; in 1991, he set up his own shop in the Wine Country, where he became a hit almost immediately. Halpert is always searching for new taste sensations; fortunately, that experimentation is backed up by thorough training in the cuisines of Provence and other locales. The food is both good and reasonably priced: try a simple sandwich of roasted vegetable with sun-dried–tomato butter, or go whole hog with such main courses as coq au vin or crusted pan-seared sea bass with oven-roasted tomatoes and thyme. There's always a fish, pasta, and risotto of the day. Be sure to try the spicy fries (a heartburn special). If your stomach can handle the wild and robust mix of flavors and food, finish your meal with the chocolate-chip crème brûlée. A dozen wines by the glass are available.

Pairs Parkside Café. 1420 Main St., St. Helena. ☎ **707/963-7566.** Reservations recommended on weekends. Main courses $12–$18; $7–$9 at lunch. AE, DC, JCB, MC, V. Wed–Mon 11:30am–3pm and 5:30–9pm. CALIFORNIA/ASIAN.

This restaurant's name refers to the *pairing* of complementary foods and wines. Hence the sophisticated menu recommends a chardonnay with the chanterelle sea bass on crab-butter mashed potatoes and sweet corn, a merlot to accompany the macaroni in a roasted garlic goat-cheese sauce with green and yellow squash, and a sauvignon blanc to wash down the miso-grilled mahimahi with crunchy green-onion rice cakes. (Vegetarian specials also are available.) Owners Craig (chef de cuisine) and Keith (pastry chef and dining-room manager) Schaueffel also seem to have a handle on matching food with atmosphere. The restaurant's 50 seats are well spaced, and the warm gold-textured walls, hardwood floors, and soft jazz set the tone for a casual evening of fun. And if the wine board's 16 by-the-glass selections have you stumped, enlist the help of the friendly staff; they know their wine. Cocktailers will have to curb their desire: No hard booze is served.

✪ **Pinot Blanc.** 641 Main St., St. Helena. ☎ **707/963-6191.** Main courses $16–$24; $9–$15 at lunch. AE, DC, DISC, JCB, MC, V. Tues–Thurs lunch 11:30am–3pm, dinner 5–9pm; Fri–Sun lunch 11:30am–4pm, dinner 4–9pm. Extended summer hours. FRENCH BISTRO.

Reviews were mixed as L.A. celebrity-chef Joachim Splichal's formal new restaurant settled in over the past 2 years. But when we dined here, nothing could be more clear: Pinot Blanc rocks! The dark-wood-paneled walls, lushly draped fabrics, and smoking-club atmosphere aren't exactly typical Wine Country, but on the flip side, it's a welcome change of pace and the kind of place where you won't feel goofy if you dress for dinner. Besides, the room's serious integrity is the appropriate setting for one hell of a good meal prepared by executive chef Sean Knight. Lunch offerings might include a delicate roasted beet salad with hazelnuts, blood oranges, and a duck prosciutto crouton; carpaccio of yellowtail hamachi; a steller foie gras with butternut squash, Oregon huckleberries, and shallots; a slew of salads; sandwiches; and pasta (ricotta cheese gnocchi with braised veal cheeks and baby artichokes—wow!). The unique menu features such unusual entrees as oxtail pot pie, squab, and Scottish wood pigeon, plus more common but equally adventurous dishes such as striped bass with celery root and brandade potatoes; grilled meats; and salmon with shallots, smoked bacon crust, baby artichokes, white beans, and arugula. Attention is paid to every detail at this restaurant, including the wine list, which features over 200 selections. Patio seating is offered during summer.

✪ **Terra.** 1345 Railroad Ave. (between Adams and Hunt sts.), St. Helena. ☎ **707/963-8931.** Reservations recommended. Main courses $14–$23. CB, DC, MC, V. Sun–Mon and Wed–Thurs 6–9pm, Fri–Sat 6–10pm. CONTEMPORARY AMERICAN.

St. Helena's restaurant of choice is the creation of Lissa Doumani and her husband, Hiro Sone, a master chef who hails from Japan and once worked with Wolfgang Puck at L.A.'s Spago. Sone makes full use of the region's bounty; he seems to know how to coax every nuance of flavor from his fine local ingredients. The simple dining room is a perfect foil for Sone's extraordinary food. Among the appetizers, the terrine of foie gras with apple, walnut, and endive salad and the home-smoked salmon with beets, potatoes, and frisée are the stars of the show. The main dishes successfully fuse different cooking styles: try the grilled salmon with Thai red-curry sauce or the sake-marinated sea bass with shrimp dumplings in shiso broth. A recommended finale? The chocolate cognac mousse cake with sun-dried–cherry ice cream.

✪ **Tra Vigne Restaurant.** 1050 Charter Oak Ave., St. Helena. ☎ **707/963-4444.** Reservations recommended. Main courses $12.50–$22; cantinetta $4–$8. CB, DC, DISC, MC, V. Daily 11:30am–10pm; cantinetta daily 11:30am–6pm. ITALIAN.

Tra Vigne's combination of good food, high-energy atmosphere, and "reasonable" prices (reasonable being a relative term) makes this restaurant a longstanding favorite among visitors. The enormous dining room packs 'em in every night—and whether seated on the veranda (heated on cold nights) or in the center of the bustling scene, diners are usually thrilled just to have a seat. Even though the wonderful bread served with house-made flavored olive oils is tempting, save room for the robust California dishes, cooked Italian-style, that have made this place everyone's favorite. The menu features about five or so pizzas, including a succulent caramelized onion, thyme, and Gorgonzola version. The dishes of the day might include grilled Sonoma rabbit with teleme-layered potatoes, oven-dried tomatoes, and mustard pan sauce, and a dozen or so antipasti. Equally tempting are the pastas—which include ceppo with sausage, spinach, potatoes, sun-dried tomatoes, and pecorino—and the delicious desserts. When ordering, plan wisely: Most dishes are very rich.

The adjoining Cantinetta offers a small selection of sandwiches, pizzas, and lighter meals (see below).

Wine Spectator Greystone Restaurant. At the Culinary Institute of America at Greystone, 2555 Main St., St. Helena. ☎ **707/967-1010.** Reservations strongly recommended. Tapas daily $3–$7; main courses $14–$19 (same prices at both lunch and dinner). AE, CB, DC, MC, V. Daily 11:30am–3pm; Mon–Thurs 5:30–9pm, Fri–Sat 5:30–10pm; 3:30pm–5:30pm tapas at the bar. MEDITERRANEAN.

This place offers a combination visual and culinary feast that's unparalleled in the area, if not the state. The room itself is an enormous stone-walled former winery, but the festive decor and heavenly aromas warm the space up. Cooking islands—complete with scurrying chefs, steaming pots, and rotating chicken—provide edible entertainment. The tapas menu focuses on Mediterranean-inspired dishes, including an excellent pork kebab and a grilled calamari that contradicts the sea dweller's rubbery reputation with every moist and peppery bite. Tapas portions are small but affordable; pastas and salads are a bit heftier. Main courses, such as a Moroccan spiced roasted lamb with apricot, pearl onion, and pine-nut relish, are well portioned and darn good, but we recommend you opt for a barrage of appetizers for your table to share. You should also order the "Flights of Fancy," where for $14 to $20 you can sample three 3-ounce pours of local wines such as white rhones, pinot, or zinfandel. While the food is serious, the atmosphere is playful—casual enough that you'll feel comfortable in jeans or shorts. If you want to ensure a meal here (which we recommend you do), reserve far in advance.

INEXPENSIVE

✪ **The Cantinetta.** Tra Vigne Restaurant, 1050 Charter Oak Ave., St. Helena. ☎ **707/963-8888.** Main courses $4–$8. CB, DC, DISC, MC, V. Daily 11:30am–6pm. ITALIAN.

Regardless of where we dine while in the valley, we always make a point of stopping at the Cantinetta for an espresso and a snack. Part cafe, part shop, it's a casual place with a few tables and a counter. The focaccias (we've never had better in our lives!), pasta salads, and pastries are outstanding, and there's also a selection of cookies and other wonderful treats, flavored oils (free tastings), wines, and an array of gourmet items, many of which were created here. You also can get great picnic grub to go.

Gillwoods Cafe. 1313 Main St. (at Spring St.), St. Helena. ☎ **707/963-1788.** Breakfast $4.60–$8; lunch $6–$9. Daily 7am–3pm. AE, MC, V. AMERICAN.

In a town like this—where if you order mushrooms on your burger, the waiter's likely to ask, "What kind?"—a plain old American restaurant can be a godsend, especially to anyone who doesn't know or care about the difference between porcinis and portobellos. In St. Helena, the land of snobs and fancy rabes, Gillwoods is that place. At this homey haunt, with its wooden benches and original artwork, it's all about the basic American meal: a breakfast of bakery goods, fruit, pancakes, omelets (with pronounceable ingredients), a decent eggs Benedict, and an egg scramble with bacon, chives, tomato, cheese, and plain old mushrooms. While the lunch menu (burgers, sandwiches, lots of salads, veggie lasagna, chicken-fried steak, and meat loaf) is available starting at 10:30am, late risers can still order from the breakfast menu until 3pm.

Green Valley Cafe & Trattoria. 1310 Main St. (between Hunt Ave. and Adams St.), St. Helena. ☎ **707/963-7088.** Reservations recommended on weekend nights. Lunch main courses $5.75–$7; most dinner main courses $9–$12. MC, V. ITALIAN.

When locals want a casual, inexpensive night out, they convene at this small, casual Italian restaurant. Its long green bar and row of tightly arranged tables offer casual neighborhood appeal that many of the valley's restaurants lack, and chef/owner Delio's cooking is backed by big-city experience at hole-in-the-wall prices. After launching and presiding over San Francisco's beloved Caffe Sport, in 1985 he and his wife, Cherie, packed up their pots and pans, traveled for 2 years, and then settled in Napa, where they've been satiating the town's residents ever since. One St. Helena store owner simply must have the lasagna once a week. Others lean toward the eggplant topped with tomato and béchamel sauce and Parmesan, fried calamari with garlic mayo, braised lamb shank with polenta, or freshly made ravioli. Lunch offerings include a spinach salad and a few other appetizers, a selection of cold and hot sandwiches (Italian sausage; burger; and grilled eggplant, tomato, cheese, peppers, onions, and olives), and, of course, a few pasta dishes.

Napa Valley Coffee Roasting Co. 1400 Oak Ave. (between Main and Adams sts.), St. Helena. ☎ **707/224-CAFE.** Most items $2.75–$4.50. MC, V. Daily 7:30am–6pm. COFFEEHOUSE.

With a reputation for some of the world's best wine and food, heaven forbid Napa residents serve a bad cup of coffee. Ensuring that each blend is as complex in its composition as a well-aged cabernet is Napa Valley's favorite coffee connoisseur, the Napa Valley Coffee Roasting Co. Though the beans are actually roasted at its sister store in Napa, blends available here include some you've probably tasted in nearby restaurants: Pinot Blanc Blend, Tra Vigne Blend, and Great Chefs at Robert Mondavi Blend. Other reasons to visit this aromatic shop: its inexpensive breakfast (eggs on toast, pastries, etc.) and congenial atmosphere.

The Napa branch is located at 948 Main St. (☎ **707/224-CAFE**).

Tomatina. At The Inn at Southbridge, 1016 Main St., St. Helena. ☎ **707/967-9999.** Pasta $6–$8; pizza $8–$19. DC, DISC, MC, V. Daily 11:30am–10pm. ITALIAN.

After we've been in the Wine Country for about a week, we usually can't stand the thought of one more decadent wine and foie-gras meal. That's when we race to Tomatina for a $3.50 chopped salad, a welcome respite from all the gluttonous excess. Families and locals come here for another reason: Though the menu is limited, it's a total winner for anyone looking for freshly prepared, wholesome food at atypically cheap Wine Country prices. A Caesar salad, for example, costs a mere $4.50. "Apizzas"—pizzas folded like a soft taco—are the house specialty, and come filled with such delights as fresh Maine clams and oregano. Pizzas are of the build-your-own variety with gourmet toppings like sautéed mushrooms, fennel sausage, baby spinach, sun-dried tomatoes, and homemade pepperoni. The 26 respectable local wines are served by the glass at a toast-worthy cost of $3.75, or $18 per bottle. As for dessert, at less than $4 a pop for gelato, biscotti, or pound cake, it's an overall sweet deal. Everything is ordered at the counter and brought to the small or family-style tables in the very casual dining area or the outdoor patio. Kids especially like the pool table and big-screen TV.

CALISTOGA
MODERATE

Alex's. 1437 Lincoln Ave. (between Washington and Main sts.), Calistoga. ☎ **707/942-6868.** Main courses $12–$25. MC, V. Tues–Fri 4–10pm, Sat 2–10pm, Sun 1–9pm (3–9pm in winter). CONTINENTAL

Alex's is for people who prefer dining the old-fashioned way—pre–cholesterol-counting red-meat eaters who get excited at the sight of a big double-cut of prime rib oozing with au jus and served with the requisite side of pungent horseradish, mashed potatoes, and plenty of French bread. Sure, the menu has the standard pasta, seafood, and poultry dishes, but they're all done far, far better at Catahoula or All Seasons Café down the street. Nope, none of that fancy-schmancy stuff for you; it's the perfectly aged, hand-cut God Bless America New York steak you're hankering for, served on a plain white tablecloth slightly soiled by your second glass of scotch. In an era in which the life expectancy of most restaurants is counted in months, Alex's has been around since 1969, so you know he must be doing something right.

All Seasons Café. 1400 Lincoln Ave. (at Washington St.), Calistoga. ☎ **707/942-9111.** Reservations recommended on weekends. Main courses $10.25–$19 at dinner. MC, V. Mon–Tues and Thurs–Fri 11am–3pm; daily 5:30–10pm. Wine shop, Thurs–Tues 11am–7pm. CALIFORNIA.

Wine Country devotees often wend their way to the All Seasons Café in downtown Calistoga because of its extensive wine list and knowledgeable staff. The trick here is to buy a bottle of wine from the cafe's wine shop, then bring it to your table; the cafe adds a corkage fee of around $7.50 instead of tripling the price of the bottle (as they do at most restaurants). The diverse menu ranges from pizzas and pastas to such main courses as braised lamb shank "osso bucco" in an orange, Madeira, and tomato sauce. Anything with the house-smoked salmon or spiced sausages is also a safe bet. Chef John Coss saves his guests from any major *faux pas* by matching wines to his dishes on the menu, so you know what's just right for smoked salmon and Crescenza cheese pizza.

✪ Catahoula. 1457 Lincoln Ave. (between Washington and Fairway sts.), Calistoga. ☎ **707/942-2275.** Reservations recommended. Main courses $11–$20. MC, V. Breakfast Sat–Sun 8:30–10am in winter, Fri–Sun 8:30–10am in summer; lunch Mon and Wed–Fri noon–2:30pm, Sat–Sun noon–3:30pm; dinner daily 5:30–10:30pm. AMERICAN/SOUTHERN.

The domain of chef Jan Birnbaum, formerly of New York's Quilted Giraffe and San Francisco's Campton Place, this restaurant is the current favorite in town. And for good reason: It's the only place in Napa where you can get a decent rooster gumbo. You'd have to travel all over Louisiana to find another pan-fried jalapeño-pecan catfish like this one. Catahoula's funky and fun, and the food that comes out of the wood-burning oven—like the roast duck with chili cilantro potatoes or the whole roasted fish with lemon broth, orzo, and escarole—is exciting (and usually spicy). Start with the spicy gumbo ya ya with andouille sausage, and finish with what may be a first for many non-Southerners: buttermilk ice cream.

INEXPENSIVE

Bosko's. 1364 Lincoln Ave. (between Cedar and Washington sts.), Calistoga. ☎ **707/942-9088.** Main courses $5–$10. MC, V. Daily 11am–10pm. ITALIAN.

It's hard not to like a place that keeps sawdust on its floors, because you immediately know that you won't encounter any snooty waiters or jacked-up prices. Bosko's formula is simple: Serve good, cheap Italian food hot and fast, and make sure nobody leaves hungry. It's a homey place, with red-and-white–checkered tablecloths, an exposed beam ceiling, and a huge U-shaped counter that's always occupied by a least one or two locals. All 16 versions of pasta are cooked to order, as are the 10 or so pizzas and hot sandwiches. Order at the counter, scramble for a table, and then wait for your food to be delivered. The lunch special is a great deal: half a sandwich or plate of pasta, salad, and a darn good bowl of minestrone soup (needs salt, however). Even more brilliant is the method of wine selection: Simply choose a bottle from the wine rack, pay retail for it at the counter, and drink it with your meal. Why don't they all do it this way?

Café Sarafornia. 1413 Lincoln Ave. (at Washington St.), Calistoga. ☎ **707/942-0555.** Main courses $5–$9. MC, V. Mon–Fri 7am–3pm, Sat–Sun 7am–4pm. AMERICAN.

When Calistoga locals want a quick, cheap fix for breakfast or lunch, this is where they come. Café Sarafornia is pleasantly homey, a clean, bright, cheery bastion for late risers like us who prefer to eat their huevos rancheros at noon (breakfast is served all day). The cafe consists of little more than a U-shaped counter, a few booths, wood and tile floors, a few ceiling fans, and a series of bucolic wall murals. The menu is a lesson in simplicity—burgers, hot dogs, pastas, sandwiches, salads, and the requisite small-town specials such as chicken-fried steak with red-eye gravy. And if you like to sweat and holler, be sure to sample the five-alarm chili. The cafe also offers kids' meals for a mere $3.95.

Pacifico. 1237 Lincoln Ave. (between Myrtle and Cedar sts.), Calistoga. ☎ **707/942-4400.** Main courses $6.75–$14.50. MC, V. Mon–Fri 11am–10pm, Sat–Sun 10am–10pm; brunch Sat–Sun 10am–3pm. MEXICAN.

If you're in the mood for Mexican food, Pacifico is the place. The rather mundane-looking facade opens up into a surprisingly festive interior, complete with brilliantly colorful Mexican artwork and pottery, huge potted palm trees, and the requisite south-of-the-border bar complete with faux tile roof and waterfall. The menu is *muy grande*, covering just about every conceivable region in Mexico from Tacos de Oaxaquenos (grilled, marinated chicken tacos topped with guajillo chili salsa) to Enchiladas del Ray (filled with Chihuahua cheese and covered with chili verde sauce) and Mole del Pueblo (chicken mole with chayote and potato, served with rice and tortillas). Fiesta Hour, Monday through Friday from 4:30 to 6pm, features special prices on margaritas and tacos. Pacifico also has the best selection of beers on tap in town.

Smokehouse Café. 1458 Lincoln Ave., Calistoga. ☎ **707/942-6060.** Main courses $8–$21. MC, V. Daily 7:30am–10pm (closed Tues–Wed Jan–Feb). REGIONAL AMERICAN BBQ.

Who would have guessed that some of the best spareribs and house-smoked meats in northern California would come from this little kitchen in Calistoga? Here's the winning game plan: Start with the Sacramento delta crawfish cakes (better than any wimpy crab cakes you'll find in San Francisco) and husk-roasted Cheyenne corn, then move on to the slow pig sandwich, a half slab of ribs, or homemade sausages—all of which take up to a week to prepare (not while you wait, luckily). The clincher is the fluffy all-you-can-eat cornbread dipped in pure cane syrup, which comes with every full-plate dinner. Kids are especially catered to—a rarity in these parts—and patio dining is available during the summer for breakfast, lunch, and dinner.

Wappo Bar & Bistro. 1226B Washington St. (off Lincoln Ave.), Calistoga. ☎ **707/942-4712.** Main courses $8.50–$14.50. AE, MC, V. Wed–Mon 11:30am–2:30pm and 6–9:30pm. INTERNATIONAL.

One of the best alfresco dining experiences in the Wine Country is under Wappo's honeysuckle-and-vine–covered arbor, but you'll also be comfortable inside this small bistro at one of the well-spaced, well-polished tables. The menu offers a wide range of choices, from Chilean sea bass with mint chutney to roast rabbit with potato gnocchi. The desserts of choice are the black-bottom coconut cream pie and the strawberry rhubarb pie.

6 Where to Stock Up for a Picnic— and Where to Enjoy It

You could easily plan your whole trip around restaurant reservations. But put together one of the world's best gourmet picnics, and the valley's your oyster. There are infinite places to spread your blanket, from grassy meadows to picnic tables at the foot of the vineyards; even your hotel room could make for a very romantic dining spot. Best of all, you don't have to count on the maître d' for the best seat in the house. Go ahead, break out that bottle of your newfound favorite cabernet, overindulge in truffle-flavored pâté, hand-feed imported chocolates to your picnic partner. It won't be cheap; in fact, the cost could compare with at least a few local restaurants. But one thing's for sure: The overall experience will be unforgettable.

One of the finest gourmet-food stores in the Wine Country, if not all of California, is the **Oakville Grocery Co.,** 7856 St. Helena Hwy. at Oakville Cross Road (☎ **707/944-8802**). Here you can put together the provisions for a memorable picnic, or, if you give them at least 24 hours' notice, the staff can prepare a picnic basket for you. The store, with its small-town vibe and claustrophobia-inducing crowds, can be quite an experience. You'll find shelves crammed with the best breads and the choicest selection of cheeses in the northern Bay Area, as well as pâtés, cold cuts, crackers, top-quality olive oils, fresh foie gras (domestic and French, seasonally), smoked Norwegian salmon, fresh caviar (Beluga, Sevruga, Osetra), and, of course, an exceptional selection of California wines. The Grocery Co., which was launched by Joseph Phelps long before food and wine were mentioned in the same breath, is open daily from 9am to 6pm; it also has an espresso bar tucked in the corner (open daily from 7am to 3pm), offering breakfast and lunch items, house-baked pastries, and 15 wines available by the glass or for tasting.

Another of our favorite places to fill a picnic basket is New York City's version of a swank European marketplace, **Dean & DeLuca,** 607 S. Main St. (Highway 29), north of Zinfandel Lane and south of Sulphur Springs Road in St. Helena (☎ **707/967-9980**). The opening of this enormous California outpost in late 1997 offered just one more indication that the Wine Country is becoming the epicenter of palatable perfection. The ultimate gourmet grocery store is more like a world's fair of foods, where everything is beautifully displayed and often painfully pricey. As you pace the barn-wood plank floors, you'll stumble upon more high-end edibles than you've ever seen under one roof: local organic produce delivered daily; 200 domestic and imported cheeses (with an on-site aging room to ensure proper ripeness); shelves and shelves of tapenades, pastas, oils, hand-packed dried herbs and spices, chocolates, sauces, and cookware; an espresso bar; one hell of a bakery section; and more. Along the back wall you can watch the professional chefs prepare gourmet takeout (such as fresh seared salmon with chanterelle mushrooms at $7.50 per 6-oz. serving, rotisserie meats, salads, and sautéed vegetables) or order their to-go fireside dinner, a four-course meal which ranges from $7.50 to $9.50 and may include a Caesar salad, rotisserie pork loin with mustard and apricot glaze, French green lentils, sun-dried tomatoes, and root veggies (two-person minimum). Wine master John Hardesty presides over the 1,200-label collection. Adjoining the wine room is a walk-in cedar humidor with over 200 cigars to choose from. Hours are Monday through Saturday from 10am to 7pm (the espresso bar opens at 8am), and Sunday from 10am to 6pm.

Also see page 75 for details on **V. Sattui Winery,** 1111 White Lane (at Calif. 29), St. Helena (☎ **707/963-7774**). Besides an enormous selection of wines and gourmet deli items—including 200 kinds of cheeses and desserts such as a sumptuous white-chocolate cheesecake—you'll also find extensive picnic facilities, making this winery one of the most popular stops along Highway 29.

If you crave a quieter, more pastoral picnic spot, head for one of the four picnic tables at **Robert Keenan Winery** in St. Helena (see p. 78), located right outside the winery and surrounded by vineyards, offering stunning views; the beautiful picnic grounds situated amidst 350-year-old moss-covered oak trees at **Cuvaison** in Calistoga (see p. 83); the spectacular grounds at **Niebaum-Coppola** in Rutherford (see p. 71); or the Wine Country's premier picnicking site, **Rutherford Hill Winery** (see p. 74), which boasts superb views of the valley.

The Sonoma Valley

Sonoma Valley is often thought of as the "other" Wine Country, forever in the shadow of the Napa Valley. Truth is, even though there are far fewer wineries here, Sonoma wines have actually won more awards than any other California wine-growing region for 7 years running (much to the chagrin of Napa vintners, no doubt).

The Sonoma Valley is also far more rural and less traveled than its neighbor to the east, offering a more genuine away-from-it-all experience than its classier cousin. The roads are less crowded, the pace slower, and the whole valley still relatively free of slick tourist attractions and big-name hotels. Commercialization has, for the most part, not yet taken hold; small, family-owned wineries are still Sonoma's mainstay, just as in the old days of wine making, when everyone started with the intention of going broke and loved every minute of it (as the saying goes in these parts, "It takes two million to make a million").

Unlike Napa Valley, you won't find palatial wineries with million-dollar art collections, aerial trams, and Hollywood ego trips (read: Niebaum-Coppola). Rather, the Sonoma Valley offers a refreshing dose of reality, where modestly sized wineries are integrated *into* the community rather than perched on hilltops like corporate citadels. If the Napa Valley feels more like a fantasyland, where everything exists to service the almighty grape and the visitors it attracts, then the Sonoma Valley is its antithesis, an unpretentious gaggle of ordinary towns, ranches, and wineries that welcome tourists but don't necessarily *rely* on them. The result, as you wind your way through the valley, is a chance to experience what Napa Valley must have been like long before the Seagrams and Moët et Chandons of the world turned the Wine Country into a major tourist destination.

1 Orientation & Getting Around

Sonoma Valley is some 17 miles long and 7 miles wide, and is bordered by two mountain ranges: the Mayacamas to the east and the Sonoma Mountains to the west. There is only one road, Highway

12 (also known as the Sonoma Highway), that passes through the valley, starting at the northern edge of the Carneros District, leading though the communities of Sonoma, Glen Ellen, and Kenwood, and ending at the southern boundary of Santa Rosa. Conveniently, most of the wineries—as well as most of the hotels, shops, and restaurants—are located either in the town of Sonoma, along Highway 12, or a short distance from it. Of the numerous side roads that branch off Highway 12, only Bennett Valley Road to the west and Trinity Road (a.k.a. Oakville Grade) to the east lead over the ranges and out of the valley, and neither is easy to navigate. If you're coming from Napa, we strongly suggest you take the leisurely southern route along Highway 12/121 rather than Trinity Road, which is a real brake-smoker.

ALONG HIGHWAY 12: SONOMA'S TOWNS IN BRIEF

As you approach the Wine Country from the south, you must first pass through the **Carneros District,** a cool, windswept region that borders the San Pablo Bay and marks the entrance to both Napa and Sonoma valleys. Until the latter part of the 20th century, this mixture of marsh, sloughs, and rolling hills was mainly used as sheep pasture (*carneros* means sheep in Spanish). After experimental plantings yielded slow-growing yet high-quality grapes—particularly chardonnay and pinot noir—several Napa and Sonoma wineries expanded their plantings here, eventually establishing the Carneros District as an American Viticultural Appellation. Though about a dozen wineries are spread throughout the region, there are no major towns or attractions—just plenty of gorgeous scenery as you cruise along Highway 121, the major junction between Napa and Sonoma.

At the northern boundary of the Carneros District along Highway 12 is the centerpiece of Sonoma Valley, the midsized town of **Sonoma,** which owes much of its appeal to Mexican general Mariano Guadalupe Vallejo. It was Vallejo who fashioned this pleasant, slow-paced community after a typical Mexican village—right down to its central plaza, Sonoma's geographical and commercial center. The plaza sits at the top of a T formed by Broadway (Highway 12) and Napa Street. Most of the surrounding streets form a grid pattern around this axis, making Sonoma easy to negotiate. The plaza's Bear Flag Monument marks the spot where the crude Bear Flag was raised in 1846, signaling the end of Mexican rule; the symbol was later adopted by the state of California and placed on its flag. The 8-acre park at the center of the plaza, complete with two ponds populated with ducks and geese, is perfect for an afternoon siesta in the cool shade. Our favorite attraction, however, is the gaggle of brilliantly feathered chickens that roam unfettered through the streets of Sonoma—a sight you'll *definitely* never see in Napa.

About 7 miles north of Sonoma on Highway 12 is the town of **Glen Ellen,** which, though just a fraction of the size of Sonoma, is home to several of the valley's finest wineries, restaurants, and inns. Aside from the addition of a few new restaurants, this charming Wine Country town hasn't changed much since the days when Jack London settled on his Beauty Ranch, about a mile west. Other than the wineries, you'll find few real signs of commercialism; the shops and restaurants, located along one main winding lane, cater to a small, local clientele—that is, until the summer tourist season, when traffic nearly triples on the weekends. If you're as yet undecided where you want set up camp during your visit to the Wine Country, we highly recommend this lovable little town.

A few miles north of Glen Ellen along Highway 12 is the tiny town of **Kenwood,** the northernmost outpost of the Sonoma Valley. Though Kenwood Vineyards' wines are well known throughout the United States, the town itself consists of little more than a few restaurants, wineries, and modest homes recessed into the wooded hillsides. The nearest lodging, the luxurious Kenwood Inn & Spa, is located about a mile south. Kenwood makes for a pleasant day trip—lunch at Café Citti, a tour of Château St. Jean, dinner at Kenwood Restaurant—before returning to Glen Ellen or Sonoma for the night.

A few miles beyond Kenwood is **Santa Rosa,** the county seat of Sonoma and home to more than 100,000 residents. Historically, it's best known as the hometown of horticulturist Luther Burbank, who produced more than 800 new varieties of fruits, vegetables, and plants during his 50-year tenure here. Unless you're armed with a map, however, it's best to avoid exploring the large, sprawling city as it's easy to get lost; plus, it has little more to offer than what you'll find in Sonoma Valley proper.

VISITOR INFORMATION

While you're in Sonoma, stop by the **Sonoma Valley Visitors Bureau,** 10 E. Spain St. (☎ **707/996-1090; www.sonomavalley. com**), right on the plaza next to the Sonoma Cheese Factory. It's open daily from 9am to 7pm in summer and from 9am to 5pm in winter. An additional visitors bureau is located a few miles south of the square at 25200 Arnold Dr. (Highway 121), at the entrance to Viansa Winery (☎ **707/996-5793**); it's open daily from 9am to 5pm.

TOURING THE SONOMA VALLEY BY BIKE

Sonoma and its neighboring towns are so small, close together, and relatively flat that it's not difficult to get around on two wheels. In fact, if you're in no great hurry, there's no better way to tour the Sonoma Valley than via bicycle. You can rent a bike at the ✪ **Goodtime Bicycle Company,** 18503 Sonoma Hwy. (Calif. 12), Sonoma (☎ **888/525-0453** or 707/938-0453). They'll happily point you to easy bike trails, or you can take one of their organized excursions to Kenwood-area wineries or to south Sonoma wineries. Not only do they provide a gourmet lunch featuring local Sonoma products, they'll also carry any wine you purchase for you and help with shipping arrangements. Lunch rides start at 10:30am and end at around 3pm. The cost, including food and equipment, is $55 per person (that's a darn good deal). Rentals cost $25 a day or $5 per hour, and include helmets, locks, and everything else you'll need (delivery is a $25 flat day rate). Bikes are also available for rent from **Sonoma Valley Cyclery,** 20093 Broadway, Sonoma (☎ **707/935-3377**), for $20 a day, or $6 per hour.

FAST FACTS: The Sonoma Valley

Hospitals   The Santa Rosa Memorial Hospital, 1165 Montgomery Dr. in Santa Rosa, about a 30-minute drive north from Sonoma (☎ **707/546-3210**), offers 24-hour emergency service, as well as complete inpatient and outpatient services, cardiac center, pediatrics, and a dental clinic.

Information   See "Visitor Information," above.

Newspapers/Magazines   The main newspaper in Sonoma Valley is the *Press Democrat,* a New York Times publication printed daily and distributed at newsstands throughout Sonoma, Lake, Napa, and Mendocino counties. Sonoma's local paper is the *Sonoma Index Tribune;* published twice a week and available at newsstands around town, it covers regional news, events, and issues. Also available around town is the *Sonoma Valley Visitors Guide,* a slender $2 publication listing just about every sightseeing, recreation, shopping, lodging, and dining option in the valley, as well as a winery map.

Pharmacy   The pharmacy at **Long's Drugs,** 201 W. Napa St., Sonoma (☎ **707/938-4730**), is open Monday through Saturday from 9am to 9pm, Sunday from 10am to 6pm. If you prefer a more personable place to get your prescription filled, **Adobe Drug,** 303

W. Napa St., Sonoma (☎ **707/938-1144**), a locally owned drug-
store, claims to be Sonoma's "Prescription Specialists" and will even
make deliveries; it's open Monday through Friday from 9am to
8pm, Saturday from 9am to 7pm.

Police   For the local police, call ☎ **707/996-3601** or ☎ **707/
996-3602,** or, in an emergency, ☎ **911.**

Post Offices   In **downtown Sonoma,** the post office is at 617
Broadway, at Patton Street (☎ **707/996-2459**). The **Glen Ellen**
post office is at 13720 Arnold St., at O'Donnel Lane (☎ **707/
996-9233**). Both branches are open Monday through Friday from
8:30am to 5pm.

Shipping Companies   **Mail Boxes, Etc.,** 19229 Sonoma Hwy.,
at Verano Street, Sonoma (☎ **707/935-3438**), which has a lot of
experience with shipping wine, claims it will ship your wine to any
state, either via UPS (which as of now only ships to a dozen states)
or Federal Express. The **Wine Exchange of Sonoma,** 452 First
St. E. (between East Napa and East Spain streets), Sonoma
(☎ **707/938-1794**), will ship your wine as well—*if* you purchase
an equal quantity of the same wine at their store (which they assured us would be in stock, and probably at a better price). For
more on the reciprocity laws associated with shipping wine out of
California, see "The Ins & Outs of Shipping Wine Home" in
chapter 3.

Taxis   Call **A-C Taxi** at ☎ **707/526-4888.**

2 Touring the Wineries

Sonoma Valley is currently home to about 35 wineries (including
California's first winery, Buena Vista, founded in 1857) and 13,000
acres of vineyards, which produce roughly 25 types of wines totaling more than five million cases a year. Chardonnay is the varietal
for which Sonoma is most noted, and it represents almost one-
quarter of the valley's vine acreage. Unlike the rigidly structured
tours at many of Napa Valley's corporate-owned wineries, tastings
and tours on the Sonoma side of the Mayacamas Mountains are usually free and low-key, and come with plenty of friendly banter between
the wine makers and their guests.

   **The towns and wineries covered below are organized geo-
graphically** from south to north, starting at the intersection of
Highway 37 and Highway 121 in the Carneros District and ending
in Kenwood. The wineries here tend to be a little more spread out

than they are in Napa, but they're easy to find. Still, it's best to decide which wineries you're most interested in and devise a touring strategy before you set out so you don't find yourself doing a lot of backtracking. (For more on this, see "Strategies for Touring the Wine Country" in chapter 3; and check out the "The Sonoma Valley Wineries" map on p. 139 to get your bearings).

We've reviewed our favorite Sonoma Valley wineries here. If you'd like a complete list of local wineries, be sure to pick up one of the free guides to the valley available at the **Sonoma Valley Visitors Bureau** (see "Visitor Information," above).

THE CARNEROS DISTRICT

Rōche. 28700 Arnold Dr. (Calif. 121), Sonoma. ☎ **800/825-9475** or 707/935-7115. Daily 10am–6pm (to 5pm in winter). No tours available.

The first winery you'll encounter as you enter Sonoma Valley, Rōche is characteristic of most Sonoma wineries—a small, family-run operation that focuses on one or two varietals and has a very limited distribution (Rōche wines, in fact, are sold exclusively through the tasting room). Situated atop a gently sloping knoll, the ranch-style winery and surrounding 25 acres of vineyards is owned by Genevieve and Joe Rōche (pronounced *Rōsh*), who originally bought the property with no intention of starting a winery. But in the early 1980s, a colleague suggested they experiment with a few vines of chardonnay—and the results were so impressive that they decided to go into business making estate-grown chardonnay and pinot noir (another berry that thrives in this cool district).

The Rōches only produce about 6,000 cases per year, some of which are bought before the wine even hits the bottle. Tastings are complimentary for nonreserve wines, and prices range from $9 for a 1995 Tamarix pinot noir blanc to $18 for the unfiltered 1994 Estate pinot noir; our favorite is the 1995 Estate chardonnay ($17), a rich, intense wine with lingering flavors of apple, pear, and butterscotch. Picnic tables overlooking the valley are available, though you'll probably prefer lunching at neighboring Viansa Winery (see below).

✪ **Viansa Winery and Italian Marketplace.** 25200 Arnold Dr. (Calif. 121), Sonoma. ☎ **800/995-4740** or 707/935-4700. Daily 10am–5pm. Guided tours by appointment only.

The first major winery you'll encounter as you enter Sonoma Valley from the south, this sprawling Tuscany-style villa is perched atop a knoll overlooking the entire lower valley. Viansa is the brainchild of Sam and Vicki Sebastiani, who left the family dynasty to create

The Sonoma Valley Wineries

Legend:

Arrowood 10
The Benziger Family Winery 7
B. R. Cohn Winery 9
Buena Vista 13
Château St. Jean 4
Glen Ellen Tasting Room 8
Gloria Ferrer
    Champagne Caves 16
Gundlach-Bundschu Winery 14
Kenwood Vineyards 5
Kunde Estate Winery 6
Landmark Vineyards 2
Matanzas Creek 1
Ravenswood Winery 11
Roche 17
St. Francis Winery 3
Schug Carneros Estate Winery 15
Sebastiani Vineyards Winery 12
Sonoma Mountain Estate
    Hopyards & Brewery 10
Viansa Winery and
    Italian Marketplace 17

Town of Sonoma

their own temple to food and wine (*Viansa* being a contraction of Vicki and Sam). While Sam, a third-generation wine maker, runs the winery, Vicky manages the marketplace, a large room crammed with a cornucopia of high-quality preserves, mustards, olive oils, pastas, salads, breads, desserts, Italian tableware, cookbooks, and wine-related gifts.

The winery, which does an extensive mail-order business through its Tuscany Club (worth joining if you love getting mail and good wine), has quickly established a favorable reputation for its cabernet, sauvignon blanc, and chardonnay, blended from premium Napa and Sonoma grapes and sold in the sexiest-shaped bottles in Sonoma. Sam is also experimenting with Italian grape varieties such as muscat canelli, sangiovese, and nebbiolo, most of which are sold exclusively at the winery. Free tastings are poured at the east end of the market- place, and the self-guided tour includes a trip through the under- ground barrel-aging cellar adorned with colorful hand-painted murals.

Viansa is also one of the few wineries in Sonoma Valley where you can purchase deli items—the focaccia sandwiches are deli- cious—and dine alfresco under the grape trellis while you admire the bucolic view.

🟢 **Gloria Ferrer Champagne Caves.** 23555 Carneros Hwy. (Calif. 121), Sonoma. ☎ **707/996-7256.** Daily 10am–5:30pm. Tours hourly from 11am–4pm.

When you have it up to here with chardonnays and pinots, it's time to pay a visit to Gloria Ferrer, the grande dame of the Wine Country's sparkling-wine producers. Who's Gloria, you ask? She's the wife of José Ferrer, whose family has been making sparkling wine for the past 5 centuries and whose company, Freixenet, is the larg- est producer of sparkling wine in the world (Cordon Negro being their most popular brand)—all of which equals big bucks, and cer- tainly a good chunk of it went into building this palatial estate. Glimmering like Oz high atop a gently sloping hill, it overlooks the verdant Carneros District; on a sunny day, it's impossible not to enjoy a glass of dry Brut while soaking in the magnificent views of the vineyards and valley below.

If you're unfamiliar with the term méthode champenoise, be sure to take the free 30-minute tour of the fermenting tanks, bottling line, and caves brimming with racks of yeast-laden bottles. Afterwards, retire to the elegant tasting room for a flute of Brut or Cuvée ($3 to $5.50 a glass, $16 and up per bottle), find an empty chair on the veranda, and say, "Ahhh. *This* is the life." There are picnic tables, but it's usually too windy up here for comfort—plus you have to purchase a bottle of their sparkling wine to reserve a table.

Schug Carneros Estate Winery. 602 Bonneau Rd. (west of the junction of Calif. 116 and Calif. 121), Sonoma. ☎ **800/966-9365** or 707/939-9363. Daily 10am–5pm. Tours by appointment only.

A native of Germany's Rhine River valley, Walter Schug (pronounced *Shewg*) comes from a long line of pinot-noir vintners. After graduating from the prestigious German wine institute of Geisenheim in 1959, he came to California and worked as wine maker for Joseph Phelps, where he established his reputation as one of California's top cabernet-sauvignon and Riesling producers. In 1980, he launched his own label from a vineyard he tended at Phelps, and left soon afterwards to build this winery. Since then, Schug's wines have achieved world-class status, with an astounding 30% sold overseas.

The winery is situated on top of a rise overlooking the surrounding Carneros District, a prime region for cool-climate grapes such as chardonnay and pinot noir (Schug's predominate wines). Its post-and-beam architecture reflects the Schug family's German heritage; the tasting room, however, is quite ordinary and small, designed more for practicality than pomp and circumstance (a radical contrast from neighboring Viansa and Gloria Ferrer). Typical of Sonoma wineries, there's no tasting fee, and bottle prices are all quite reasonable, ranging from $12 for a 1996 North Coast sauvignon blanc to $20 for a 1995 North Coast merlot. The best buy, however, is the award-winning 1995 Carneros pinot noir, a bargain at $18. The winery has no picnic facilities, probably due to steady winds upwelling from the neighboring dairy farm.

SONOMA

✪ **Gundlach-Bundschu Winery.** 2000 Denmark St. (off Eighth St. E.), Sonoma. ☎ **707/938-5277.** Daily 11am–4:30pm. Tours last 10–20 min. and are offered about every half hour, May–Sept only; no reservations necessary.

If it looks like the people working here are actually enjoying themselves, that's because they are. Gundlach-Bundschu (pronounced *Gun*-lock *Bun*-shoe) is your quintessential Sonoma winery—nonchalant about appearance, but obsessed with wine: The G-B clan are a nefarious lot, infamous for wild stunts such as holding up Napa's Wine Train on horseback and—egad!—serving Sonoma wines to their captives; their small tasting room looks not unlike a bomb shelter, the Talking Heads is their version of Muzak, and the "art" consists of a dozen witty black-and-white posters promoting their wines.

This is the oldest family-owned and -operated winery in California, going into its sixth generation since Jacob Gundlach harvested his first crop in 1858. What started out as a winery known for whites is now coveted among wine's cognoscenti for their reds, particularly the zinfandels. Prices for their 17 distinct wines range from a very reasonable $8 per bottle for the Polar Bearitage (ha, ha) white table wine to $40 for the Vintage Reserve cabernet sauvignon, though most prices are in the midteens; tastings are free. Tours include a trip into their 430-foot cave (the longest in Calif., they claim).

Gundlach-Bundschu has the best picnic grounds in the valley, though you'll have to walk to the top of Towles' Hill to earn the sensational view. And the Shakespeare plays held at the winery's adjacent outdoor theater Friday through Sunday from Memorial Day to Labor Day (general admission $18) are a real blast.

Sebastiani Vineyards Winery. 389 Fourth St. E., Sonoma. ☎ **800/ 888-5532** or 707/938-5532. Daily 10am–5pm. Tours offered 10:30am–4pm, every half hour in summer, every 45 min. to an hour in winter; no reservations necessary.

The name Sebastiani is practically synonymous with Sonoma. What started in 1904, when Samuele Sebastiani began producing his first wines, has in three successive generations grown into a small empire and Sonoma County's largest winery, producing some six *million* cases a year. Oddly enough, the winery occupies neither the most scenic setting nor structure in Sonoma Valley, yet its place in the history and development of the region is unparalleled.

The 25-minute tour is interesting, informative, and well worth the time. You can see the winery's original turn-of-the-century crusher and press as well as the world's largest collection of oak-barrel carvings, crafted by local artist Earle Brown. If you don't want to take the tour, head straight for the charmingly rustic tasting room, where you can sample an extensive selection of wines *sans* tasting fee. Bottle prices are very reasonable, ranging from $5 for a 1996 white zin to $15 for a 1994 cabernet sauvignon. A picnic area is adjacent to the cellars, though a far more scenic spot is located across the parking lot in Sebastiani's Cherryblock Vineyards.

Buena Vista. 18000 Old Winery Rd. (off E. Napa St., slightly northeast of downtown), Sonoma. ☎ **800/926-1266** or 707/938-1266. Daily 10:30am– 5pm. Self-guided tours only.

The patriarch of California wineries was founded in 1857 by Count Agoston Haraszthy, the Hungarian émigré who is universally regarded as the father of California's wine industry. A close friend of General Vallejo, Haraszthy returned from Europe in 1861 with 100,000 of the finest vine cuttings, which he made available to all winegrowers. Although Buena Vista's wine making now takes place at an ultramodern facility in the Carneros District, the winery still maintains a tasting room inside the restored 1862 Press House—a beautiful stone-crafted room brimming with wines, wine-related gifts, and accessories (as well as a small art gallery along the inner balcony).

Tastings are free for most wines, $3 for the really good stuff; bottle prices range from as low as $8.50 for a buttery 1996 sauvignon blanc to $26 for the Carneros Grand Reserve cabernet sauvignon (which was so good that we bought three). You can take the self-guided tour any time during operating hours; a "Historical Presentation," offered daily at 2pm, details the life and times of the Count. After tasting, grab your favorite bottle, a selection of cheeses from the Sonoma Cheese Factory, salami, bread, and pâté (all available in the tasting room), and plant yourself at one of the many picnic tables recessed into the lush, verdant setting.

Ravenswood Winery. 18701 Gehricke Rd. (off Lovall Valley Rd.), Sonoma. ☎ **800/NO-WIMPY** or 707/938-1960. Daily 10am–4:30pm. Tours by reservation only.

Compared to old heavies like Sebastiani and Buena Vista, Ravenswood is a relative newcomer to the Sonoma wine scene, but it has quickly established itself as the *sine qua non* of zinfandel, the versatile grape that's quickly gaining popular ground on the rapacious cabernet sauvignon. In fact, Ravenswood is the first winery in the United States to focus primarily on zins, which make up about three quarters of its 150,000-case production; it also produces a merlot, cabernet sauvignon, and a small amount of chardonnay.

The winery is smartly designed—recessed into the Sonoma hillside to protect its treasures from the simmering summers. Tours follow the wine-making process from grape to glass, and include a visit into the aromatic oak-barrel aging rooms. A gourmet "Barbecue Overlooking the Vineyards" is held each weekend (from 11am to 4:40pm, Memorial Day through Sept; call for details and reservations), though you're welcome to plop your own picnic basket down at any of their tables. Tastings are free and generous, though you may not find some of the pourers to be as witty as they think they are (ours was a jerk, though we've known people who have had great experiences here). Bottle prices range from $8.50 for a 1996 light and crisp French Colombard to $16 for a 1995 cab, but it's the kick-butt zins—priced well in the low- to midteens—that you'll want to stock up on.

GLEN ELLEN

B. R. Cohn Winery. 15140 Sonoma Hwy. (Calif. 12, just north of Madrone Rd.), Glen Ellen. ☎ **707/938-4064.** Daily 10am–5pm. No tours available.

You may not have heard of Bruce Cohn, but you've certainly heard of the Doobie Brothers, the San Francisco band he managed to fame and fortune—part of which he used to purchase this wonderfully bucolic estate with its whitewashed turn-of-the-century farmhouse and groves of rare olive trees. Cohn, a native of Sonoma County, started making his own wine in 1984 and was an immediate success. In the small, simple tasting room lined with framed gold and platinum albums (guess whose?), a friendly and informative staff pours free tastings of cabernet, pinot noir, a delicious chardonnay, and the occasional merlot. Bottle prices range from the midteens to $35, and the winery often sells selections that aren't available elsewhere, such as the estate-grown 1995 Olive Hill merlot ($24). Though best known for his cabernet sauvignon, it's a case of Cohn's reserve chardonnay you'll want to send back home along with a bottle or two of his award-winning (and pricey) olive oil. There are a few picnic tables on the cement patio fronting the tasting room, but bring along a blanket and relax on the terraced hills of plush lawn overlooking the vineyards.

Arrowood. 14347 Sonoma Hwy. (Calif. 12), Glen Ellen. ☎ **707/938-5170.** Daily 10am–4:30pm. Tours by appointment only, Mon–Fri at 10:30am and 2:30pm.

Richard Arrowood had already established a reputation as a master wine maker at Château St. Jean before he and his wife, Alis Demers Arrowood, set out on their own in 1986. Their utterly picturesque winery is perched on a gently rising hillside lined with perfectly manicured vineyards. Tastings take place in the Hospitality House, the newest of Arrowood's two stately gray-and-white buildings fashioned after New England farmhouses, complete with wraparound porches. Richard's focus is on making world-class wine with minimal intervention, and his results are impressive: four of his five current releases have scored over 90 points. Mind you, such excellence doesn't come cheaply: Prices start at $24 for a 1996 chardonnay and quickly climb to the mid- to high 30s. Arrowood is one of the very few wineries in Sonoma that charge for tastings ($3), but if you're curious what near-perfection tastes like, it's well worth it. No picnic facilities are available.

Glen Ellen Tasting Room. 14301 Arnold Dr. (at the south end of town in Jack London Village), Glen Ellen. ☎ **707/939-6277.** Daily 10am–5pm. Self-guided tours available.

While most other Sonoma County wineries are knocking themselves out to make the best wines on the planet, Glen Ellen is content with making reasonably good wines at rock-bottom prices. The story starts with Bruno Benziger, a retired New York wine-and-spirits importer who decided to move to Sonoma and start a winery aimed at the middle market—and he succeeded beyond his wildest dreams: Glen Ellen chardonnay and merlot became nationwide best-sellers, and the white zinfandel and cabernet were among the top three. The Benziger family eventually sold the Glen Ellen brand (along with M. G. Vallejo) in 1993 to pursue higher-quality, lower-volume wine (see "The Benziger Family Winery," below), though the Glen Ellen label continues to produce about 3.8 *million* cases a year.

The Tasting Room, housed in the original Glen Ellen winery built back in 1881, is a large, modern, and handsomely trimmed room with polished woods, racks of oak wine barrels, and a wide assortment of wine-related gifts for purchase. Tastings are free, and bottles are value-priced at $5 for a 1996 white zin and $7 for a Glen Ellen merlot; reserve wines run an affordable $12 or $13 per bottle. Sure, it's mediocre wine—but what do you expect at these prices? Also worth a visit is the History Center, a smartly designed self-guided tour of Glen Ellen back in its heyday (the poster-sized black-and-white photographs are truly captivating). Picnic tables with views overlooking a creek are located behind the Tasting Room.

✪ The Benziger Family Winery. 1883 London Ranch Rd. (off Arnold Dr., on the way to Jack London State Historic Park), Glen Ellen. ☎ **800/989-8890** or 707/935-3000. Tasting room daily 10am–5:30pm. Tram tours daily (weather permitting) at 11:30am, 12:30, 2, and 3:30pm.

When Bruno Benziger moved from New York, purchased the plot next to Jack London State Park, and started the Glen Ellen label (see above), he had no idea that he would become the valley's second-largest wine producer. After the Benziger family's fast track to the top, they sold the rights to that label in order to create lower-volume, higher-quality wines under this one.

A visit here confirms that you are indeed visiting a "family" winery; at any given time, three generations of Benzigers (pronounced *Ben*-zigger) may be running around tending to chores, and you're

From Grapes to Hops: The Benzigers as Brew Masters

Okay, so it's not a winery. But just as fascinating (if not more complex) is the amount of time and technology it takes to brew beer—and nowhere in the United States will you find a brewery as dedicated to educating the public about the entire beer-making process, from barley field to bottle, than the ✪ **Sonoma Mountain Estate Hopyards & Brewery,** next to Arrowood Winery at 14335 Sonoma Hwy. (Highway 12), Glen Ellen (☎ **707/ 935-4500**). The shiny new brewery is a pet project of the Benziger boys (of the Benziger Family Winery), who plowed up 2 acres of prime merlot vineyard to plant hops for their handcrafted lagers, imported an entire copper brew house from the Black Forest of Germany, tapped their own mountain spring water flowing beneath the property, and convinced master brewer Chris Atkinson to move down from Oregon to California. The result is one of the best amber ales we've ever tasted (and we've tasted a *whole* lot).

What really sold us on the brewery, though, was the Ingredient Walk, a self-guided tour of living exhibits—hops, barley, and yeast—that are necessary to brew beer, and the Living Machine, an eco-friendly water reclamation system that allows the brewery to recycle waste water for reuse in the hopyards. "It's a huge success," says lead bartender Jonathan Radin. "Environmentalists from all over are coming to see how it works."

The tasting room resembles a huge hunting lodge, complete with large fireplace, leather couches, and denim-clad men hunched over the bar watching TV. Tastings of the four brews cost $2. Currently, the only two beers available to take home are the pilsner and the amber ale, which run about $7 for a six-pack. You can take the self-guided tour during the brewery's regular open hours, daily from 11am to 6pm; guided tours of the entire eco-brew process are offered in spring and summer (call to check times).

instantly made to feel as if you're part of the clan. The pastoral, user-friendly property features an exceptional self-guided tour ("The most comprehensive tour in the wine industry," exclaims *Wine Spectator* magazine), gardens, a spacious tasting room manned by an amiable staff, and an art gallery. The free 40-minute tram tour, pulled by a beefy tractor, is both informative and fun as it winds through the estate vineyards before making a champagne-tasting pit stop on a scenic bluff. (*Tip:* Tram tickets—a hot item in the summer—are available on a first-come, first-served, basis, so either arrive early or stop by in the morning to pick up afternoon tickets.)

Tastings of the standard-release wines are free, and bottle prices range from $10 for a 1996 fumé blanc to $18 for a 1995 pinot noir. The best buy, however, is the award-winning 1995 zinfandel (Sonoma County), priced to move at $16 a bottle. You can also purchase a full glass of wine for $5 and tour the estate in style. The winery offers several scenic picnic spots.

KENWOOD

Kunde Estate Winery. 10155 Sonoma Hwy., Kenwood. ☎ **707/833-5501.** Tastings daily 11am–5pm. Cave tours Fri–Sun approximately every half-hour from 11am–4pm.

Expect a friendly, unintimidating welcome at this scenic winery, run by four generations of the Kundes since 1904. One of the largest grape suppliers in the area, the Kunde family (pronounced *Kun*-dee) has devoted 800 acres of their 2,000-acre ranch to growing ultrapremium-quality grapes, which they provide to about 30 Sonoma and Napa wineries. It's this abundance that allows them to make nothing but estate wines (wines made from grapes grown on the Kunde property, as opposed to grapes purchased from other growers).

The tasting room is located in a spiffy new 17,000-square-foot wine-making facility, which features specialized crushing equipment that enables the wine maker to run whole clusters to the press—a real advantage in white-wine production. Tastings of the dozen or so releases are free; bottle prices range from $11 for a 1996 Magnolia Lane sauvignon blanc to $24 for a 1993 Reserve cabernet sauvignon; most labels sell in the mid- to high teens. The tasting room also has a gift shop and large windows overlooking the bottling room and tank room.

The tour of the property's extensive wine caves includes a history of the winery. Private tours are available by appointment, but most folks are happy to just stop by for some vino and to relax at one of the many picnic tables placed around the man-made pond. Animal lovers will appreciate Kunde's preservation efforts; the property has a duck estuary with more than 50 species (seen by appointment only). The Kunde Estate also happens to be where actress Geena Davis and director Renny Harlin tied the knot in 1993.

Kenwood Vineyards. 9592 Sonoma Hwy. (Calif. 12), Kenwood. ☎ **707/833-5891.** Daily 10am–4:30pm. Tours by appointment only.

Kenwood's history dates back to 1906, when the Pagani brothers made their living selling wine straight from the barrel and into the jug. In 1970 the property was bought by the Lee family, who dumped a ton of money into converting the aging winery into a modern, high-production facility (though they have cleverly concealed most of it within the original barnlike buildings). Since then, Kenwood's wines have earned a solid reputation for consistent quality with each of their varietals: cabernet sauvignon, chardonnay, zinfandel, pinot noir, merlot, and their most popular wine, sauvignon blanc—a crisp, light wine with hints of melon.

Though the winery looks rather modest in size, its output is staggering: 275,000 cases of ultrapremium wines fermented in 60 steel tanks and 7,000 French and American oak barrels. Popular with wine collectors is wine maker Michael Lee's Artist Series cabernet sauvignon, a limited production from the winery's best vineyards featuring labels with original artwork by renowned artists. The tasting room, housed in one of the old barns, offers free tastings of most varieties as well as gift items for sale. Wine prices are moderate, ranging from $7.50 for a bottle of 1995 Vintage Red table wine to $20 for a 1995 Sonoma County merlot; the Artist Series, on the other hand, runs anywhere from $50 to $250.

Château St. Jean. 8555 Sonoma Hwy. (Calif. 12), Kenwood. ☎ **800/ 543-7572** or 707/833-4134. Self-guided tours daily 10am–4pm; tasting room daily 10am–4:30pm. At the foot of Sugarloaf Ridge, just north of Kenwood and east of Hwy. 12.

Château St. Jean is notable for its exceptionally beautiful buildings, well-landscaped grounds, and elegant tasting room. Among California wineries, it's a pioneer in vineyard designation—the procedure of making wine from, and naming it for, a single vineyard. A private drive takes you to what was once a 250-acre country retreat built in 1920; a well-manicured lawn overlooking the meticulously maintained vineyards is now a picnic area, complete with a fountain and picnic tables. There's a self-guided tour with detailed and photographic descriptions of the wine-making process. When you're done, be sure to walk up to the top of the faux medieval tower for a magnificent view of the valley.

Back in the elegant tasting room—split into three areas to better handle the traffic—you can sample Château St. Jean's wide array of wines ranging from chardonnays and cabernet sauvignon to fumé blanc, merlot, Johannisberg Riesling, and gewürztraminer (don't miss a rare tasting of their late-harvest wines as well—you'll be amazed what a little more time on the vine can do to a wine). Tastings are complimentary, and prices range from $8 for a Sonoma County fumé blanc to $27 for a Durell Vineyards pinot noir; most wines, though, are priced around $20. If you can find a bottle of the 1991 Sonoma County Reserve cabernet, buy it—it's won more awards than Pete Sampras.

St. Francis Winery. 8450 Sonoma Hwy. (Calif. 12), Kenwood. ☎ **800/ 543-7713** or 707/833-4666. Daily 10am–4:30pm. No tours available.

Although St. Francis Winery makes a commendable chardonnay, zinfandel, and cabernet sauvignon, it's their highly coveted merlot that they're best known for. Wine maker Tom Mackey, a former high-school English teacher from San Francisco, has been hailed as the Master of Merlot by *Wine Spectator* magazine for his uncanny ability to craft the finest merlot in California (although we prefer the one at Matanzas Creek; see below). Seventy percent of the estate's vineyards yield merlot grapes, used to make Mackey's Estate Reserve merlot—the one bottle you don't want to leave without (in fact, they'll only *let* you leave with one bottle).

The property itself has an interesting history: The original vineyard was planted in 1910 as part of a wedding gift to Alice Kunde (scion of the local Kunde family), but it wasn't until 1979 that Joe Martin and Lloyd Canton—two white-collar executives turned vintners—completed their long-awaited dream winery on the site and christened it after Saint Francis of Assisi. It has a small but cozy tasting room complete with the requisite wine-related gift items. Tastings are free for most wines, and $1 for the reserve reds. A good buy is the 1996 chardonnay ($12), barrel-fermented in American and French oak for 6 months with hints of oak and fruit. Otherwise, prices range from $18 to $20 a bottle, and $30 for the reserve reds. A few picnic tables overlooking the vineyards are set out behind the tasting room.

Landmark Vineyards. 101 Adobe Canyon Rd. (off Hwy. 12), Kenwood. ☎ **800/452-6365** or 707/833-1144. Daily 10am–4:30pm.

California's oldest exclusively chardonnay estate was first founded in 1972 in the Russian River area of Sonoma County. When new-housing development started encroaching on the winery's territory, proprietor Damaris Deer W. Ethridge (great-great-granddaughter of John Deere, the tractor baron) moved her operation to northern Sonoma Valley in 1990. The winery, which produces about 30,000 cases annually, is housed in a modest mission-style building set on 20 acres of vineyards. The tasting room offers complimentary samples of their award-winning chardonnay, as well as a recently introduced pinot noir. (The wall-to-wall mural behind the granite-topped tasting counter, by the way, was painted by noted Sonoma

County artist Claudia Wagar.) Wine prices range from $11 for a 1996 Adobe Canyon sauvignon blanc to $20 for a 1996 Overlook chardonnay.

The winery has a pond-side picnic area, as well as what is probably the only bocce court in the valley (yes, you can play, and yes, they provide instructions). Also available from Memorial Day to Labor Day are Belgian Horse–drawn wagon tours through the vineyards, offered every Saturday and Sunday from 11am to 3pm ($5, which includes a tasting of Landmark's reserve wines).

JUST UP FROM THE VALLEY

✪ **Matanzas Creek.** 6097 Bennett Valley Rd. (off Warm Springs Rd.), Santa Rosa. ☎ **707/528-6464.** Daily 10am–4:30pm. Tours daily by appointment only at 10:30am, 1, and 3pm. From Hwy. 12 in Kenwood or Glen Ellen, take Warm Springs Rd. turnoff to Bennett Valley Rd.; the drive takes 15–20 min.

Okay, so it's not technically in Sonoma Valley—but if there's one winery that's worth the detour, it's Matanzas Creek. After a wonderfully scenic 20-minute drive along Bennett Valley Road, you'll arrive at one of the prettiest wineries in California, blanketed by fields of lavender and surrounded by rolling hills of well-tended vineyards.

The winery itself has a rather unorthodox history. In 1978, Sandra and Bill MacIver, neither of whom had any previous experience in the worlds of wine making or business, set out with one goal in mind: to create the finest wines in the country. Actually, they've overshot their mark. With the recent release of their Journey 1990 chardonnay, they've been hailed by critics as the proud parents of *the* finest chardonnay ever produced in the United States, comparable to the finest white wines in the world.

This state-of-the-art, environmentally conscious winery produces only three varietals—the above-mentioned chardonnay, plus sauvignon blanc and merlot—all of which are available for tasting free of charge. Prices for current releases are, as you would imagine, at the higher end, ranging from $18 for a 1996 sauvignon blanc to a whopping $75 for the 1993 Estate merlot—but it's easily the finest merlot you'll sample in the Wine Country. Also available for purchase is culinary lavender from Matanzas (pronounced Mah-*tan-z*as) Creek's own lavender field, the largest outside of Provence and a breathtaking sight when it's in bloom in June—purchase a glass of wine and bring it outside to savor as you wander through these wonderfully aromatic gardens. Picnic tables hidden under groves of oak have pleasant views of the surrounding vineyards. On the return trip, be sure to take the Sonoma Mountain Road detour for a real backcountry experience.

3 More to See & Do

When you've had it up to your gills in Sonoma Valley wineries, it's time to explore the valley's numerous other sites and attractions, ranging from biplane rides to golf courses. The majority of activities are centered around the town of Sonoma, which is small enough to explore on foot (the picturesque town plaza is truly worth checking out). If the weather's warm, we strongly recommend a guided tour of the Sonoma Valley via horseback or bicycle, two of our favorite things to do in the Wine Country.

THE CARNEROS DISTRICT

BIPLANE RIDES   For the adrenaline junkie in your group, ✪ **Aeroschellville Biplane & Glider Rides** will help you lose your lunch on one of their authentic 1940 Boeing-built Stearman biplanes. Rides range from the "Scenic" (a leisurely flight over Sonoma Valley) and "Aerobatic" (loops, rolls, and assorted maneuvers) to—drum roll, please—the "Kamikaze," an intensely bowel-shaking aerobatic death wish that's (and we quote) "not for the faint of heart." Prices range from $70 for the Scenic to $90 for the Kamikaze. A second passenger is welcome to join the fun for an additional fee.

Safe and saner types should opt for the **glider rides,** which soar over the bay and offer breathtaking views of the Sonoma and Napa valleys and, on a clear day, the Sierra mountain range. Prices range from $80 to $145 for one passenger, $120 to $195 for two.

Reservations are recommended for both biplane and glider rides, though drop-ins are welcome. Aeroschellville is located at the Sonoma Valley Airport, 23982 Arnold Dr. (on Calif. 121, across from Gloria Ferrer Champagne Caves), Sonoma Valley (☎ **707/938-2444**).

SONOMA

The best way to learn about the history of Sonoma is to follow the self-guided *Sonoma Walking Tour* map, provided by the Sonoma League for Historic Preservation. Tour highlights include General Vallejo's 1852 Victorian-style home; the Sonoma Barracks, erected in 1836 to house Mexican army troops; and the Blue Wing Inn, an 1840 hostelry built to accommodate travelers—including John Fremont, Kit Carson, and Ulysses S. Grant—and new settlers while they erected homes in Sonoma. You can purchase the $2.75 map at the **Vasquez House,** 414 First St. E., between East Napa and East Spain streets (☎ **707/938-0510**), open Wednesday through Sunday from 1:30 to 4pm.

The Super Spa

There's no question about it: ✪ **Sonoma Mission Inn & Spa,** 18140 Sonoma Hwy. (☎ **800/862-4945** or 707/938-9000), is the most complete—and the most luxurious—spa in the whole Wine Country. At this elegant pink Spanish Mission–style palace, you can pamper yourself in myriad ways: Take a soak in mineral baths; get a facial, body wrap, or massage; aerobicize; work out with weights and cardio machines or let go of your tension in a yoga class; relax with a steam or a sauna; play tennis; or just lounge or lunch by the pool. Or you can opt for our (okay, Erika's) personal favorite—the Rejuvinator, a 1-hour-40-minute megatreatment: First you're wrapped in blankets on a massage table. Then comes an "oil drip" onto your hair and scalp, followed by a scalp massage and a hair mask that smells so much like cookie dough that you'll be tempted to nibble on it. Next comes a face mask and a rinse. Finally, the crowning glory—a stress-relieving back massage.

   The Rejuvenator's $174 price tag is steep, but if you can swing it, this package of pampering is well worth the cost—it really does the trick. Be prepared to also fork over the $35 spa fee that all nonhotel guests have to pay (hotel guests pay $10 on weekdays, $20 on weekends to use the facilities). But even if you don't go for any of the spa selections, consider spending the 35 bucks just to hang out here—a perfect poolside day followed by a workout in the exercise room and a sauna, steam, and mineral plunge is one of our favorite ways to unwind in the Wine Country.

   Also worth a look is the **Mission San Francisco Solano de Sonoma,** located on Sonoma Plaza at the corner of First Street East and Spain Street (☎ **707/938-1519**). Founded in 1823, this was the northernmost—and last—mission built in California. It also was the only one established on the northern coast by the Mexican government, who wanted to protect their territory from expansionist Russian fur traders. It's now part of Sonoma State Historic Park. Admission is $2 for adults, $1 for children 6 to 12, and free for children 5 and under. It's open daily from 10am to 5pm except New Year's Day, Thanksgiving, and Christmas.

SHOPPING   Most of Sonoma's shops, which offer everything from food and wine to clothing and books, are located around the plaza. **The Mercado,** a small shopping center at 452 First St. E., houses several good stores selling unusual wares. The **Arts Guild of Sonoma,** 140 E. Napa St. (☎ **707/996-3115**), showcases the works of local artists in a wide variety of styles and media. It's open Wednesday through Monday from 11am to 5pm, and admission is free.

Our favorite stop along the plaza, however, is the ✪ **Wine Exchange,** 452 First St. E. (☎ **707/938-1794**), which carries more than 700 domestic wines, books on wine, wine paraphernalia, olive oils, and a small selection of cigars. It's a great place to begin your wine experience: browse though the numerous racks of bottles, ask questions of the wine-savvy staff, and be sure to check out the stack of wines in open cases to the right of the front door as you enter—they're almost all priced under $10. Even the beer connoisseur who's feeling displaced in the Wine Country will be happy to find more than 300 beers from around the world here, including a number of exceptional domestic beers. There are $1 wine and beer tastings daily at the small bar in back, which is occupied most evenings by a gaggle of friendly locals. The Exchange is open Monday through Saturday from 10am to 6pm, Sunday from 11am to 6pm. Shipping is available to anywhere in the United States.

THE LOCAL FARMER'S MARKET   Obsessed with farm-fresh produce, Sonomans host a year-round **Sonoma Valley Farmer's Market** every Friday morning from 9am to noon at the Depot Park on First Street West (just north of East Spain Street). Dozens of growers offer fresh fruits, vegetables, flowers, homemade jams, honey, barbecued turkey, baked goods, and handmade crafts from local artists. It's such a popular gathering place for locals and visitors alike that they've added a Saturday-morning market from 1 to 3:30pm November through December, and a Tuesday-night market from 5:30pm to dusk April through October. Both Saturday and Tuesday markets are held at the plaza in front of City Hall.

GLEN ELLEN

Hikers, mountain bikers, horseback riders, and picnickers will enjoy a day spent at ✪ **Jack London State Historic Park,** 2400 London Ranch Rd. off Arnold Drive (☎ **707/938-5216**). On its 800 acres, which were once home to the renowned writer, you'll find 10 miles of trails, the remains of London's burned-down dream house (as well as some preserved structures), and plenty of ideal picnic spots. An on-site museum, called the House of Happy Walls, was built by Jack's wife to display a collection from the author's life. The park is open daily from 9:30am to 7pm in summer, from 9:30am to 5pm in winter; the museum is open daily from 10am to 5pm. Admission to the park is $6 per car, $5 per car for seniors 62 and over. Pick up the $1 self-guided tour map on arrival to help acquaint you with the grounds. In summer, golf-cart rides also are offered from noon to 4pm on weekends for those who don't want to hoof it.

SHOPPING   Gourmands might want to stop by **The Olive Press,** 14301 Arnold Dr., in Jack London Village (☎ **800/ 9-OLIVE-9** or 707/939-8900). With olive trees abounding in the area and the locals' penchant for gourmet foods, it's no surprise that fresh-pressed olive oil has become a lucrative business in this neck of the woods. Everyone from large commercial growers to small-volume growers and hobbyists can pile their olives in the hopper and watch the state-of-the-art Italian-made olive press in action as it conveys the fruit up a belt, cleans it, and begins the pressing process. There's also a nifty gift shop, but don't expect a bargain here; even if you bring your own bottle, a gallon of oil can go for $100 (you'd be surprised how many olives it takes to make a gallon). The Press also carries numerous varieties of olive oils, imported olive-tree varietals, cured olives, and olive-related foods, gifts, and books. Open daily from 10am to 5:30pm.

HORSEBACK RIDING   Long before the Sonoma Valley became part of the Wine Country, it was better known as cattle country— and there's no better way to explore the land's old roots than with a guided horseback tour provided by the ♦ **Sonoma Cattle Company** (☎ **707/996-8566; www.thegridnet/trailrides/**). After you've been instructed in the basics of horse handling, you'll be led on a leisurely stroll—with the occasional trot thrown in for thrills— through beautiful Jack London State Historic Park. The ride takes you past vineyards owned by London's descendants, across meadows blanketed with lupine, around a lake originally dammed by London, and up to enjoy Sonoma Mountain's panoramic views. The Sonoma Cattle Company also offers regular, sunset, and full-moon rides at Sugarloaf Ridge at the northern end of Sonoma Valley. This route also winds through deep, shady forests and up to ridge tops with spectacular 360° views. At either location you can also opt for the Western Barbecue Ride ($75 for 3 to 4 hr.) or the Gourmet Boxed Lunch Ride and Tour of the Benziger Family Winery ($55 for 3 hr.).

SANTA ROSA

GOLF   Thanks to the valley's mild climate, golf is a year-round pursuit here. At the northern end of the Sonoma Valley is the semi-private **Oakmont Golf Club,** 7025 Oakmont Dr., off the Sonoma Highway, Santa Rosa (☎ **707/539-0415**), which has two 18-hole championship courses, both designed by Ted Robinson, as well as a driving range, clubhouse, and locker rooms. The par 63 East course is considered the most challenging, while the par 72 West course is for higher handicapped golfers. Greens fees range from $21 to $26 on weekdays, $26 to $33 on weekends; carts are $22. Reservations are recommended at least a day in advance on weekdays, and at least 1 week on weekdays.

Originally designed by Sam Whiting in 1926, the **Sonoma Golf Club,** 17700 Arnold Dr., off Boyes Drive (pro shop ☎ **707/996-0300**), was completely remodeled in 1991 by Robert Muir Graves. Its par 72, 18-hole championship course is considered one of the top public courses in the state. It's mostly flat, with several tight doglegs around an armada of redwoods and oaks. A driving range was added in the $10-million renovation; a clubhouse and locker rooms are also provided. Greens fees ($45 Mon through Thurs, $55 Fri, $65 weekends) include cart. A strict dress code is enforced.

If you're a beginner or just want to bone up on your irons game, the **Los Arroyos Golf Club,** 5000 Stage Gulch Rd. off Arnold Drive, a short drive from downtown Sonoma (pro shop ☎ **707/938-8835**), is for you. Its small, 9-hole course is fairly flat and inexpensive—$12 on weekdays, $15 on weekends. Pull carts are an extra $2; a driving range, practice greens, and club rentals are also available. It's open on a first-come, first-play basis.

4   Where to Stay

We've arranged the listings below first by area and then by average room price during the high season, using the following categories: **Very Expensive,** more than $250 per night; **Expensive,** $200 to $250 per night; **Moderate,** $150 to $200 per night; and **Inexpensive,** less than $150 per night.

When planning your trip, keep in mind that during the high season—between June and November—most hotels charge peak rates and sell out completely on weekends; many have a 2-night minimum. Always ask about discounts, particularly during midweek, when most hotels and B&Bs drop their rates by as much as 30%. During the off-season, you will have far better bargaining power and may be able to get a room at almost half the summer rate.

HELPING HANDS If you are having trouble finding a room, try calling the **Sonoma Valley Visitors Bureau** (☎ **707/996-1090**). They'll refer you to a lodging that has a room to spare, but they won't make reservations for you. The **Bed and Breakfast Association of Sonoma Valley** (☎ **800/969-4667**) will refer you to one of their member B&Bs, and can make reservations for you as well.

SONOMA
EXPENSIVE

✪ **Sonoma Mission Inn & Spa.** 18140 Sonoma Hwy. (Calif. 12; P.O. Box 1447), Sonoma, CA 94576. ☎ **800/862-4945** or 707/938-9000. Fax 707/ 935-1205. 198 units. A/C MINIBAR TV TEL. May–Oct $180–$285 Historic Inn room; $245–$345 Wine Country room; $395 suite. Nov–Apr $170–$255 Historic Inn room; $200–$360 Wine Country room; $285 suite. AE, CB, DC, MC, V. From central Sonoma, drive 3 miles north on Calif. 12.

As you drive through Boyes Hot Springs, you may wonder why someone decided to build a multimillion-dollar spa resort in this ordinary little town. There's no view to speak of, and it certainly isn't within walking distance of any wineries or fancy restaurants. So what's the deal? It's the water, of course, the lifeblood of every Wine Country spa—naturally heated artesian mineral water, to be precise, piped from directly underneath the spa and into the temperature-controlled pools and whirlpools. Set on 12 meticulously groomed acres, the Sonoma Mission Inn consists of a massive three-story replica of a Spanish mission (well, aside from the pink paint job), an array of satellite wings housing 30 superluxury suites, and, of course, the spa facilities. It's a popular retreat for the wealthy and the well-known, so don't be surprised if you see Barbra Streisand or Harrison Ford strolling around in their skivvies.

The modern rooms are furnished with plantation-style shutters, ceiling fans, down comforters, and such extra amenities as bathroom scales, hair dryers, and oversize bath towels. The Wine Country rooms, in a newer building, feature king-size beds, desks, refrigerators, and huge limestone and marble bathrooms; some offer woodburning fireplaces, and many have balconies. The older, slightly smaller Historic Inn rooms are sweetly appointed with homey furnishings, and most have queen-size beds; they are, however,

Sonoma Valley Accommodations

Sugarloaf Ridge State Park
Adobe Canyon Rd.

0 ___ 1 mi
0 ___ 1.6 km
N

Annadel State Park

Sonoma Hwy.
Goff
Randolph
Kenwood

Matanzas Creek

Bennett Valley Rd.

1

12 **2**

Warm Springs Rd.

Nuns Canyon Rd.

Trinity Rd.

Sonoma Mtn. Rd.

3 **4**

Bouverie Wildflower Preserve

VALLEY OF THE MOON

NAPA COUNTY

SONOMA COUNTY

Glen Ellen

Crane Creek Reg. Pk.

Jack London State Historic Park

London Ranch Rd.

Sonoma Cr.

Arnold Dr.

Petaluma Rd.

Sonoma Mtn.

Agua Caliente
Fetters Hot Springs

Gehricke Rd.

SONOMA MOUNTAINS

Petaluma Res.

Boyes Hot Springs

Verano Ave.

Sonoma State Historic Park

El Verano

W. Napa St.   E. Napa St.

Castle Rd.

Buena Vista

5

Rodgers Creek

Petaluma Adobe State Hist. Pk.

Sonoma

Napa Rd.

Vineburg

Adobe Rd.

Adobe Rd.

See map below

SONOMA VALLEY

12

116

121

Bonneau Rd.

Beltane Ranch	**2**
Best Western Sonoma Valley Inn	**9**
El Dorado Hotel	**12**
El Pueblo Inn	**8**
Gaige House Inn	**4**
Glenelly Inn	**3**
Kenwood Inn & Spa	**1**
Sonoma Chalet	**6**
Sonoma Hotel	**11**
Sonoma Mission Inn & Spa	**5**
Thistle Dew Inn	**10**
Trojan Horse Inn	**7**
Victorian Garden Inn	**13**

Town of Sonoma

0 ___ .5 mi
0 ___ .8 km
N

El Verano

12

6

Salvador Vallejo Home

Norrbom Rd.

Ravenswood Winery

Gehricke Rd.

Mountain Cemetery

Buena Vista Rd.

7

8

Sonoma State Historic Park

W. Spain St.

Mission San Francisco Solano

Buena Vista Winery

Castle St.

Lowell Valley Rd.

Old Winery Rd.

Petaluma Ave.

W. Napa St.

11

10 **12**

Sebastiani Vineyards

E. Spain St.

9

Sonoma Plaza/ City Hall

13

E. Napa St.

5th St. E.

7th St. E.

8th St. E.

Arroyo Seco

Riverside Dr.

Sonoma Creek

Dowdall Creek

W. Mac Arthur St.

E. Mac Arthur St.

Broadway

Denmark St.

Carriger Creek

Leveroni Rd.

Felder Creek

Creek Park

12

Napa Rd.

Gundlach-Bundschu Winery

157

overpriced for what you get and in serious need of renovation. All rooms have video access on command and come with a complimentary bottle of wine. The new Texan owners have plans to expand the resort even further, including a whole new spa menu.

Dining: The Grille, run by chef Jeff Jake, is known for its low-calorie, low-sodium, and low-cholesterol California cuisine as well as its 200 varieties of Napa and Sonoma wines (see "Where to Dine," below). The casual cafe, serving American cuisine at lunch, is renowned for its bountiful breakfasts.

Amenities: Room service, concierge, laundry, dry cleaning, newspaper delivery, baby-sitting, secretarial services, valet parking, complimentary refreshments. Health club, tennis courts. Full spa facilities with a wide range of treatments and nutritional consultation (individual spa and salon services range from $35 to $134); see "The Super Spa" on p. 152. The spa's bathhouse includes a sauna, steam room, whirlpool, outdoor exercise pool, and gym with weight equipment ($10 weekdays, $20 weekends, complimentary with any spa service).

MODERATE

Thistle Dew Inn. 171 W. Spain St., Sonoma, CA 95476. ☎ **800/382-7895.** Fax 707/996-8413. 6 units. A/C TEL. Summer $120–$195 double; winter $110–$170 double. Rates include full breakfast and afternoon hors d'oeuvres. AE, MC, V.

Innkeepers Larry and Norma Barnett will be the first to admit that they don't run the fanciest B&B in town, but they'll just as quickly tell you that you'd be hard-pressed to find a better deal for your dollar in Sonoma than the Thistle Dew Inn. Six rooms—all with private baths, queen beds, and phones with voice mail—are split between two turn-of-the-century homes, both handsomely furnished with an impressive collection of original Arts and Crafts furniture. If you're looking to save a few dollars, opt for a room in the main house; otherwise, you'll want one of the four larger and quieter rooms in the rear house. Each has its own deck overlooking Larry's cactus garden and is furnished with either a gas fireplace, a two-person whirlpool tub, or both. Luxury perks include breakfast (the French toast we had was excellent), which can be delivered to your room for an additional fee; afternoon hors d'oeuvres; free use of their bicycles and utensil-filled picnic baskets; passes to the nearby health club; and use of the garden hot tub. We guarantee you'll like the location—just half a block from Sonoma's plaza—as well as your hosts Larry and Norma and their very low-key, help-yourself approach toward innkeeping.

INEXPENSIVE

Best Western Sonoma Valley Inn. 5550 Second St. W. (1 block from the plaza), Sonoma, CA 95476. ☎ **800/334-5784** or 707/938-9200. Fax 707/938-0935. 75 units. $79–$179 double. Rates include continental breakfast. AE, CB, DC, MC, V.

There are just two reasons to stay at the Sonoma Valley Inn: 1) it's the only place left with a vacancy, or 2) you're bringing the kids along. Otherwise, unless you don't mind staying in a rather drab room with thin walls and small bathrooms, you're probably going to be a little disappointed. Kids, on the other hand, will love the place: there's plenty of room to run around, plus a large pool and gazebo-covered spa to play in. The rooms *do* come with a lot of perks, however, such as continental breakfast delivered to your room each morning, a gift bottle of white table wine from Kenwood Vineyards (chilling in the fridge), cable TV with HBO, and either a balcony or deck overlooking the inner courtyard. It also has a good location, just a block from Sonoma's plaza.

✪ **El Dorado Hotel.** 405 First St. W., Sonoma, CA 95476. ☎ **800/289-3031** or 707/996-3030. Fax 707/996-3148. 26 units. A/C TV TEL. Summer $130–$160 double; winter $100–$130 double. Rates include continental breakfast and a split of wine. AE, MC, V.

This place may look like a 19th-century Wild West relic from the outside, but inside it's all 20th-century deluxe. Each modern, handsomely appointed guest room—designed by the same folks who put together the ultraexclusive Auberge du Soleil resort in Rutherford (see chapter 4)—has French windows and tiny terraces; some offer lovely views of the plaza, while others overlook the hotel's private courtyard and heated lap pool. All rooms (except those for guests with disabilities) are on the second floor, and have private baths with plush towels and hair dryers. The two rooms on the ground floor are off the private courtyard, and each has its own partially enclosed patio. Services include a concierge, laundry, in-room massage, bicycle rental, and access to a nearby health club. Breakfast, served either inside or out in the courtyard, includes coffee, fruits, and freshly baked breads and pastries. Within the hotel is Piatti, a popular restaurant serving regional Italian cuisine (see "Where to Dine," below).

El Pueblo Inn. 896 W. Napa St., Sonoma, CA 95476. ☎ **800/900-8844** or 707/996-3651. 38 units. A/C TEL. May–Oct $80–$94 double; Mar–Apr and Nov $69–$80 double; Dec–Feb $65–$80 double. AE, DISC, MC, V.

Located on Sonoma's main east-west street 8 blocks from the center of town, this isn't Sonoma's fanciest hotel, but it offers some of the best-priced accommodations around. The rooms here are pleasant enough, with post-and-beam construction, exposed brick walls, light-wood furniture, and geometric prints. The coffeemaker should be a comfort to early risers, and an outdoor heated pool will cool you off in hot weather. Reservations should be made at least a month in advance for the spring and summer months.

Sonoma Chalet. 18935 Fifth St. W., Sonoma, CA 95476. ☎ **707/938-3129.** 4 units, 3 cottages. Apr–Oct $85–$160 double; Nov–Mar $85–$150 double. Rates include continental breakfast. AE, MC, V.

This is one of the few accommodations in Sonoma that's truly secluded; it's on the outskirts of town, in a peaceful country setting overlooking a 200-acre ranch. The accommodations, housed in a Swiss-style farmhouse and several cottages, are all delightfully decorated by someone with an eye for color and a concern for comfort. You'll find claw-foot tubs, country quilts, Oriental carpets, comfortable furnishings, and private decks; some units have woodstoves or fireplaces. The two least expensive rooms share a bathroom, while the cottages offer the most privacy. A breakfast of fruit, yogurt, pastries, and cereal is served either in the country kitchen or in your room (and the gaggles of ducks, chickens, and ornery geese will be glad to help you finish off the crumbs). If you like country rustic (and farm animals), you'll like the Sonoma Chalet.

Trojan Horse Inn. 19455 Sonoma Hwy., Sonoma, CA 95476. ☎ **800/899-1925** or 707/996-2430. Fax 707/996-1689. 6 units. $120–$140 double. Rates include full breakfast and afternoon hors d'oeuvres. AE, MC, V.

This turn-of-the-century Victorian-style farmhouse, located at the west end of town, was once the home of one of Sonoma's pioneer families. Innkeepers John and Doris Leonard have maintained the old-world ambiance, furnishing their guest rooms with period antiques such as brass beds, armoires, handmade quilts, and century-old high oak beds. In the winter, the Bridal Veil room's old-fashioned wood-burning fireplace helps ward off the chill, as does the Jacuzzi tub in the Grape Arbor room—two amenities that are definitely worth the $20 upgrade. A hearty country breakfast is served between 8 and 9:30am, after which you can walk into town, lounge on the landscaped grounds alongside Sonoma Creek, relax in the outdoor hot tub, or borrow one of the inn's bikes for a ride through the Wine Country. The only caveat is the busy traffic along the highway; light sleepers should request a room away from the street.

Victorian Garden Inn. 316 E. Napa St., Sonoma, CA 95476. ☎ **800/ 543-5339** or 707/996-5339. Fax 707/996-1689. 4 units. $95–$165 double. Rates include breakfast and afternoon wine and sherry. AE, DC, MC, V.

Proprietor Donna Lewis runs what is easily the cutest B&B in Sonoma Valley. A small picket fence and a wall of trees enclose an adorable Victorian garden brimming with bowers of violets, roses, camellias, and peonies, all shaded under flowering fruit trees. It's truly a marvelous sight in the springtime. Four guest rooms—three in the century-old water tower and one in the main house, an 1870s Greek Revival farmhouse—are in keeping with the Victorian theme: white wicker furniture, floral prints, padded armchairs, and claw-foot tubs. The most popular rooms are the Top o' the Tower, which has its own entrance and view overlooking the garden, and the Woodcutter's Cottage, which also has its own entrance and garden view, plus a sofa and armchairs set in front of the fireplace. A breakfast of croissants, muffins, gourmet coffee, and fruit picked from the garden is served at the dining table, in the garden, or in your room; evening wine and sherry are served in the parlor. After a hard day's wine tasting, spend the afternoon cooling off in the pool or on the shaded wraparound porch, enjoying a mellow merlot while soaking in the sweet garden smells.

Sonoma Hotel. 110 W. Spain St., Sonoma, CA 95476. ☎ **800/468-6016** or 707/996-2996. Fax 707/996-7014. 17 units, 5 with bathroom. Summer $75– $85 double without bathroom, $115–$125 double with bathroom. Winter Sun– Thurs $59 double without bathroom, $90 double with bathroom; Fri–Sat $75 double without bathroom, $115–$125 double with bathroom. Rates include continental breakfast. AE, MC, V.

This cute little historic hotel on Sonoma's tree-lined town square places an emphasis on European-style elegance and comfort. Each room is decorated in early California style, with antique furnishings, fine woods, and floral-print wallpapers; some feature brass beds, and all are blissfully devoid of phones and TVs. Five of the third-floor units share immaculate baths (and significantly reduced rates), while rooms with private baths have deep claw-foot tubs with overhead showers. Perks include continental breakfast and a bottle of wine on arrival. Also within the hotel is Le Bistro, a small restaurant serving Mediterranean cuisine for lunch, dinner, and Sunday brunch.

GLEN ELLEN
EXPENSIVE

✪ **Gaige House Inn.** 13540 Arnold Dr., Glen Ellen, CA 95442. ☎ **800/ 935-0237** or 707/935-0237. Fax 707/935-6411. 11 units. A/C TEL. Summer

$170–$295 double. Winter $155–$255 double. Rates include full breakfast and evening wines. AE, DISC, MC, V.

When you review hotels and B&Bs for a living—and we've reviewed thousands of them—it's hard to be impressed. When we visited the Gaige House Inn, however, we were not only impressed, we didn't want to leave. The inn's new owners, Ken Burnet, Jr., and Greg Nemrow, have managed to turn what was already a fine B&B into *the* finest in the Wine Country, and they've done it by offering a level of service, amenities, and decor normally associated with outrageously expensive resorts (and without the snobbery). Breakfast is made with herbs from the inn's garden and prepared by a chef who commutes daily from San Francisco. Firm mattresses are graced with wondrously silk-soft linens and premium down comforters, and even the furniture and artwork are of museum quality.

But wait, it gets better. Behind the inn is a 1.5-acre oasis with perfectly manicured lawns, a 40-foot-long pool, and an achingly inviting creek-side hammock shaded by a majestic Heritage oak. All 11 rooms, each artistically decorated in a plantation theme with Asian and Indonesian influences (trust us, they're beautiful), have private bathrooms, direct-dial phones, and king- or queen-size beds; two rooms have Jacuzzi tubs, and several have fireplaces. The Gaige Suite is their finest room, bright and airy with large windows, a private balcony overlooking the lawn, a fireplace, and a Jacuzzi tub so large you could swim in it. Personally, we prefer Garden Room no. 10, exquisitely decorated with mahogany trim and flooring, a corner fireplace, a private deck, a huge glass-walled shower with dual heads, and a Jacuzzi tub for two. On sunny days, breakfast is served at individual tables on the large terrace. Evenings are best spent in the reading parlor sipping premium wines. Future plans include two additional suites in the creek-side house and an outdoor hot tub.

INEXPENSIVE

Beltane Ranch. 11775 Sonoma Hwy. (Hwy. 12), Glen Ellen, CA 95442. ☎ 707/996-6501. 5 units. TEL. $110–$145 double. Rates include full breakfast. No credit cards (though checks are accepted).

The word "Ranch" conjures up the impression of a big ol' two-story house in the middle of hundreds of rolling acres, the kind of place where you laze away the day in a hammock watching the grass grow or pitching horseshoes in the garden. Well, friend, you can have all that and more at the Beltane Ranch, a century-old buttercup-yellow manor that's been everything from a bunkhouse to a brothel to a turkey farm. You simply can't help but feel your tensions ease away as you kick your feet up on the shady wraparound porch overlooking the vineyards, sipping a cool, fruity chardonnay while reading *Lonesome Dove* for the third time. Each room is uniquely decorated with American and European antiques; all have private baths, sitting areas, and separate entrances. Innkeeper Deborah Mahoney serves a big country breakfast in the garden or on the porch overlooking the vineyards. For exercise, you can play tennis on the private court or hike the trails meandering through the 1,600-acre estate. *Tip:* Request one of the upstairs rooms, which have the best views.

✪ **Glenelly Inn.** 5131 Warm Springs Rd. (off Arnold Dr.), Glen Ellen, CA 95442. ☎ **707/996-6720.** Fax 707/996-5227. 8 units. $115–$150 double. Rates include full breakfast and afternoon hors d'oeuvres. MC, V.

The Glenelly Inn is one of our favorite places to stay in the Wine Country. First off, the rates are reasonable, particularly when you factor in breakfast and afternoon snacks. But more important, this former 1916 railroad inn is positively drenched in serenity. Located well off the main highway on an oak-studded hillside, the peach-and-cream inn comes with everything you would expect from a country retreat—long verandas with comfy wicker chairs and views of the verdant Sonoma hillsides; a hearty country breakfast served beside a large cobblestone fireplace; and bright, immaculate rooms with old-fashioned claw-foot tubs, Scandinavian down comforters, and ceiling fans. But innkeeper Kristi Hallamore, a native San Franciscan of Norwegian descent (and a darn good cook), also understands that it's the little things that make the difference. Hence, the firm mattresses, good reading lights, and a simmering hot tub well ensconced within a grapevine- and rose-covered arbor. All rooms, decorated with antiques and country furnishings, have queen beds, private baths with showers, terry-cloth robes, and private entrances. Top picks are either the Vallejo or Jack London cottages, both with large private patios, though we also like the rooms on the upper veranda—particularly in the spring when the terraced gardens below are in full bloom.

KENWOOD
VERY EXPENSIVE

✪ **Kenwood Inn & Spa.** 10400 Sonoma Hwy., Kenwood, CA 95452. ☎ **800/353-6966** or 707/833-1293. Fax 707/833-1247. 12 units. Apr–Oct $255–$395 double (2-night minimum on weekends); Nov–Mar $225–$365 double. Rates include gourmet breakfast and bottle of wine. AE, MC, V.

Inspired by the villas of Tuscany, the honey-colored Italian-style buildings, flower-filled flagstone courtyard, and pastoral views of vineyard-covered hills are enough to make any northern Italian homesick. We were immediately impressed with the friendly staff who made us feel right at home. Every spacious room here is lavishly and exquisitely decorated with imported tapestries, velvets, and antiques; each has a fireplace, balcony (unless you're on the ground floor), feather bed, CD player, and down comforter—but no phone or TV, so you can relax. A minor caveat is road noise, which you're unlikely to hear from your room, but can be slightly heard over the tranquil pumped-in music around the courtyard and pool.

An impressive two-course gourmet breakfast is served poolside or in the Mediterranean-style dining room; ours consisted of a poached egg accompanied by light, flavorful potatoes, red bell peppers, and other roasted vegetables, all artfully arranged, followed by a delicious homemade scone with fresh berries and a small lemon tart.

Amenities: The inn's own full-service spa offers aromatherapy, massage (including one of the best we've had in a long time), and various skin and body treatments such as a Mediterranean salt scrub of lemon rind, rosemary, and salt.

5 Where to Dine

In the past decade the Sonoma Valley has experienced a culinary revolution. In response to the saturation of restaurants in the Bay Area, both budding and renowned chefs and restaurateurs have pulled their San Francisco stakes and resettled in the Sonoma Valley to craft culinary art from the region's bounty of organic produce and meats. The result is something longtime locals never dared to dream of when it came to fine dining in Sonoma: a choice.

Granted, the selection of fine restaurants in Sonoma pales in comparison to that found in Napa Valley, but the overall dining experience is certainly equivalent—enough so that even New York restaurateur Drew Nieporent, who brought Rubicon to San Francisco and Montrachet, Nobu, and Tribeca Grill to New York, agreed that Sonoma was sophisticated enough to host a Big Apple–style restaurant, and opened Freestyle. Yet even the big players are forced to concede to Sonoma's small-town code by keeping their restaurants simple and unpretentious, hence the absence of ostentatious eateries such as Napa's Tra Vigne or Pinot Blanc.

Instead, as you travel through the valley, you'll find a few dozen modestly sized and privately owned cafes, often run by husband-and-wife teams who pour their hearts and bank accounts into

Dining in the Town of Sonoma

Babette's Café **8**
Basque Boulangerie Café **7**
Della Santina's **5**
Depot Hotel Restaurant
  and Italian Garden **1**
The Feed Store Again! **3**
Freestyle **4**
The General's Daughter **12**
La Casa **9**
Lo Spuntino **10**
Pasta Nostra **6**
Piatti **2**
Swiss Hotel **11**

keeping their businesses thriving during the off-season. In fact, don't be surprised if the person waiting your table is also the owner, chef, host, sommelier, and retired professor from Yale. It's this sort of combination that often makes dining in Sonoma a very personable experience, and one that you'll relish long after you leave the Wine Country.

Note: Though Sonoma Valley has far fewer visitors than Napa Valley, its restaurants are often equally as crowded, so be sure to make reservations as far in advance as possible. Also bear in mind that the food is usually on the rich side, served in large portions, and washed down with copious amounts of wine—enough so that we make a point of eating at only one restaurant a day lest we explode.

The restaurants below are organized first by area, then by price, using the following guide: **expensive,** more than $45 per person; **moderate,** $25 to $45 per person; and **inexpensive,** less than $25 per person. These categories reflect the price of the majority of dinner menu items and include an appetizer, main course, coffee, dessert, tax, and tip.

SONOMA
EXPENSIVE

✪ **Babette's Cafe.** 464 First St. E. (at the square), Sonoma. ☎ **707/939-8921.** Reservations recommended for both cafe and dining room. Cafe, main courses $10.25–$15.95; dining room, fixed-price menu $59. MC, V. Cafe, daily noon–1pm; dining room, Tues–Sat 6–10pm. FRENCH.

After it was voted the "Best Best-Kept Secret" by the *San Francisco Bay Guardian,* Babette's Cafe soon became one of the hottest places to dine in Sonoma. Thankfully, this quaint little spot across from Sonoma's plaza has managed to maintain its homey atmosphere despite its newfound success. Like most of Sonoma's restaurants, Babette's is both intimate and casual; its front-room cafe feels like a cozy French bistro, while the main dining room is a smaller, more formal space. But its down-home appeal doesn't extend to the food, which continues to garner rave reviews while remaining affordably priced. Along with soups, salads, and sandwiches (all less than $8), main courses include cassoulet baked with duck confit, house-made pork sausage, lamb, and white beans; and Moroccan spiced vegetables on couscous. Chef Daniel Patterson (formerly of Domaine Chandon and Mustards Grill) also offers a fantastic five-course fixed-price dinner with tempting selections ranging from a caviar starter to roasted quail with garden cress, quinoa, and blood-orange vinaigrette; roasted monkfish on a sauce of smoked ham hocks, leeks, and red wine; and pan-roasted veal on vegetables and black chanterelles. Be sure to start your feast with the fresh goat cheese on toast (served with an endive-and-herb salad), and end with the warm-peach-and-blueberry napoleon. Wines can be paired with each course for an additional $39.

✪ **The Grille.** At Sonoma Mission Inn, 18140 Sonoma Hwy., Sonoma. ☎ **707/938-9000.** Reservations recommended. Main courses $18–$28. AE, MC, V. Sat 11:30am–2pm, Sun brunch 10am–2pm; daily 6–9:30pm. CALIFORNIA/SPA.

The Grille, one of the most well-known restaurants in the Wine Country, has long suffered from a solid reputation for serving high-caliber spa cuisine. The problem, of course, is the word "spa," which conjures up visions of blue-haired ladies eating boiled vegetables and soybean salads. Fortunately, the Grille has found a solution: Jeffrey Jake, a wondrously talented chef with a reputation for turning no-name restaurants into award-winning success stories. One bite of his corn risotto flavored with wild mushrooms and molten Reggiano Parmigiano cheese and you'll see why: it's one of the best we've ever tasted, and we're risotto addicts. About half of Jake's menu is spa-conscious, with the calorie and cholesterol percentages listed below selected entrees ranging from roasted medaillons of ostrich in apple sauce (11mg cholesterol, 18.1g fat) to oven-roasted breast of Petaluma chicken in a Crimini-mushroom cabernet sauce (105mg cholesterol, 4.6g fat). He mercifully spares us the fine print, how-ever, for the dishes we *really* want, such as the seared Sonoma foie gras with caramelized apples, white truffle oil, and a zinfandel reduc-tion sauce (yes, it's as good—and as bad for you—as it sounds), or the rack of herb-marinated lamb, roasted in Levain crumbs and pistachios and served with garlic mashed potatoes. Pastry chef Steve Fischer is equally adept at making more from less, working wonders with low-cal lemon desserts such as the tart lemon chiffon topped with a sweet berry puree. The pleasant decor features peach-colored walls, bentwood chairs, and just the right amount of elbow room. Service is professional yet friendly, and though jackets are re-quested, few were seen. The wine list is extensive and expensive.

MODERATE

✪ **Della Santina's.** 133 E. Napa St. (just east of the square), Sonoma. ☎ **707/935-0576.** Reservations recommended. Main courses $8.95–$14.75. DISC, MC, V. Daily 11:30am–9:30pm. ITALIAN.

Those of you who just can't take another expensive, chichi Califor-nia meal should follow the locals to this friendly, traditional Italian restaurant. How traditional? Just ask father/son team Dan and Robert: when we last dined here they pointed out Señora Santina's hand-embroidered linen doilies as they proudly told us about her Tuscan recipes. And their pride is merited: Every dish we tried was refreshingly authentic and well flavored—without overbearing sauces or one *hint* of California pretentiousness. Be sure to start with tra-ditional antipasti, especially the sliced mozzarella and tomatoes or the delicious white beans. The nine pasta dishes are, again, wonder-fully authentic (gnocchi lovers, rejoice!). The spit-roasted meat dishes are a local favorite (though we found them to be a bit over-cooked), and for those who can't choose between chicken, pork, turkey, rabbit, or duck, there's a selection that offers a choice of three. Don't worry about breaking your bank on a bottle of wine, as most of the savory choices here go for under $25. Portions are huge, but save room for dessert—they're wonderful, too.

Depot Hotel Restaurant and Italian Garden. 241 First St. W. (off Spain St.), Sonoma. ☎ **707/938-2980.** www.depotel.com. Reservations recommended. Main courses $7–$16. AE, CB, DC, DISC, MC, V. Wed–Fri 11:30am–2pm; Wed–Sun 5–9pm. NORTHERN ITALIAN.

Michael Ghilarducci has been the chef and owner here for the past 13 years, which means he's either independently wealthy or a darn good cook. Fortunately, it's the latter. Located a block north of the plaza in a handsome, historic 1870 stone building, the Depot Hotel offers pleasant outdoor dining in an Italian garden complete with a reflection pool and cascading Roman fountain. The menu is unwaveringly Italian, filled with a plethora of classic dishes such as spaghetti bolognese and veal alla parmigiana. Start with the bounteous antipasto misto and end the feast with a dish of Michael's handmade Italian ice cream and fresh-fruit sorbets.

Freestyle. 522 Broadway, Sonoma. ☎ **707/996-9916.** Main courses $12–$18. AE, CB, DC, DISC, MC, V. Wed–Sun 11:30am–2:30pm; Wed–Mon 5:30–10pm. SONOMA CUISINE.

New York restaurateur Drew Nieporent, who brought Rubicon to San Francisco and Montrachet, Nobu, and Tribeca Grill to New York, finally decided that Sonoma was sophisticated enough to host a Big Apple–style restaurant ("I've finally made it to Broadway," he quipped). Local residents apparently agree: Freestyle has been humming right through the slow season since it opened in late 1997. After hearing all the hype, we entered the restaurant with high hopes for a memorable evening; unfortunately, that wasn't the case. We found the seating awkward and cramped, the portions entirely too small, the acoustics deafening, and the decor—a monochrome profusion of lacquered plywood and burgundy fabrics—cheap and unimaginative. Yes, Steven Levine is a talented chef (his grilled Sonoma foie gras paired with toasted hazelnuts, huckleberries, and a corn-quinoa salad is outstanding), but it was too little, too late. If you're going to spend this kind of money on a meal, you'll probably have a more enjoyable dining experience at Della Santina's or Babette's Cafe around the corner. Sorry, Mr. Nieporent, but considering your past successes, we felt you could have done a lot better.

The General's Daughter. 400 W. Spain St., Sonoma. ☎ **707/938-4004.** Reservations recommended in summer. Main courses $8.75–$21.50. MC, V. Daily 11:30am–2:30pm; Sun–Fri 5:30–9pm, Sat 5:30–10pm. CALIFORNIA.

Ask almost any local about the General's Daughter and they'll give you pretty much the same answer: "It's a beautiful building, but I've never eaten there." And for good reason: This fully restored 1883 farmhouse—built by General Vallejo for his daughter Natalia—is gorgeous both inside and out. Unfortunately, such compliments rarely apply to the cuisine, which is both unimaginative and unspectacular. All the standards are here—roast chicken, grilled salmon, rib-eye steak, rack of lamb, and the requisite vegetarian dish of grilled vegetables—along with the occasional bizarre attempt at Mexican/Asian fusion (sorry, readers, but we just didn't have the stomach to sample the seared rare ahi tostada). The food isn't *bad*, really—it's just not good, and if you're going to spend $21.50 on a steak, you might as well dine at the Grille (see above). The general consensus, from what we've gathered, is that the General's Daughter is best admired from a distance.

Pasta Nostra. 139 E. Napa St., Sonoma. ☎ **707/938-4166.** Main courses $7.50–$16. AE, MC, V. Mon–Sat 11:30am–2:30pm; Mon–Thurs 5–9pm, Fri–Sat 5–10pm, Sun 4:30–9pm. ITALIAN.

Very few restaurants in Sonoma Valley cater to families with children, but Pasta Nostra is the exception. It's not the best restaurant in Sonoma by far, but on a sunny day with kids in tow you won't find a better—and cheaper—place to dine. Inside the converted Victorian home are semiformal settings with white tablecloths and fine tableware; outside on the ivy-walled patio are a dozen or so tables shaded by trees. Expect big portions of hearty Italian-American fare such as freshly made fettuccine carbonara, mostaccioli with house-made Sicilian-style sausage, and roasted lamb loin with a hazlenut-dijon crust and mint balsamic glaze. Kids have their own short menu, featuring all-time favorites such as lasagna and spaghetti with meatballs—at childlike prices. *Tip:* Few people know about the small parking lot in the rear.

✪ **Piatti.** 405 First St. W., Sonoma. ☎ **707/996-2351.** Reservations recommended. Main courses $9.95–$18.95. AE, DC, MC, V. Sun–Thurs 11:30am–10pm, Fri–Sat 11:30am–11pm. ITALIAN.

Part of a northern-California chain that originated in Napa, Piatti has built a steadfast and true clientele by consistently serving large portions of good Italian food at a fair price in a fun and festive setting (got all that?). The restaurant occupies the ground floor of the El Dorado Hotel at the northwest corner of Sonoma Plaza (just follow your nose). Good pizzas and braised meats—such as the superb lamb shank flavored with a rich port-wine sauce and fresh mint—emerge from a wood-burning oven. Also offered is an array of satisfying pastas, our favorite being the cannelloni stuffed with roasted veal, spinach, porcini mushrooms, and ricotta. Other recommended dishes include a wonderful roast-vegetable appetizer, the teeming pile of fresh mussels in a tomato-and-herb broth, the rotisserie chicken with garlic mashed potatoes, and the veal scaloppini. Granted, there are fancier and more intimate restaurants in the valley, but none that can fill you up with such good food at these prices. And if the sun is out, there's no prettier place in Sonoma to dine alfresco than Piatti's courtyard.

Swiss Hotel. 18 W. Spain St., Sonoma. ☎ **707/938-2884.** Reservations recommended. Main courses $10–$20. AE, MC, V. Daily 11:30am–2:30pm and 5–9:30pm. (Bar, daily 11:30am–2am.) CONTINENTAL/NORTHERN ITALIAN.

The historic Swiss Hotel, located right in the town center, is a Sonoma landmark, complete with slanting floors and aged beamed ceilings. The turn-of-the-century long oak bar at the left of the entrance is adorned with black-and-white photos of pioneering Sonomans. The bright white dining room and rear dining patio are pleasant spots to enjoy lunch specials like penne with chicken, mushrooms, and tomato cream; sandwiches; and California-style pizzas fired in a wood-burning oven. Dinner might start with a warm winter salad of radicchio and frisée lettuce with pears, walnuts, and bleu cheese. Main courses run the gamut; we like the linguine and prawns with garlic, hot pepper, and tomatoes; the filet mignon wrapped in a bleu-cheese crust; and the duck in an orange-honey sauce.

INEXPENSIVE

Basque Boulangerie Cafe. 460 First St. E., Sonoma. ☎ **707/935-7687.** Menu items $3–$7. MC, V. Daily 7am–6pm. BAKERY/DELI.

If you want a big breakfast with eggs, sausage, and the works, head to the Feed Store (see below), but if you prefer a lighter morning meal and strong coffee, stand in line with the locals at the Basque Boulangerie Cafe, the most popular gathering spot in the Sonoma Valley. Most everything—sourdough Basque breads, pastries, quiche, soups, salads, desserts, sandwiches, cookies—is made in-house, and made well. Daily lunch specials, such as a grilled-veggie sandwich with smoked mozzarella cheese ($4.75), are listed on the chalkboard out front. Seating is scarce, and if you can score a sidewalk table on a sunny day, consider yourself one lucky person. A popular option is ordering to go and eating in the shady plaza across the street. The cafe also sells wine by the glass, as well as a wonderful cinnamon bread by the loaf that's ideal for making French toast.

The Feed Store, Again! 529 First St. W., Sonoma. ☎ **707/939-7147.** Main courses $4.50–$8.25. MC, V. Wed–Mon 7:30am–2:30pm, Sat–Sun 8am–3pm. AMERICAN.

Owners Drake and Madeline Dierkhising tried to retire from the restaurant business, but after seeing how poorly their baby was being run by the new owner, they decided to buy it back. Hence, the "Again!"—and once again the locals are back for their daily sustenance. It's a bright, roomy, cheerful place with plenty of windows, high ceilings, an open kitchen, and a tasteful Southwestern color scheme. The wait staff is as nice as can be, and prices are very reasonable. For breakfast, try the cheese blintzes or apple crepe, both topped with seasonal fruit, blueberry sauce, and yogurt, or the zesty huevos rancheros with guacamole, salsa, and black beans. Bestsellers on the lunch menu are the Jalisco Club (charbroiled chicken, smoked bacon, cheese, avocado, and salsa rolled in a flour tortilla), grilled-veggie sandwich, and classic burger ("Best in town," says Drake, who also says the same about his muffins, made elsewhere at a bakery he also owns). A small brewery has recently been added to the cafe, but Drake—ever the perfectionist—is still searching for the right brew master for the job, so it may not be in service.

La Casa. 121 E. Spain St., Sonoma. ☎ **707/996-3406.** Reservations recommended on weekends and summer evenings. Main courses $6–$11. AE, CB, DC, DISC, MC, V. Daily 11:30am–10pm (bar appetizers until midnight). MEXICAN.

This no-nonsense Mexican restaurant, on the Sonoma Plaza across from the mission, serves great enchiladas, fajitas, and chimichangas. To start, try the black-bean soup or the ceviche made with fresh snapper, marinated in lime juice with cilantro and salsa, and served on crispy tortillas. Follow that with tamales prepared with corn husks spread with corn masa, stuffed with chicken filling, and topped with a mild red-chili sauce. Or you might opt for the delicious *suiza*—deep-dish chicken enchiladas—or fresh snapper Veracruz if it's available. On a sunny afternoon or a clear night, choose to dine patio-style, where you can sip cerveza under the warmth of heat lamps.

✪ **Lo Spuntino.** 400 First St. E., Sonoma. ☎ **707/935-4743.** Deli items $5–$9. AE, CB, DISC, MC, V. Sun–Thurs 10am–6pm, Fri–Sat 10am–9pm. ITALIAN DELI.

Lo Spuntino, Italian for "snack" or a tiny taste, is the sexiest thing going in Sonoma, a suave deli and wine bar owned by Sam and Vicki Sebastiani, who also run Viansa Winery. It's a visual masterpiece, with shiny black-and-white–checkered flooring, long counters of Italian marble, track lighting, and a center deli and wine bar where a crew of young men slice meats, pour wines, and scoop gelato. Start by sampling the preserves and jams near the entrance, then wander the aisle and choose among the armada of cured meats, cheese, fruit, pastas, salads, and breads lining the deli. Popular choices are the hefty sandwiches on herbed focaccia bread or the herb-marinated rotisserie chickens served by the half with your choice of pasta or salad. Roasted turkey, duck, pork, lamb, and rabbit also are available. Opposite the deli is the wine bar, featuring all of Viansa's current wine releases for both tasting and purchase, as well as a small selection of microbrewed beers on tap. On your way out, stop at the gelateria and treat yourself to some intense Italian ice cream. *Note:* Lo Spuntino also hosts live jazz bands every Friday night from 6 to 9pm.

GLEN ELLEN
MODERATE

✪ **The Girl & The Fig.** 13690 Arnold Dr., Glen Ellen. ☎ **707/938-3634.** Reservations recommended. Main courses $12–$19. AE, MC, V. Daily 5:30–9pm; Sun brunch 10am–2:30pm. COUNTRY FRENCH.

This modern, attractive cafe with mustard-yellow walls, tile floors, and an open kitchen is the creation of Sondra Bernstein (The Girl), who, after spending the past 4 years working at Viansa Winery and Italian Marketplace, left to open her own restaurant in August 1997. The coup de grâce was convincing San Francisco chefs/couple Gina Marie Armanini and John Gillis to come work for her. "They make a fantastic team," boasts Bernstein, and if the ever-crowded dining room is any indication, both tourists and locals agree. The cuisine is nouveau-country with French nuances, and yes, figs are sure to be on the menu in one form or another, such as the wonderful winter fig salad made with arugula, pecans, dried figs, Laura Chenel goat cheese, and a fig-and-port vinaigrette. Garden-fresh produce and local meats, poultry, and fish are used whenever possible, in dishes such as the pan-roasted medaillons of lamb served with braised winter greens, mashed potatoes, and fresh mint sauce (when's the last time you had fresh mint sauce?), or the hearty winter vegetable stew over couscous—a bargain at $11.95. For dessert try the warm pear galette topped with gingered crème fraîche, a glass of the Quady Essensia Orange Muscat, and a sliver of raclette from the cheese cart. Sondra knows her wines, and will be happy to choose the best accompaniment to your meal. *Note:* Monday nights in Glen Ellen are a whole lot more fun since Sondra introduced Fondue Night.

Sonoma Valley Dining

Glen Ellen Inn Restaurant. 13670 Arnold Dr., Glen Ellen. ☎ **707/ 996-6409.** Reservations recommended. Main courses $12–$22. AE, MC, V. Off-season Thurs–Tues 5:30pm–closing (depending on reservations); summer daily 5:30pm–closing. CALIFORNIA.

Christian and Karen Bertrand run this popular Glen Ellen restaurant. The dining room is so small and cozy that you feel as if you're dining in their home, but that's exactly the place's charm. Garden seating is the favored choice on sunny days, but the covered, heated patio is always welcoming. First courses from Christian's open kitchen might include a wild-mushroom–and-sausage "purse" served in a brandy cream sauce and warm goat-cheese croquettes. Main courses change with the seasons, but might range from linguine with artichoke hearts and feta to a stellar late-harvest ravioli stuffed with pumpkin, walnuts, and sun-dried cranberries on a bed of butternut squash. Other favorites include the marinated pork tenderloin on smoked mozzarella polenta, topped with roasted pepper onion compote; and, of course, the classic filet mignon accompanied by a full-bodied cabernet sauvignon. On our last visit, the Sonoma Valley mixed green salad, seared ahi tuna, and homemade French vanilla ice cream floating in bittersweet caramel sauce made a perfect meal. The wine list offers numerous Sonoma selections, as well as more than a dozen wines by the glass.

Mes Trois Filles Restaurant. 13648 Arnold Dr., Glen Ellen. ☎ **707/938-4844.** Reservations recommended. Main courses $14.50–$20.50. AE, DC, MC, V. Wed–Sun 5pm–9pm. FRENCH.

Matching the intimacy of Glen Ellen is this sweet little restaurant named after the owner's *trois filles* (three daughters). The decor consists of little more than 10 romantically set tables dispersed throughout a bright, peach-colored room. Locals love this place, but it's not only because of the small-town atmosphere. Chef/owner Len Moriyama cooked at Campton Place Restaurant—one of the most highly regarded dining rooms in San Francisco—before taking his talents north. Moriyama is in the kitchen nightly, preparing such dishes as his popular wild-mushroom ravioli in herbed beurre blanc, roasted breast of duck in bing-cherry sauce, and rack of lamb in merlot sauce. Ever mindful of health-conscious Californians, he can prepare lower-calorie variations of his heavier dishes. While the menu changes to reflect seasonal ingredients, desserts might include cheddar cheesecake with a wild-berry sauce, chocolate Grand Marnier mousse, and poached pear in phyllo with a zinfandel zambiglione.

INEXPENSIVE

Jack's Village Café. 14301 Arnold Dr., Glen Ellen. ☎ **707/939-6111.** Main courses $5.75–$9.50. AE, DISC, MC, V. Daily 8:30am–4pm; Wed–Sun 6–9pm. CALIFORNIA COUNTRY.

Hidden behind the Glen Ellen Tasting Room in Jack London Village is this small cafe run by Debra De Martini, a pretty and vivacious woman who greets guests, waits tables, and works the grill if need be ("all hats" is her job description). Century-old wood beams create a rustic ambiance inside, while the outdoor patio is surrounded by trees, flowers, and soothing sounds from a nearby creek. When the weather is pleasant, there's no better place in Glen Ellen to sit outside with a good glass of wine, a bowl of steamed mussels, and a roasted-eggplant–and-mozzarella sandwich. Other menu items range from a wild-mushroom risotto with braised leeks and sun-dried tomatoes (a bargain at $9.50) to a roasted pork-loin sandwich with sautéed onions and Jack's special barbecue sauce. Breakfast is taken seriously here: Chef Jon Brzycki makes his French toast with thick slices of sourdough bread sprinkled with cinnamon and nutmeg. The smoked salmon with toasted bagel and cream cheese is the perfect light breakfast for two, and the hot oatmeal and house-made granola are good choices as well. Be sure to check the Daily Specials board above the grill before you order.

KENWOOD
MODERATE

Kenwood Restaurant & Bar. 9900 Sonoma Hwy., Kenwood. ☎ **707/ 833-6326.** Reservations recommended. Main courses $12.50–$24.50. MC, V. Tues–Sun 11:30am–9pm. CALIFORNIA/CONTINENTAL.

This is what California Wine Country dining should be (but what it often, disappointingly, is not). From the terrace of the Kenwood Restaurant, diners enjoy a view of the vineyards set against Sugarloaf Ridge as they imbibe Sonoma's finest at umbrella-covered tables. On nippy days you can retreat inside to the Sonoma-style roadhouse, with its shiny wood floors, pine ceiling, vibrant artwork, and cushioned rattan chairs set at white-cloth–covered tables. Chef Max Schacher serves first-rate cuisine, perfectly balanced between tradition and innovation, and complemented by a reasonably priced wine list. Great starters are the Dungeness crab cake with herb mayonnaise; the superfresh sashimi with ginger, soy, and wasabi; and the wonderful Caesar salad. Main-dish choices might include poached salmon in a creamy caper sauce, prawns with saffron Pernod sauce, or braised Sonoma rabbit with grilled polenta. But the Kenwood doesn't take itself too seriously: Sandwiches and burgers also are available.

INEXPENSIVE

Café Citti. 9049 Sonoma Hwy., Kenwood. ☎ **707/833-2690.** Main courses $6–$9.50. MC, V. Daily 11am–3:30pm; Sun–Thurs 5–8:30pm, Fri–Sat 5–9pm. ITALIAN.

If you're this far north into the Wine Country, then you're probably doing some serious wine tasting. If that's the case, then you don't want to spend half the day at a fancy, high-priced restaurant. What you need is Café Citti (pronounced *Cheat*-ee), a roadside do-it-yourself Italian trattoria that is both good and cheap. You order from the huge menu board displayed above the open kitchen. Afterwards you scramble for a table (the ones on the patio, shaded by umbrellas, are the best on warm afternoons), and a server will bring your meal. It's all hearty, home-cooked Italian. Standout dishes are the green-bean salad, tangy Caesar salad, focaccia sandwiches, and the roasted rotisserie chicken stuffed with rosemary and garlic. The freshly made pastas come with a variety of sauces; our favorite is the zesty marinara. Wine is available by the bottle, and the espresso is plenty strong. Everything on the menu board is available to go, which makes Café Citti an excellent resource for picnic supplies.

6 Where to Stock Up for a Picnic— and Where to Enjoy It

Sure, Sonoma has plenty of restaurants, but when the weather's warm there's no better way to have lunch in the Wine Country than by toting a picnic basket to your favorite winery and basking under the sweet Sonoma sunshine. Even Sonoma's central plaza, with its many picnic tables, is a good spot to set up a gourmet picnic. But first you need grub, so for your picnicking pleasure, check out Sonoma's top spots for stocking up for an alfresco fete.

If you want to pick up some specialty fare on your way into town, stop at **Angelo's Wine Country Deli,** 23400 Arnold Dr. (☎ **707/ 938-3688**), where you'll find all types of smoked meats, special salsas, and homemade mustards. The deli is known for its half-dozen types of homemade beef jerky. It's open in summer daily from 9am to 6pm; off-season, Monday through Thursday from 9am to 5pm and Friday through Sunday from 9am to 6pm.

The venerable **Sonoma Cheese Factory,** on the plaza at 2 Spain St. (☎ **707/996-1000**), offers award-winning house-made cheeses and an extraordinary variety of imported meats and cheeses; a few are set out for tasting every day. The factory also sells caviar, gourmet salads, pâté, and homemade Sonoma Jack cheese. Good, inexpensive sandwiches are also available, such as fire-roasted pork loin or New York steak. While you're there, you can watch a narrated slide show about cheese making. The factory is open Monday through Friday from 8:30am to 5:30pm, Saturday and Sunday from 8:30am to 6pm.

At 315 Second St. E., a block north of East Spain Street, is the **Vella Cheese Company** (☎ **800/848-0505** or 707/938-3232), established in 1931. The folks at Vella pride themselves on making cheese into an award-winning science, their most recent victory being "U.S. Cheese Championship 1995–96" for their Monterey Dry Jack. Other cheeses range from flavorful High Moisture Jack to a razor-sharp Raw Milk Cheddar. Vella has also become famous for their Oregon Blue, made at their southern Oregon factory—it's rich, buttery, and even spreadable, one of the few premier bleus produced in this country. Any of these fine handmade, all-natural cheeses can be shipped directly from the store. Hours are Monday through Saturday from 9am to 6pm and Sunday from 10am to 5pm.

Three other highly recommended picnic outfitters include **Lo Spuntino** and **Basque Boulangerie Cafe** in Sonoma, and **Café Citti** in Kenwood (see "Where to Dine" above), and **Viansa Winery & Italian Marketplace,** which makes fabulous focaccia sandwiches—and has a lovely picnic area for noshing on them, too (see p. 138).

Gundlach-Bundschu (see p. 141), located on the outskirts of Sonoma, also has a wonderful picnic area perched on the side of a small hill overlooking the Sonoma countryside (though you'll have to earn the sensational view with a trek to the top). On the opposite side of the valley, our favorite picnic picks are **Château St. Jean's** (see p. 148) big, beautiful lawn overlooking the vineyards (bring a blanket) or the blissfully quiet pond-side picnic area at **Landmark Vineyards** (see p. 149), which also sports a bocce court if you're feeling restless.

If you'd rather have someone else provide the picnic grub for you, **Ravenswood Winery** (see p. 143) offers a gourmet "Barbecue Overlooking the Vineyards," held each weekend from 11am to 4:40pm from Memorial Day through the end of September. It's a really good time for not much money.

Index

See also separate Accommodations and Restaurant indexes, below.

ACCOMMODATIONS

FROMMER'S® COMPLETE TRAVEL GUIDES

*(Comprehensive guides to destinations around the world, with
selections in all price ranges—from deluxe to budget)*

Acapulco, Ixtapa &
  Zihuatenejo
Alaska
Amsterdam
Arizona
Atlanta
Australia
Austria
Bahamas
Barcelona, Madrid &
  Seville
Belgium, Holland &
  Luxembourg
Bermuda
Boston
Budapest & the Best
  of Hungary
California
Canada
Cancún, Cozumel &
  the Yucatán
Cape Cod, Nantucket
  & Martha's Vineyard
Caribbean
Caribbean Cruises &
  Ports of Call
Caribbean Ports of Call
Carolinas & Georgia
Chicago
China
Colorado
Costa Rica
Denver, Boulder &
  Colorado Springs
England
Europe

Florida
France
Germany
Greece
Hawaii
Hong Kong
Honolulu, Waikiki &
  Oahu
Ireland
Israel
Italy
Jamaica & Barbados
Japan
Las Vegas
London
Los Angeles
Maryland & Delaware
Maui
Mexico
Miami & the Keys
Montana & Wyoming
Montréal &
  Québec City
Munich & the
  Bavarian Alps
Nashville & Memphis
Nepal
New England
New Mexico
New Orleans
New York City
Northern New England
Nova Scotia, New
  Brunswick & Prince
  Edward Island
Oregon

Paris
Philadelphia & the
  Amish Country
Portugal
Prague & the Best of the
  Czech Republic
Provence & the Riviera
Puerto Rico
Rome
San Antonio & Austin
San Diego
San Francisco
Santa Fe, Taos &
  Albuquerque
Scandinavia
Scotland
Seattle & Portland
Singapore & Malaysia
South Pacific
Spain
Switzerland
Thailand
Tokyo
Toronto
Tuscany & Umbria
USA
Utah
Vancouver & Victoria
Vienna & the
  Danube Valley
Virgin Islands
Virginia
Walt Disney World &
  Orlando
Washington, D.C.
Washington State

FROMMER'S® DOLLAR-A-DAY GUIDES

(The ultimate guides to comfortable low-cost travel)

Australia from $50 a Day	Ireland from $50 a Day
California from $60 a Day	Israel from $50 a Day
Caribbean from $60 a Day	Italy from $50 a Day
Costa Rica & Belize from $35 a Day	London from $60 a Day
England from $60 a Day	Mexico from $35 a Day
Europe from $50 a Day	New York from $75 a Day
Florida from $50 a Day	New Zealand from $50 a Day
Greece from $50 a Day	Paris from $70 a Day
Hawaii from $60 a Day	San Francisco from $60 a Day
India from $40 a Day	Washington, D.C., from $60 a Day

FROMMER'S® PORTABLE GUIDES

(Pocket-size guides for travelers who want everything in a nutshell)

Bahamas	Dublin	Puerto Vallarta,
California Wine	Las Vegas	Manzanillo &
Country	London	Guadalajara
Charleston & Savannah	Maine Coast	San Francisco
Chicago	New Orleans	Venice
		Washington, D.C.

FROMMER'S® NATIONAL PARK GUIDES

(Everything you need for the perfect park vacation)

Grand Canyon	Yosemite & Sequoia & Kings Canyon
National Parks of the American West	Zion & Bryce Canyon
Yellowstone & Grand Teton	

FROMMER'S® IRREVERENT GUIDES

(Wickedly honest guides for sophisticated travelers)

Amsterdam	New Orleans	Santa Fe
Chicago	Paris	Walt Disney World
London	San Francisco	Washington, D.C.
Manhattan		

FROMMER'S® BY NIGHT GUIDES

(The series for those who know that life begins after dark)

Amsterdam	Madrid & Barcelona	Paris
Chicago	Manhattan	Prague
Las Vegas	Miami	San Francisco
London	New Orleans	Washington, D.C.
Los Angeles		

THE COMPLETE IDIOT'S TRAVEL GUIDES

(The ultimate user-friendly trip planners)

Cruise Vacations	New York City	San Francisco
Las Vegas	Planning Your Trip to	Walt Disney World
New Orleans	Europe	